THE EXTRAORDINARY DECADE
Literary Memoirs

THE EXTRAORDINARY DECADE

Literary Memoirs

by
P. V. Annenkov

———

Edited by Arthur P. Mendel

———

Translated by Irwin R. Titunik

Ann Arbor
THE UNIVERSITY OF MICHIGAN PRESS

Introduction

By Arthur P. Mendel

Time came out of joint in Russia in the early decades of the nine-teenth century. Rather than mingling naturally, past, present, and fu-ture were fixed in mutual contradiction. Although Peter the Great had rudely broken the present from the past by his violent abuse of cus-tom, the fracture had seemed to heal during the eighteenth century. By the end of that century, in the reign of Catherine the Great, and during the first years of the reign of her grandson Alexander I, a ten-uous but workable compromise was reached between the force of tra-dition and the appeal of change. Each received its due. The past found ample scope in the present, and those who felt that scope too large and who urged more ambitious reforms and heavier borrowing from the West were confident that in time the infirm present would grow organically into the robust future they desired. In the meantime, they would bear their proper responsibilities as part of the governing elite arguing fervently with the traditionalists, of course, but main-taining the essential unity of the elite, the homogeneous landed aris-tocracy, that set the tone and the direction of Russia's political, social, and cultural life.

The Napoleonic Wars and the deepening tsarist conservatism that accompanied them destroyed this unity, together with the sense of fundamental well-being, pride, and hope that nurtured it. Had Russia suffered the devastating and humiliating defeat that Napoleon dealt Prussia, Alexander I and his younger brother and successor Nicholas I might have learned the lesson that defeat so forcefully taught Prussia, the lesson that Peter the Great had learned a century before from a no less disastrous rout at Narva: a great power must be as advanced as its neighbors. Unfortunately for Russia, the decisive military success of the French in Russia, climaxed by the prolonged occupation of Mos-cow, was obscured by Napoleon's retreat, which was mistakenly at-tributed to Russian strength, and by the ensuing occupation of Paris

by Russian troops. Alexander I and Nicholas I drew simple but peri-
lously wrong conclusions from this deceptive glory. Russia had won,
so it need not change. Russia faced renewed conflict at any time with
the West, so it dare not change, either serfdom, the traditional Russian system of economic mobilization for war, or autocracy, the tried
and tested instrument for this mobilization and for the police order
indispensable for a society of mass servitude. The influence of old Russia, in other words, overwhelmed completely the promise of a new
Russia which had reconciled the reformers to the system.

If the conclusions drawn from the war by the state upset the pre-
carious balance between past and future by promoting this rededica-
tion to tradition, the conclusions drawn by the reformers drove them
to the opposite extreme. There were, for example, young army officers
who had fought the war in the belief that victory would bring a new
surge of progress and who had seen impressive examples of the kind
of society they wanted as they chased Napoleon westward and occupied his country. For these young men, and, no doubt, for countless
other members of the educated elite, it was the future, not the past,
whose claim on the present should have been mightily enhanced.

A significant part of the educated and creative elite was thus
alienated from the governing elite. Instead of contributing their
talents, so rare in this underdeveloped society, to the improvement of
the existing system, they became the leaders of efforts to destroy it.
The state, in turn, drew still more tightly into itself and became even
more inflexibly hostile to reform, more firmly attached to the ever
more sanctified past. The outcome was predictable: an abortive revolution by the reformers in December 1825 and the bleak, obscurantist, and frozen conservatism of Nicholas I.

Excluded by choice and by force from government, in which they
had earlier participated in the hopes of gradual change, the intelligentsia, as the alienated elite came to be called, lost faith in gradual-
ism and turned increasingly to radical and total solutions that would
wipe the slate clean and allow fresh beginnings. Some looked to an
idealized West, to liberalism or pre-Marxian socialism, for their inspiration. Others sought models for their utopias in a no less idealized
Russian past. But both groups, Westerners and Slavophiles, shared a
common disaffection from the present and from those who administered it. The most eminent and gifted of these utopian critics, Alexander Herzen, caught the essence of the schism perfectly when he
called the period of Nicholas I one of outer slavery and inner freedom. The slavery was that of the governing elite, terrified of any
change. The inner freedom was that of the intelligentsia, who thought,
talked, and wrote of nothing but change. It was a boundless, anarch-

ical freedom of mind. Everything was to be decided anew. Nothing could be taken for granted. The moorings in the past had been cut once and for all. The past could give nothing, show no goal, outline no path. What was Russia? Was it of the East? Was it European? Should Western institutions be adamantly rejected, or assimilated whole, or modified to suit inherently Russian attributes? But what were these attributes? Was the peasant commune, for example, a uniquely Russian phenomenon that revealed a uniquely Russian Christian (or socialist) folk spirit or was it simply an archaic institution that all societies share in their early years, and, therefore, a sign of depressing backwardness, not of inspiring potential? And if Russia was to go to school in the West, what should be learned? Political and economic liberalism? Socialism? Catholicism?

Themes such as these—free-floating toward ideal futures, oblivious of the weight of established social forms or the pressure of social inheritance—obsessed the intelligentsia in these years that separated the illusory victory over Napoleon from the all-too-true disaster at Crimea. Fundamentally, the issues merged into a single question that was to be asked repeatedly from that time to the present and that was used as the title of influential books by Herzen, Chernyshevsky and Lenin: *What Is to Be Done?* Here was the ultimate, perhaps the sole, concern of the Russian intelligentsia throughout its long search for a program that would at last pull time together again and thereby end the schism that tore them from their home and wasted their lives in endless, futile anguish.

In his superb memoirs of the decade beginning in 1839, Pavel V. Annenkov has preserved for us the thoughts and moods, the kaleidoscopic shifts of alliances and enmities, the petty failings, and the nobility of this small but vastly influential band of seekers that made this the "extraordinary decade," the period, in Plekhanov's words, "into which converge and from which branch off all currents of Russian social thought." Annenkov was the very close contemporary and intimate friend of those who wrestled so desperately with these "accursed questions." Birth dates are significant here, for at that time a few years one way or the other made all the difference, defined radically opposed styles and sentiments. It is more than coincidence that so many of the new intelligentsia who, to one extent or another, forsook the past and the present in the name of the future were born between 1811 and 1814, in the years of the Napoleonic Wars and the depressing aftermath—V. G. Belinsky (1811), A. I. Herzen (1812), M. A. Bakunin (1814), T. N. Granovsky (1813), N. P. Ogarev (1813), V. P. Botkin (1811), and P.V. Annenkov (1813).

Yet, Annenkov does not really belong to the list. True, he knew the others intimately and he read, thought, and wrote much about the issues that so profoundly disturbed them. But the issues did not disturb him. He seemed, somehow, to remain above it all, to observe and record the passions of others rather than to experience them himself. Belinsky said of him: "He is one of the happiest persons I have ever met, a healthy, integrated nature, not spoiled by that vile intellectualism that has become a sickness in our Moscow circle." "Annenkov has a remarkable characteristic," the memoirist who reported Belinsky's comment went on to add, "no matter what an argument was about, it was absolutely impossible to tell which authorities he agreed with, since he agreed now with one, now with another, and seemed to share the views of whomsoever he was eye to eye with in discussion." Turgenev, Annenkov's closest friend among the eminent men of the period, was similarly bothered by this distressing lack of conviction. "Have you noticed," he once asked, "that you never hear Annenkov stating his own views about anything. He limits himself to agreement. . . . Often, just for fun, I tell him one thing, to which he thoughtfully and solemnly agrees, and then, after a while, something else, to which he also agrees." Turgenev and V. P. Botkin both felt that this showed something of the bureaucrat in Annenkov, although Botkin quickly added that there was really "not a drop" of the bureaucrat in him.

Botkin was certainly right in retracting the comparison, for it is doubtful that Turgenev or any other of the illustrious writers and rebels of the time would have maintained life-long friendship with a bureaucratic yes-man. Something else lay behind this apparent indifference, so strikingly out of place in these decades of fervent, indeed fanatic, dedication to abstract ideas. Belinsky's reference to his "integrated nature" points in the right direction, for Annenkov's sanguine balance really belonged to the preceding period, to the years before time fragmented. It is significant that his one serious contribution to scholarship was editing an edition of Pushkin's works. It was the Pushkin era with which he felt comfortably at home, not the extraordinary decade he portrayed. He was a self-satisfied aristocrat, a connoisseur, amateur and dilettante, in the best sense of those words, one who was passionately absorbed, not in this or that cause or program, but in whatever pleasures and fascination life afforded a well-bred man of independent means, in literature, art, travel, and—as spectator only—in the game of politics.

He was born into a middle-level gentry family with estates in Simbirsk province; he took courses (significantly as an auditor) in humanities at St. Petersburg University; and he dabbled briefly in government service, but soon quit in order " to live the way I want to." From then on he devoted himself to the arts and to the various literary and political (discussion) circles that flourished in Moscow, St. Petersburg, and among Russians abroad, particularly in Paris. He knew everyone—Gogol, Turgenev, Tolstoy, Belinsky, Herzen, Bakunin, Granovsky, and the other leaders of Russian art and thought—and in his incessant trips abroad, lasting for years on end, he developed comparable friendships with eminent European writers and radicals—Marx, George Sand, Heine, Proudhon, Herwegh, Leroux, as examples. Marx clearly saw through Annenkov's attraction to these European radicals: it was simply an "Epicurean" fascination with extremism typical of the aristocracy. This was, of course, as intolerable for dedicated Russian radicals as it was for Marx. The Populist leader, Peter Lavrov, in a stinging article attacking Annenkov, dismissed him as "an aesthetic tourist," one of the sort that "toured the world, took fleeting glances into various social classes, became acquainted with stockbrokers and proletariat, with serious scholars and modish café habitues along Parisien boulevards, with the secretary of Napoleon III and the followers of Garibaldi, and who emerged from all these studies and associations joyful, content, and euphorically optimistic, without a trace of a frown on their face, a care in their heart, or a thought in their head."

What Marx and Lavrov found so objectionable, however, was just what appealed to those who shared Annenkov's cultural and social background. Turgenev, notwithstanding the criticism quoted earlier, considered him "extremely intelligent, with fine, sure taste"; and Leo Tolstoy described him in 1857 as "happy and well, just as intelligent and, even more than before, eager to grasp the living, contemporary quality in everything, fearful of being left behind. It would be really awful for him to be left behind by the times, for it is only in what is contemporary that he unfalteringly believes."

This zest for diverse experiences and this fascination with everything contemporary in the world of culture and politics, combined with an absence of rigid commitments that would have narrowed his range of empathy and perception, made him an ideal biographer of his age. Precisely because he had so few axes of his own to grind, he could freely indulge his pleasure in watching his more impassioned friends grind theirs, usually on each other, and in describing both the objecive spectacle and the subjective thoughts and moods of the combatants. He was, in Turgenev's words, "a master at crystallizing the specific character of a period," at capturing unique traits of personality and subtle combinations or shifts in mind and sentiment. What politics he had were those one would have expected, those of a moderate, prudent liberal. However much he was attracted as a spectator to flamboyant personalities and their radical politics, he would have no radicalism for himself and rejected all extremism, whether that of "vile conservatism" or "barbaric nihilism," to quote Annenkov (1874). Reflecting attitudes prevalent before the schism, before the Westerners who defended the future severed relations from the government, he continued to hope for gradual reforms from above and was, consequently, overjoyed by the Great Reforms of the 1860's. As a result, he found himself more out of place among the middle- and lower-class nihilists, materialists, and revolutionaries of the 1860's and 1870's than he had been, by temperament, among the upper-class radicals of the preceding decades. By this later period, he had come to regard Bakunin's extremism, his penchant for violence and gargantuan destruction, as unbelievably monstrous, to denounce revolutionary Populism, the dominant ideology of the 1860's and 1870's as barbarism, and to help lead the attack against those in the period who would reduce art and literature to forms of social service.

Since these conservative sentiments grew stronger as Annenkov grew older, it is no doubt true, as Soviet critics claim, that by the time Annenkov wrote these memoirs he had lost some of the empathy for radicalism that he had as a younger man. All memoirists suffer fallible memory and the effects of hindsight and altered attitudes, however, and all are, to one degree or another, culpable for the inadvertent distortions these cause. It is significant, moreover, and further testimony to the quality of Annenkov's observations and reflections, that Soviet Russian scholars continue to regard this conservative and "Epicurean" account as among the finest records of this extraordinary decade.

But there is a more fundamental response to Soviet criticism of Annenkov for his portraits of the radicals. In the half-century since the October Revolution, Soviet writers have focused, for obvious reasons, on the most radical tendencies in groups and individuals, and Western scholarship has tended to echo this emphasis. Thus, both inside and outside of Soviet Russia, a vast literature has accumulated around the extremists, while people like Granovsky, Kavelin, Botkin, Ketcher, and Korsh remain virtually unknown. Certainly one of the main contributions of Annenkov's memoirs is to help us gain a more balanced perspective of the period by showing us the views and sentiments of the moderates as well as the less extreme attitudes of the radicals, particularly, in this connection, Belinksy. It is unfortunate that Annenkov did not realize his intentions to write a sequel to these memoirs, one that would cover the following decade. Had he done so, he would have been able to trace the fruitful connection between these moderate liberals and the hopeful reforms of the 1860's in which some of them were to play important roles. It was, finally, this group,

the "party of progress" as Annenkov calls it, that through collaboration on the Great Reforms of Alexander II came nearest to ending the
fateful schism that divorced the intelligentsia from the governing elite.

Annenkov began his reminiscences of the "extraordinary decade"
in the fall of 1875, although preliminary work on them was begun at the
time of Herzen's death, in 1870. The memoirs were first published in
the liberal periodical *Vestnik Evropy* (*Herald of Europe*), Nos. 1–5
(1880). Both in this first publication and in Annenkov's *Memoirs and
Critical Sketches,* published in 1881, Chapters XXI and XXII are missing. Judging from the context of the concluding paragraphs in Chapter XX, the missing chapters, assuming they were indeed written or
planned, concerned the Natural or Gogol School of Russian literature.
The two Soviet editions used in this translation, those published in
1928 and 1960, retain the original chapter numbers, with the lacunae,
and this has been the policy in the present volume. The concluding
section of this volume, "Two Winters in the Provinces and the Country," contains a sketch of the first part of what Annenkov hoped would
be the volume covering the years 1849–58, "the second extraordinary
epoch" of Russian literary history, as he described these years. The
sketch was first published in *Byloe* (*The Past*), No. 18 (1922).

Translator's Note

A translator of Russian expository prose of the second half of the nineteenth century faces the fact that such writing, generally speaking, is characterized by a certain chronic inelegance and a tendency to turn ponderous or obscure. P. V. Annenkov's *Memoirs* fall wholly under the rule, and not among the exceptions, of this writing tradition. It must be remembered, however, that this was the style *par excellence* of the Extraordinary Decade itself and bore the authority of V. G. Belinsky, whose own writing practice first popularized or even "canonized" it. Annenkov's *Memoirs*, written more than twenty years after Belinsky's death, vividly testify to the strength and durablity of that authority.

It would be presumptuous, to say the very least, to attempt, in translation, to gloss over or edit away the characteristic features of that style for the sake of greater smoothness and readability. Instead, the translation offered here endeavors expressly to represent the Russian text with all its original features intact, insofar as it is possible to do so in English. The honesty of that intention does not, of course, automatically guarantee accuracy, but the interests of accuracy, I believe, *are* served thereby.

I should like to express my deep appreciation to Professor Gleb Struve of The University of California, Berkeley, for his kind help in elucidating for me a number of puzzles and byways in the Russian text. Professor Arthur Mendel, the editor of this volume, read the whole of the manuscript and I am very indebted to him for innumerable suggestions and corrections. Needless to say, any errors that might still be found in the translation, any misconstructions or stylistic faults not traceable to the original, are entirely the responsibility of the translator.

I should also like to acknowledge the aid rendered me by a grant from the Faculty Research Fund of the Horace H. Rackham School of Graduate Studies of The University of Michigan for the preparation of the typescript.

The Russian text used for translation was the most recent edition of P. V. Annenkov's memoirs, *Literaturnye vospominaniya* (Moscow, 1960), under the editorship of V. P. Dorofeev. B. M. Eykhenbaum's edition under the same title (Leningrad, 1928) was consulted, as were earlier editions and printings of Annenkov's works. Russian words and names appearing in the translation have been transliterated according to the popular system now commonly used in nonspecialized publications; exception, as customary, was made in the case of well-known Russian names of foreign origin which are spelled in their original, foreign form (e. g., *Herzen* instead of *Gertsen,* Alexander instead of Aleksandr, and Nicholas in reference to the Emperor Nicholas I). A list of translated titles of Russian periodical publications mentioned throughout the text and their corresponding Russian originals is appended below.

I. R. Titunik

Translations of Names of Journals

Athenaeum—*Ateney*
Colloquium—*Beseda*
Contemporary—*Sovremennik*
Library for Reading—*Biblioteka Dlya Chteniya*
Lighthouse—*Mayak*
Literary Supplements to the Russian Invalid—*Literaturnye Pribavleniya k Russkomu Invalidu*
Moscow Miscellany—*Moskovsky Sbornik*
Moscow News—*Moskovskie Vedomosti*
Moscow Observer—*Moskovsky Nablyudatel*
Moscow Telegraph—*Moskovsky Telegraf*
Muscovite—*Moskvityanin*
Northern Bee—*Severnaya Pchela*
Notes of the Fatherland—*Otechestvennye Zapiski*
Police News—*Politseyskie Vedomosti*
Report—*Molva*
Russian Herald—*Russky Vestnik*
Simbirsk Miscellany—*Simbirsky Sbornik*
Son of the Fatherland—*Syn Otechestva*
Telescope—*Teleskop*

Contents

CHAPTER

[I]

IT WAS IN THE FALL OF 1839, a year before I left to go abroad, that I made the acquaintance of Vissarion Grigorevich Belinsky.[1] He had by that time come to Petersburg, brought from Moscow by I. I. Panaev,[2] to work on *Notes of the Fatherland;* his career was then already in the second or third stage of its development.

Belinsky made his professional debut, as is common knowledge, with an article bearing the title "Literary Reveries—An Elegy in Prose," published in the *Report* in 1834.[3] This article, a survey of Russian literature, attracted attention owing to the verve with which it was written and the way it characterized periods and personalities, making them quite unlike their usual and, so to speak, canonical presentation in our literature courses. The lyrical tone of the article plus a philosophical coloring borrowed from Schelling's system gave it particular originality. It was all youth, daring, fervor, as well as full of blunders which the author himself subsequently acknowledged. But everything about it did reveal the fact that new intellectual demands on Russian literature and on Russian life in general had arisen. Old Kachenovsky [4]—no doubt captivated by the critic's free and easy treatment of authorities and his frequent digressions into the realm of history and philosophy—the old professor summoned Belinsky—a student only very recently expelled for substandard abilities, as the University council phrased it—shook his hand warmly and said, "We didn't think like that, we didn't write like that in my day." [5]

Of course, the article made less of a stir in Petersburg, where the notorious saturnalias of the recently founded *Library for Reading,*[6] with its mockery of learning and conviction of any sort, were already coming to a head. But even in Petersburg the article did not pass without notice. Precisely at that time, N. P. Grech,[7] being a man more endowed with a sense of decency than were his brother literary journalists of the period, arrived at a way of regarding Belinsky which was still comparatively favorable. To these views he gave utterance publicly on numerous occasions: "An intelligent fellow but a confirmed drunkard, and he writes his articles without sobering up." Belinsky the drunkard was about as conceivable as Lessing on a tightrope or something of the sort. At the very same time, F. V. Bulgarin,[8] who, as his contribution, dubbed Belinsky "the bulldog," began his seemingly endless diatribe on intellectual perversion, his nearly twenty-year long assault on the new spirit in literature threatening Russia, to the shame of her descendants and to her disgrace before Europe, with the loss of all her intellectual treasures.[9]

Still, however provocative Belinsky's article may have been in the way it was composed, especially for the self-proclaimed notables of Petersburg—whom the critic, on his own admission, found it *indescribable bliss* and *boundless delight* to expose and humiliate—the article did not actually strike out at a single one of our old authorities, maintaining for them an attitude of the highest enthusiasm throughout. The boldness of the article consisted not so much in its investigations as in the principles and postulates to which the critic gave voice and which underlay his investigations. The article tended, rather, to place persons and things under threat of exposure, making good that threat with respect only to a very few of them.

Belinsky had not yet introduced the slightest discord into that young circle,[10] founded in the shadow of Moscow University in the early 1830's, from which were to emerge the most extraordinary personalities of the years following. The germs of disparate and antagonistic views were already present in the circle, as the list of names composing its membership readily proves (K. Aksakov,[11] Stankevich, *et al.*), but these germs had not yet become active, remaining latent, for the time being, behind a friendly exchange of ideas and an identity of scientific purpose. One need only recall that K. S. Aksakov was at that time a philosopher in the German style no less than was Stankevich; that P. Kireevsky [12] was as avid a European and Westerner as was T. N. Granovsky; [13] that the latter, who joined the circle soon after having collaborated on Senkowski's *Library for Reading*, shared with them all a poetic outlook on Russia's past and present.

Belinsky, later on to contribute so much toward effecting a dissolution of the circle into its component parts, toward a delimitation and definition of factions which issued from it, was in these early stages still just an echo of all the views, judgements, and criticisms existing at the core of the circle and existing without the slightest suspicion of their disparity and incompatibility. That is why Belinsky's ecstatic article, with its distinctive erraticalness, its tendency to fly off in all directions, and lack of central focus, could constitute a mixture, still unconscious, of states of mind having the least possible affinity with and resemblance to one another. A purely Slavophile idea and an idea of a purely Western variety advanced side by side; the aphorisms of our skeptical historical school of those days jostled against hyperboles worthy of Sergey Glinka [14] in his most exalted moments of patriotic rapture; liberalism and conservative doctrine (if one can use these terms when dealing with an era ignorant of the very things the terms designate) alternated raising their voices, not the least bit uneasy about being neighbors. As an example, it is enough to make mention of certain of the article's theses to show how our fledgling critic could at that time stand simultaneously both for Peter I's reforms and for the Muscovite opposition to those reforms.

For the Belinsky of 1834 the significance of folk customs and their staunch preservation in the ethnic milieu still constituted a matter of the first importance, and precisely the same kind of importance as they subsequently were for the most rabid of the young critic's opponents from the Slavic party. He was inclined to find, as did the latter, glimmers of poetry in simple and rude folkways, merely qualifying the life they created as, albeit indigenous and true to character, still one-sided and isolated. On the other hand, the future Slavophiles apparently fully shared at that time an opinion of Belinsky's, namely, that Peter the Great was absolutely right in his reforms and not one bit less national-spirited than any Muscovite tsar of olden times. Particularly characteristic of this duality is that passage in his article where, while shifting to a position in favor of the great reformer, Belinsky first, nevertheless, addresses a doleful apostrophe of farewell to the olden ways in their demise. And he does this, moreover, in words and images that for us now, with our definitive picture of Belinsky's personality, constitute something of an unbelievable and spurious characteristic, distorting his true visage. "Hence venerable flowing beards!" he wrote. "Farewell also to you, simple and noble bowl-shaped cut of hair, so suited to those estimable beards! You have been replaced by flour-dusted wigs! . . . Farewell to you, also, comely and poetic *sarafan*, mantle of our noble dames and damsels, and to you, muslin tunic, with your sumptuous sleeves, and to you, *povoynik*, high-peaked and pearl-strung tiara—simple, enchanting costume so becoming to the high bosoms and rosy-red cheeks of our fair-faced and dove-eyed beauties. . . . Farewell also to you, heart-rending Russian songs, and to you, noble and graceful dance: no more will be heard the cooing of our fair maids, our turtle doves. . . ." It was from such beginnings that a Belinsky was emerging.

The liberalism of the amorphous circle of friends was also represented in the article, and represented quite fully by the proposition ly-

ing at its very basis, according to which our literature was a matter of
the chance emergence and conjunction of a few people, some more,
some less talented, of whom society had no special need and who
themselves could get along materially and morally without society.
The consequences were a paltry literature and debilitated writers, no
matter what their merits, talents and zeal. One may surmise that, in
addition, the European idea of the importance for the state of the
bourgeoisie and the *tiers-état* had successful currency in the circle,
seeing that Belinsky, searching among the diverse classes of our country for people whose enterprise could reconcile European enlightenment with the fundamental bases of Russian national life, designated
for this role the clergy, the merchant class, the urban dwellers, the art-
isans, and even the small businessmen and manufacturers.[15] However,
immediately thereupon he made a qualification, in the face of possible
objections from the opposite point of view, to the effect that "the
highest life of a people expresses itself preeminently in its upper strata
or, *what is most likely the real truth, in the whole idea of a people.*"

In short, Belinsky's famous first article, his maiden speech, perfectly expressed the intellectual condition of the young people of the
time, in whom trends of every description lived at close quarters with
one another as if in some primordial paradise, seeing no cause for dis-
association and having no apprehensions about their mutual cordiality
and intimacy. The bond uniting them was an identical love of learning, of the world, of free thought, of homeland. Their condition may
be likened to a sizable natural reservoir in which the waters of future
rivers mingle peacefully together until such time as a geological upheaval divides them and channels them off in opposite directions. Belinsky was precisely the subterranean blaze that hastened an upheaval.

I shouldn't wonder that it has occurred to someone to ask: Is it
worthwhile to dwell at such length on a mere journal article, one not
entirely free of contradictions and one, furthermore, containing definitions which the author himself later repudiated? The question is easily
dismissed when we call to mind the fact that the article made an extraordinary impression as a first attempt to include the cultural history
of our society in the evaluating of literary periods. Need we mention
how it was received by the young minds of Petersburg attempting to
preserve themselves in the face of the *conspiracy* against literature being hatched before their very eyes?[16] For them the article did away
with a great number of convictions and notions derived from their
school days. That the article had, in this regard, an aspect of protest
was plain to see, not only for the coryphaei of the *Library for Reading*
party, of whom we have already spoken, but also for people inclined

to agree with many of its theses but loath to see traditions unceremoniously challenged, and challenged, what is more, on the grounds of alien philosophical systems. Among such people were Pushkin and Gogol.

Both Pushkin and Gogol were regarded with extreme favor by the critic, but they maintained an obstinate silence about him practically throughout their lives. The former, as reported by Belinsky himself, merely secretly sent him issues of his *Contemporary* [17] and remarked about him: "That strange fellow for some reason is very fond of me." [18] I myself heard the latter's judgement: "His is no ordinary head, but it always has this way about it that the sounder its first thought, the sillier its second." The remark had to do with conclusions Belinsky drew from his aesthetic and philosophical principles and the application of those conclusions directly and without qualification to facts and personages of Russian origin. Yet, later on, this very same Gogol referred to Belinsky's articles about his (Gogol's) own work as articles exemplary for their compelling truth and masterly exposition.

In Petersburg, to resume, Belinsky's first article and the articles that followed it found a most emphatic response among the young teachers of Russian language and literature assembled in the capital for the state-run boarding schools and military academies (which were expanding, in accordance with the system adopted, more and more into special educational institutions for the entire *well-born* Russian youth). No claim is being made that the article in the *Report* instantly revoked the official doctrine on literature: the latter persisted for a long while and still figured prominently on examinations straight up to the time the boarding schools and military academies were reformed. Nevertheless, owing to the young teachers of these institutions and, next to them, teachers of the majority of our secondary schools, it did happen, once Belinsky's articles began to appear, that alongside the approved program of teaching Russian literature there took shape another, inconspicuous current of teaching which stemmed in its entirety from the definitions and outlook of the new critic and which relentlessly washed away from young minds everything that scholasticism, pedantry, rote, antique traditions and well-meaning exaggeration had caused to lodge there. The vitalizing effect of this inconspicuous current increased with the further progress made by the critic, who, it can be said, was held in constant focus by these teachers and young people in general during this period. As a result, Belinsky's name was already a byword among the up-and-coming generation, in the schools and in the lecture halls, before it was even recognized among the literary factions, before it had been endorsed for pure or ulterior motives by some and had provoked the contemptuous retorts of others, before it had so much as attracted the notice of even the most vigilant guardians of Russia's intellectual life.

Belinsky's work, the work of his thought inspired to seek constantly ideals of morality and the grand philosophical solution to life's problems—this work went on without abating while he himself was modestly numbered among the second-rate Russian writers and journalists under the eyes of the censors. For the Bureau of Censorship of the time, the only first-rate writers long remained the editors Senkowski, Grech, and Bulgarin exclusively, though Pushkin and Gogol were far too prominent not to constitute an exception. It must be accounted a piece of extreme good fortune that the censors of the day missed seeing in the Belinsky of those early stages a moral philosopher who, under pretext of analyzing works of Russian literature, was concerned exclusively with attempts to discover sound conceptual bases on which a rationally ordered personal and social existence could be built. Later the censors did recognize in him an influential writer and tried in every way to prevent application of his ideas to historical personages and to the contemporary scene, but even with such an understanding of Belinsky's activity, they still continued, to a certain extent, to regard him as—echoing the *Northern Bee* [19]—a man who was turning out predominantly abstruse and obscure inanities, tolerable by virtue of their bizarre originality, and the more innocuous, the greater the force and detail with which they were expressed. It is to this state of affairs that we owe the preservation of certain central theses and ideas of Belinsky's which reached the light of day under the name of monstrosities and absurdities. This same state of affairs does much to elucidate subsequent features in the life of our society that might otherwise appear curious, unforeseen, and unexpected surprises.

CHAPTER

[II]

I CAME IN CONTACT with Belinsky for the first time at the home of A. A. Komarov,[20] a teacher of Russian literature with the Second Cadet Corps School. Komarov occupied quarters within the corps' buildings.

As I have already said, Belinsky's arrival in Petersburg had special significance for a small circle of young people who saw in the literary triumvirate of O. I. Senkowski, N. P. Grech, and F. V. Bulgarin (which rose upon the rich soil of Smirdin's [21] capital, ultimately exhausting it) something like an incarnation of surreptitious scorn for the cause of education on Russian native soil, a model of cunning, calculating, but limited, practical sagacity and, finally, an ingenious scheme of using good intentions and patriotism to dupe people who could not be duped in any other way. One must avow that this three-handed enterprise was carried on with extraordinary skill. Senkowski's inexhaustible wit, often apt and almost always caustic, endeavored, at the same time that it mocked Russian quasi-science, to preclude any serious attempt at independent work and to poison with ridicule the sources to which that work might have recourse. Grech spread the word about depravity of mind and conscience in Europe, while sentimentalizing over the spectacle of moral salubrity that obtained in our country. His colleague, meanwhile, relentlessly called attention to those subtle effluvia of poison and venom which, despite the efforts of the triumvirate, were nevertheless finding their way through to us from abroad and were corrupting the public's judgments about Russian writers and men active in Russian affairs generally.

It is a remarkable fact that these worthies of Petersburg journalism in the 1830's did, on occasion, quarrel among themselves, without reaching the point of open dissension, however. They quarreled over the right to patronize writers, each of them desiring to have patronage exclusively in his own hands. Patronage had become the basic motif in

7

criticism, the guide lines for evaluating men and works. Patronage distributed positions in literature in exactly the same way as it did in the government administration: it promoted to the rank and title of "talents" people such as Messrs Masalsky, Stepanov, Timofeev, *et al.*, and several times even saw fit simply to appoint "geniuses," as was done, for example, with Kukolnikov [22] and "Baron Brambeus." [23] It is hard for the present generation to comprehend the degree of indignation which the organs of this self-appointed custodianship over literature aroused in people who wanted to preserve some semblance of freedom and human dignity, at least in this sector of social life.

With no recourse to social or political interests, to combat the triumvirate became virtually a matter of honor: according to whether a person was well or ill disposed toward the triumvirate, so would the young people of certain circles—very limited in number, to be sure—ascertain his moral qualities. Enmity toward the triumvirate further intensified when practical consequences brought to light a ruling, made at about that same time, to forbid rivalry among journals and to tolerate only already existing publications. This turned the organs of the triumvirs into the equivalent of our present-day railroad concessions with their *government guarantees*.

Belinsky's arrival was, as I have stated, particularly important in that it signaled a new attempt at combating the literary concessionaires after three other attempts had failed. Two attempts had been made in Moscow in 1835—the earlier one undertaken by the *Telescope* [24] and the later one by the *Moscow Observer*,[25] a journal actually founded precisely for that purpose.[26] Pushkin's *Contemporary*, in Petersburg, was responsible for making the third attempt, which also was unsuccessful.[27] With the new regulation on journals in force, all campaigns against the monopolists of public opinion, it seemed, had to come to a halt. This regulation greatly resembled a later ruling with regard to the Raskolniki [28] which allowed them to keep their old chapels and oratories but strictly forbid them to erect new ones nearby. However, it differed from that ruling inasmuch as the Bureau of Censorship of those days did concede the possibility of allowing official renovation of old literary chapels—something the Raskolniki could not do with theirs other than by clandestine measures or through bribery.

It was at this time that A. A. Kraevsky,[29] still a comparatively young man, exerted every effort to win the chance of clearing a place for himself within the ranks of the journalist-concessionaires of the period; and he did this, one must acknowledge, not merely because of the obvious material advantages but also out of moral promptings—to set in opposition to an evil armed force another force, likewise armed, but founded on different principles and with different aims. He set about on a thoroughgoing search with truly remarkable persistence, tenacity, and resolution to find himself a position as editor. The fruit of his efforts was the appearance under his editorship, first of all, of *Literary Supplements to the Russian Invalid* (the license to publish was obtained by the then notable Plyushar from that rather petty, sly and stingy old man, Voeykov), a journal to which Belinsky contributed, as we know. Later, in 1838, A. A. Kraevsky discovered *Notes of the Fatherland* and bought up the rights to renew publication from the well-known P. Svinin,[30] now dealing directly in his own name. Upon coming to terms with Svinin, but without yet leaving the *Supplements*, Kraevsky announced the appearance of his new-old journal, which shortly thereafter did become genuinely his own. The rallying cry he then sounded, with the approval of the most respected members of the Petersburg literary world, to all who had not yet fallen beneath the ignominious yoke of the feudal lords of journalism, was distinguished by a combination of unerring shrewdness and indications of complete sincerity and integrity of purpose. "Should this new effort," the new editor declared to his supporters, "to oppose the entrenchment of the Smirdin clique also fail, then all that will remain for us to do is to resign ourselves and proclaim its triumph."

Poor A. F. Smirdin could hardly have imagined that he was to give his name as an appellation for a far from dignified literary period. An honest, kind, guileless man, though without any education, he had come unexpectedly into the bookseller Plavilshchikov's rather substantial fortune and had taken a fancy to the role of a moving force behind contemporary letters and learning. He had also been prompted to precisely this whim, it appears, by the Petersburg journalists who had purposely won over the ambitious businessman for their own ends. Cowed by their authority, the bookseller-Maecenas looked upon the world with their eyes, lavished money at their advice, and in the speech of his class and trade referred to any initiative, any talent failing to seek the protection of the triumvirs with the words: "They're the gentlemen that mean us no good!" But what was done to him by those well-meaning gentlemen of his, who later managed to ruin yet another, similarly improvised, moving force behind Russian learning—the bookseller Plyushar, editor of the *Encyclopedic Dictionary*—that is something almost beyond belief.

I myself heard from Smirdin's own lips, in that period of his life when he was already an impoverished and saddened old man, the story of his undertaking, on Bulgarin's advice, to bring out a work entitled, I believe, "An Illustrated Journey Through Russia." The text was to be written by the author of *Ivan Vyzhigin*, who made himself also responsible for ordering the engravings from London. A formal contract to this effect was signed between them, Smirdin agreeing to allot 30,000 rubles for the project. The pictures were long in coming, and when they did arrive, Smirdin saw with horror that they consisted of shoddy engravings produced, not in London, but in Leipzig. To Smirdin's bitter complaints about the contract's having been violated Bulgarin replied that there was no question of any violation since the contract merely stated: order abroad. The trap had been crudely and brazenly fashioned, but the bookseller had fallen into it. When Smirden related this incident to me, his tired and enflamed eyes filled with tears, his voice began to tremble—"I am going to write my memoirs," he muttered, "I am going to write 'Memoirs of a Bookseller'!"

As the first, enormous issue of *Notes of the Fatherland* (1839) proved, the galvanizing effect of that new rallying cry brought together under the banner of the rehabilitated journal many new and old forces that had been shunning literature. The issue was filled with articles remarkable for the time, and all from the pen of either well-established or novice writers. Rich and poor undertook to work for Kraevsky's journal almost entirely without remuneration or for piddling remuneration, if only they could furnish the editor the means to carry on the struggle against the capitalists who had taken over literary affairs. This situation lasted somewhat longer than might have seemed necessary, as some people felt afterward; but that is a matter of suppositions which must remain suppositions and about which there is nothing more one can say. However, a story which circulated throughout the city at the time is curious. F. V. Bulgarin, by dint of his instinct for self-preservation, soon surmised the new power which had appeared in journalism with the coming out of *Notes of the Fatherland* and the danger which threatened the authority of the captains of the press, should that power turn decisively against them. At a meeting with the editor of the new journal, F. V. Bulgarin made him the proposal pure and simple that he join the coalition of journalist-magnates and *direct* the affairs of literature in common with them. This proposal, needless to say, was turned down by its addressee.

To return to the matter at hand, it should be noted that successive issues of the journal displayed, as did the first, many superb verses, competent articles, and even intelligent critical reviews. Yet, there was nothing to be discovered in its editorial policy tantamount to clear-cut precepts, to literary standpoints and trends, for which no sheer skill in running a journal and rallying supporters, no sheer hard work or even implacable hatred for enemies, could successfully compensate. With *Notes of the Fatherland* Petersburg found itself in possession of a magnificent depository for articles and belles lettres but with no program or doctrine which could oppose the depraved creed of the directors of *Library for Reading* and the *Northern Bee*.

The only recourse was to look to Moscow, which indeed was the center of upcoming forces and talents, where people pored over philosophical systems in the search precisely for *principles* and did not balk at the trenchant tone of polemics or even an abstract and abstruse style of speech, provided only they could give their thoughts and accrued conviction full expression. The story goes that, when I. I. Panaev proposed the name of Belinsky, Kraevsky failed to recognize in him the man who was to lay the foundation of his importance to society.[31] Circumstances dictated, nevertheless, that he turn to Belinsky. When, after preliminary negotiations, expedited considerably by the fact that, having left the *Moscow Observer* in 1838, Vissarion Grigorevich no longer had an outlet for his work or means to support himself, when, we said, the critic did appear in Petersburg in 1839 to live there and to work on Kraevsky's journal, there was a general feeling of expectation within the circle of opponents to the Petersburg trend that, with Belinsky, dynamic thought had appeared on the scene, and an arm strong enough to demolish or, at least, to weaken the coalition of literary entrepreneurs who fundamentally despised Russian society with all its ambitions and hopes, and with its express intent to work out its own spiritual life.

CHAPTER

[III]

UNDER THE EFFECT of the impassioned tone of his philosophical articles and, especially, the ardor of his polemics, one could be excused for imagining Belinsky a man of categorical opinions who tolerated no objections and who relished lording it over everything and everybody in conversations. I was, I confess, astonished when, at that evening get-together at A. A. Komarov's, I had pointed out to me as the bearer of the name Belinsky a man of small stature, stoop-shouldered, with sunken chest and rather large, pensive eyes, who very modestly, simply, and in a kind of spontaneously intimate way responded to the greetings of people being newly introduced to him. Needless to say, I did not find the slightest sign of any awesomeness, affectation, or dictatorial temperament such as I had feared. On the contrary, one could discern signs of timidity and shyness in Belinsky, but of a kind not the least bit evocative of any condescending aid or rash solicitude on the part of some overanxious sympathizer. It was obvious that underneath that exterior lived a proud and indomitable nature which could at any moment burst forth. Altogether, Belinsky's awkwardness, his habit of becoming tongue-tied and flustered when meeting strangers—things at which Belinsky himself laughed so much—had, as did his whole person altogether, much that was expressive and engaging about them: behind them shone the steady glow of his noble, integrated, and independent character.

We had been regaled with stories about Belinsky's transports and outbursts of feeling, but he gave vent to no outbursts, no transports, that first evening of my acquaintance with him at any rate. He was subdued, preoccupied and—what particularly struck me—unhappy. Judging the impressions I felt at that first meeting in the light of all that has been learned and discussed since, I can assert with complete confidence that all Belinsky's thought and conversation were still cast over with the romantic-philosophical attitude of mind to which he had submitted in 1835 and persistently adhered over the course of four years, despite his exchanging Schelling for Hegel in 1836–37, despite bidding a final farewell to illusions concerning the unique beauty of the old Russian way of life or, more generally, simple, unaffected life, and despite turning to the worship of "Reason in Reality." He was now living out the last days of that romantic-philosophical attitude of mind.

On the evening described, a conversation was struck up about a certain burlesque tale in the Hoffmann manner, then circulating in manuscript, written by several collaborators during their get-togethers, for amusement's sake and as a way of killing time. "Be that as it may," remarked Belinsky, "still, Hoffmann is a great name. I fail to understand why it is that Europe has yet to rank Hoffmann together with Shakespeare and Goethe. They are writers of the same power and category." This assertion and others like it were part of what Belinsky had inherited and retained from the period of his Schellingian outlook, an outlook which held, as we know, that the external world was a component of the grand evolutions of the Absolute Idea, expressing in each manifestation of its own the moment and stage of development of that Idea. Therefore, the fantastic element of Hoffmann's stories seemed to Belinsky a particle of revelation or disclosure of the omnific Absolute Idea, and had for him exactly the same quality of realness as did, for instance, an accurate depiction of character or a report of any real-life occurrence.

During the period described, Belinsky was already wholly under the sway of Hegel and had fully possessed himself of the idealistic manner of construing the phenomena of the surrounding world, people, and events, as a result of which the latter two were almost always imbued on his lips with a certain grandiose aura, often entirely out of keeping with their actual merits. Petty and practical-minded explanations of any fact or question standing out, however slightly, from the ordinary run of things disgusted him, and it was only by adopting a special attitude, which he purposely made the effort to do in Petersburg, that he was able to bring himself to abide them at all. He had, of course, relinquished his former, indeed quite recent, ecstatic credo concerning "the great mysteries of life" *without apprehension and ascertainment of which man's existence would become,* as he had maintained, *not merely insipid, but positively the greatest calamity imaginable for the earthborn.* Yet, despite this change, our Russian world, our contemporary life, even certain of its particularities could not otherwise find reflection in his mind than in weighty images, in sweeping generalizations which amazed and fascinated his new listeners. On the whole, the roots of all the old doctrines and ways of thinking through which he had passed remained covertly alive in him after his arrival in Petersburg, were liable, on any provocation, to sprout and put forth shoots and did at times come openly alive, blossoming in full flower. This, in the milieu of the mundane circle of Belinsky's Petersburg acquaintances, comprised his greatest originality and, concomitantly, his irresistible power of attraction.

An outstanding and exciting event of the time was the appearance of Pushkin's posthumous works, which the *Contemporary* (now in the hands of P. A. Pletnev) [32] published in installments from 1838 to 1839. They—these marvellous works—found in Belinsky an enthusiast, as one might put it, and connoisseur such as had never before fallen to the lot of our great poet. This was not the same Belinsky who some two years earlier, still during Pushkin's lifetime, had considered the poet's career definitively culminated, and who, notwithstanding his recognition of the imprint of Pushkin's genius on his latest works, declared them all to be something less than might have been expected from his pen. Now, however, it was a case of homage without reservation, almost prostration in the dust before the divinity of Poetry Revealed and before the artist who had summoned it forth. An overwhelming impression had been made on Belinsky by Pushkin's "Stone Guest" in particular. He proclaimed it a universal and incalculably prodigious work. When we once asked him to elucidate wherein the universal significance of this creation of Pushkin's lay and what he found in it beside exquisite imagery, poetically realized characters, and amazingly simple handling of very profound drama, Belinsky undertook to elaborate the notion that all such things comprise merely the work's external excellence, whereas the subterranean springs running underneath it were far more important than its beauty, which everyone could see and feel. He undertook an inquiry into these vital well-springs but faltered on the very first steps of the argument and exclaimed in embarrassment: "That's just the sort of thing that always happens to me! I get a grip on something, get carried away God knows where, and get stumped. I don't know how to express my idea, though the idea is absolutely clear for me, just the same." He threw up his hands and walked away, his face expressing pain or anguish. It was apparent that Pushkin's drama contained for him a new revelation of the "mysteries of life," an emanation of one of the "substances"—as they used to say those days—of the human spirit. But Belinsky was unable or unwilling to enlarge on these topics before a circle of people ill-prepared to understand abstractions and not notably inclined to "philosophize."

On my third or fourth meeting with Belinsky, I became aware of that particular good-natured humor of his, brought on sometimes by the most trivial, even banal, sallies of his companions (something that a little surprised me at first), which was always connected in him with a kind of innocuous, almost tender ridicule, with a gentle irony directed at himself and at those around him. For all that, Belinsky's humorous mood of those days was pierced through with a constant and irrepressible strain of melancholy. He was sad, and not merely on occasion, but somehow deep down, at heart. It required no especially perceptive observer or especially adept psychologist to detect this strain in him; it struck one squarely between the eyes. And there was ample reason why this should be so. Belinsky was experiencing the distress of his break with his Moscow friends which had come into the open only just on the eve of his departure from Moscow, and he must have been feeling the bitterness of that circumstance all the more keenly now that he found himself far away from home, in an unfamiliar and inhospitable city.

People quite unjustly supposed, and still do suppose, that Belinsky thought nothing of parting company and altering relationships on the basis of a difference of conviction. At the time, it was popularly held and very nearly stated in print that he even found a certain benefit in doing so, inasmuch as each such change of position enabled him to give vent to his spleen, to vicious instincts, to a propensity to revile and offend that might otherwise have suffocated him! I can say, on the contrary, that rarely have I met people who would have suffered more than Belinsky, being compelled by consequence of the irrevocable, logical, and dialectical development of their principles to forsake former confederates in thought and strike off in another direction. Belinsky suffered prolonged torment over the loss of his old associates just as he did over the loss of his old way of thinking. And it was only when he was firmly convinced of the strict validity of his change of position that he freed himself of all anxieties and took on new character, namely, that of anger and indignation against those who held up his progress and importuned his attention to no purpose.

The first attempt to treat the constituents of the Moscow intellectual circle critically and to subject the circle to an analysis that would have the result of sorting out the diverse elements composing it was laid down, as is well known, by Belinsky in an article printed in the *Telescope* of 1836, under the title "On the Literary Criticism and Views of the *Moscow Observer*." As a polemic, this article belongs among the masterpieces of the author; with respect to the vividness of its colors and the high relief of its conclusions, it has not lost, we believe, a certain degree of interest even today. The whole article was directed aaginst the chief critic of the *Moscow Observer*, S. P. Shevyrev.[33] Belinsky inquired of Shevyrev what it was he believed in, what laws of creativity, what basic philosophical-aesthetic or ethical ideas he professed, and, in the course of this questioning, revealed Shevyrev's dilettantism with regard to all theories of art and his habit of improvising laws and rules of taste in order to justify his own personal tastes, to gratify a few select bosom friends of his, and to map out society's goals in terms of his own random and ephemeral impressions. Belinsky took particular exception to the critic's views on the importance of the *genteel* and *feminine genteel* element in literature which supposedly could elevate literature's tone and even make the lives of the authors themselves more refined. "Artistic and *genteel*," retorted Belinsky, "are not synonyms, as is equally true of 'nobleman' and 'noble man.' Artistry is something accessible to people of all classes, of all stations in life, provided only they have intelligence and feeling; gentility is the property of caste. . . . Gentility has some coincidence with education of the kind which consists in knowing a little bit about everything, but it can never coincide with science and creativity," etc. All in all, the article was one of those customarily written to break off old ties and allegiances and to seek out new ones. Of special importance in it for us are its somber concluding lines: "What is most exasperating is that people here are still unable to view a man's thought apart from the man himself, to conceive of a man losing his time, ruining his health, and *making enemies* out of fidelity to a deeply felt opinion, out of love for an abstract idea instead of one of importance in his practical life. But what is the use!" He brings this thought to a close with the exclamation: "But if you are a person susceptible of thinking and holding convictions, go forward, and may you not be swerved from your path either by the reckonings of self-interest, or by considerations of personal or social life, or by fear of popular disdain, or by the seductions of people's perfidious friendship intent on depriving you, in exchange for their paltry offerings, of your most precious treasure—independence of mind and pure love of truth!"

Unless we are utterly mistaken, a profound and sincere cry of pain, uttered by a soul on the verge of losing certain of its sympathies and beliefs, is distinctly heard in the solemn tone of that passage. Belinsky's words also held a prophecy. His forebodings did not deceive him. Breaking off with Shevyrev and his party had seemed to him, not without good reason, an act of courage: from that moment up to and including the present time, Belinsky incurred the reputation, in certain circles, of an irresponsible vilifier of all that was held in respect and esteem on Russian soil; and attempts to sustain this alleged reputation of Belinsky for posterity are still repeated from time to time even in our very midst.

Beside the article which gave powerful impetus to the dissolution of the placidly flourishing community of friends of science and learning, there were at the same time many other occasions where Belinsky openly invited battle and enemies. For instance, he did not hesitate to call Pushkin's *Contemporary,* from its second issue on, "The St. Petersburg *Moscow Observer,*" having detected in its tendency (correctly or not is another matter) a covert intention of finding its readers and connoisseurs within a single, exclusively genteel circle. We recall that Belinsky's polemic with the *Contemporary* produced, in its time, almost as great an outburst of protest and indignation as did a comment of his made somewhat later and drawn from a different set of ideas. In "On the Tales of Gogol"—the article I have in mind—Belinsky proffered the thought, which he was not even the first to express, that all ancient and modern epic poems patterned after the *Iliad,* such as the *Aeneid, Jerusalem Liberated, Paradise Lost,* the *Russiad,* and the like, wherein live, genuine folk traditions and conceptions are replaced by others cleverly fabricated to imitate them, belonged to a specious kind of literature. No words can express the horror of our former pedagogical world for whom this comment appeared the epitome of unpardonable ignorance and a heresy beyond anything imaginable.

Thus, our critic propagated and surrounded himself with enemies whose numbers multiplied practically with each new comment of his about our writers of the past that differed from traditional conceptions. Bulgarin, a venal specimen of those whose displeasure Belinsky incurred, remarked in the *Northern Bee* that, with the way of reasoning he had discovered, Belinsky would have no trouble proving any proposition whatsoever, including the following: *"Treason is not a bad thing, it is even something laudable."* Making accusations which had at that time almost the character of a criminal indictment and drawing particularly on Belinsky's critiques of Derzhavin, Karamzin, Zhukovsky, and Batyushkov,[34] Bulgarian proceeded to upbraid the critic for possessing the same feelings as were harbored against Russia by "envious foreigners, renegades, *beardless* youths and the like." That is how the literary argument was formulated from the very start and how it was carried on to a certain extent—in this instance, with less brazenness, of course—even by people totally unlike Bulgarin and his ilk.

Things had become even more serious now in view of Belinsky's having fallen out with that circle of people to which he had wholeheartedly belonged, with those very few people whose minds he had valued and by withdrawing from whom he risked becoming truly alone in the world.

What happened between them?

Leaving aside private and personal squabbles between friends about which we have, and especially then had, a very dim and scant notion, I turn to their controversy in the realm of ideas. When, in that same year of 1839, Belinsky published in Kraevsky's journal (of which he was not yet an acknowledged permanent staff member) two articles of his—a review of F. N. Glinka's book, *Sketches of the Battle of Borodino* and a bibliographical account of Zhukovsky's "The Anniversary of Borodino"—he believed that he was merely making logically correct deductions from Hegel's basic principles and impeccably applying them to living fact, to reality. It must be mentioned that from his very first attempt at defining the meaning of *reality* in the life of nations and individuals, he had already encountered opposition on the part of many of his friends who were loath to concede their right to be full-fledged and first-hand judges of any reality. But the argument that broke out did not reach the point of severing relations until 1839. In the summer of that year, Moscow, and all Russia with Moscow, was, of course, celebrating a great patriotic event—the unveiling of the monument on the field of Borodino. High feeling was rife, and understandably so. I happened to be in Moscow in the summer of 1839 and from the window of a certain relation's house across from the Kremlin, I viewed the magnificent procession circling the Kremlin walls with Metropolitan Filaret walking at its center and accompanied by the emperor himself, Nicholas Pavlovich, on horseback. It was the forerunner, so to speak, of the ceremonial unveiling of the Borodino monument which was to take place in August of the same year. A great deal of heated discussion and high patriotic feeling had already been aroused at that point, but as I was not acquainted then with a single person belonging to the circle I am describing, I was in no position to sense how powerfully echoes of that event would engross me in time to come.

Belinsky had the idea of using the unveiling of the Borodino monument to affirm the wisdom of the Hegelian aphorism on the identity of Reality with Truth and Reason and to analyze the fertile sum and substance of that postulate. But from the very first article it became apparent that excessive generalization of the rule could lead to outlandish conclusions, to stark and egregious misconceptions. Belinsky's friends tried to show him all the dangers of making a direct and unqualified application of his idea to the Russian world, but in vain: being a person who never knew how to make concessions and com-

promises or how to maintain a judicious silence, Belinsky became all
the more resolute for their misgivings. He had either to repudiate the
whole theory or remain faithful to it all the way. He even came to feel
that precisely the moment he had written about earlier had arrived,
the moment when he must decide on an open break with persons
closest to him for the sake of preserving his own thought and conscience.

In his widely known memoirs, the late Herzen [35] recounts an argument between himself and Belinsky which took place shortly before
the latter left Moscow and after which a coolness ensued in their
friendship with one another, lasting, however, but a short time—a
year or so—and ending in complete reconciliation, since the original
cause of the quarrel—blind glorification of reality—was acknowledged
by its advocate, Belinsky, to be a fallacy in terms both of philosophy
and life. Herzen's description of the argument is of unusual interest as
it points up the first storms we experienced in Russia in consequence of
the clash of philosophical systems and abstractions with the real order
of things. Herzen orally supplemented his description with the following detail. When he was in Petersburg a year after his first run-in with
Belinsky, Herzen found Belinsky already there and, needless to say, renewed his dispute with him over the matter of Belinsky's new doctrine. "And it was then," Herzen related, "in the heat of his argument
with me, that Belinsky had recourse to a position which sounded particularly bizarre coming from him: 'Look, friend,' the critic said, 'it's
time we curbed our meager and upstart little minds and admitted to
ourselves that they always will be nothing but rubbish in the face of
events where nations and their leaders, and the history that they em-
body, play the roles.'" Herzen, as he himself acknowledged, was horrified at these words, instantly fell silent and withdrew. He felt that
what had occurred amounted to an abrogation of one's rights to one's
own reason, an incomprehensible and monstrous form of self-annihi-
lation. Two years later, upon his return to Petersburg from his second
banishment to Novgorod (1841), Herzen no longer had any cause to
squabble with the critic: they were exactly of the same opinion on all
questions.

Thus, Belinsky appeared in this city alien to him with a deep
wound in his heart; but he kept on hoping to adapt his friends' views
to his own theories, once given the chance to have his full say on the
issue dividing them. In early 1840, he came out with his article "Menzel as a Critic of Goethe" in *Notes of the Fatherland*. In it, subduing
with all the force of his contempt the low-caliber minds that minutely
picked over what pleased and what displeased them in the panorama
of history, Belinsky established special rights and privileges, even a

special morality, for great artists, great lawmakers, for geniuses in general, who were empowered to devise special roads for themselves and to lead their contemporaries and all mankind along those roads without regard for their protests, perturbations, sympathies and antipathies. No more complete a withdrawal in favor of the privileged and elect of Fate could possibly be professed. Admittedly, the article was written with vigor and expertise and did contain a number of valid comments, now part of our common fund of knowledge, such as, for instance, his comment on the aptness and historical importance of unpremeditated feeling among the masses of the people and his comment about the intimate connection always obtaining between the strivings of great minds and the instincts of society, and the like. However, all this could not mitigate the article's fundamental, sophistical character as an attempt at complete suppression of critical attitudes toward social questions. All this was of short duration. By the fall of the same year, Belinsky recovered from his intoxication with a trend of thought which threatened to end his career at its very beginning.

A great deal has already been written about this period in Belinsky's development, and written with a variety of purposes in mind Nevertheless, it is a subject still not altogether clarified, owing, perhaps, precisely to the fact that it has occupied the investigators excessively and has been magnified by them into a full-blown spiritual crisis—a view for which Belinsky's own latter-day explanations supplied corroboration. In fact, it was simply boundless *optimism* of the kind the Hegelian system often engendered, and not on Russian soil alone. It had already produced the same results in other countries, such as Prussia, on account of its inherent ambiguity. One needed merely to take its definition of the state as a concrete phenomenon in which the individual personality was supposed to find peace and the resolution of all its strivings, one needed merely, we say, to give this definition a particular, official meaning in order to arrive at the deification of any existing order of things. Curiously enough, Belinsky's first mentor in this field of self-delusion then was none other than the present-day negator of all forms of government ever known, the enemy of fully established states, of self-contained nationalisms and their social traditions and beliefs—M. Bakunin.[36] The first error in dialectical reckoning, about which we have been speaking and which had such consequences for Belinsky, belongs to him.

CHAPTER

[IV]

THERE IS GOOD REASON to believe that 1836–37 were onerous years in Belinsky's life. I had frequent occasion afterward to hear hints from him about the misery of those years of young manhood when he was living out the torments and the attachments of his soul. But he never would divulge the details of his life at that time, as if ashamed of his own wounds and feelings. Only once did he observe that there were times when, behaving like a temperamental child, he would spend whole nights crying over imaginary distress. One could only suppose that that distress was not quite as imaginary as he maintained. Remarkably enough, both these years, years filled for him with excruciating agitations and perturbations, were employed simultaneously also for the study of Hegel's philosophy.

Hegel's philosophy had found a unique and eloquent proselytizer in the person of a certain ex-artillery officer who had rapidly attained a proficiency in German and who, in general, possessed an aptitude for readily mastering languages and abstract concepts. This person was M. Bakunin. In 1835, at a time when he knew not what to do with himself, Bakunin came into contact with N. Stankevich who, surmising his talents, brought him to take up the study of German philosophy. The work went swiftly. Bakunin revealed to a superlative degree a facility for dialectics, so indispensable if one is to infuse life into abstract, logical formulas and to obtain conclusions from them applicable to life. He was the one consulted whenever any obscure or difficult point in the master's system required elucidation. Belinsky much later on, ten years afterward, in 1846, could still say that he had not come upon anyone more adept than Bakunin at extirpating, one way or another, any doubt as to the inevitability and grandeur of all the postulates in a system of thought. Indeed, none who approached Bakunin failed to obtain a satisfactory response, sometimes in keeping with the main tenets of the doctrine but sometimes of a factitious nature, made up and improvised by the commentator himself, inasmuch as his dialectical facility, as often is the case with dialecticians in general, was not overnice in its choice of means to achieve its ends.

Be that as it may, the fact is that, beginning in 1836, infatuation with Hegel's philosophy was rife in the young circle which banded together in Moscow in the name of the great German master and attempted to solve by logical progression from one set of antinomies to another all the mysteries of creation, the origin and history of all the phenomena of life, including all the phenomena of the human spirit and consciousness. A person unacquainted with Hegel was considered by the circle virtually a nonentity, a fact which gave rise to desperate efforts on the part of many whose mental resources were scant to become full-fledged human beings at the price of grueling and brain-wracking work which stripped them of the last vestiges of any natural, simple, spontaneous feeling and understanding about things. The circle had a constant entourage of such people. Belinsky, once having been exposed to the basic postulates of Hegel's Logic and Aesthetics, primarily in Bakunin's exposition and exegesis of them, very soon became one of the circle's leading lights.

Bakunin's approach, it should be observed, was to promulgate Hegel's postulates as a universal revelation recently achieved by man, as a compulsory law of human mentality, the postulates wholly and completely exhausting that mentality without any residue and without any possibility whatsoever of correction, addition or change. One had either to submit to them without question or to turn one's back on them, thereby renouncing light and reason. Submit to them without question was just what Belinsky did do at first, repressing, in his endeavor to achieve the ideal of dispassionate existence in "Spirit," all the stirrings and strivings of his moral character and organic nature, and constantly falling short and despairing of ever being able to forge himself a life of perfect radiance in accordance with the master's precepts.

Of course, there was no avoiding strong protests on the part of the neophyte. Belinsky's gift for grasping the essence of philosophical theses, even on merely a hint of them, and thereupon disclosing aspects of the theses such as had never occurred to specialists in the matter—this gift of Belinsky's astounded many of his philosophizing friends. It was something he did not lose even when he had apparently given himself over heart and soul to one single, specific interpretation of the Hegelian system. This ability of his to take at times a completely original and independent stand toward that system was what occasioned Herzen's remark that in all his life he had come across only two persons who really understood Hegel's doctrine, and neither one of them knew a word of German. One was the Frenchman Proudhon and the other a Russian—Belinsky. Belinsky's objections to certain dogmas of the system could sometimes throw its weak and scholastical aspects into striking relief, but they could not shake his *faith* in the system and liberate him from its tyranny over him.

There is that famous exclamation of Belinsky's, an extremely characteristic one, whereby he made known his opinion that it was ignominious for man to serve merely as an instrument for the "Universal Idea" to achieve through him its own imperative self-determination. This exclamation can be translated to mean: "I have no desire to serve merely as the arena for the peregrinations of the 'Absolute Idea' around me and the universe." Of course, objections of this sort, however momentary they may have been, could not help but disgruntle his friend, Bakunin, whose character, as is the case with all proselytizers, was not without a streak of despotism. Sharp altercations came about subsequently, precisely in consequence of Belinsky's protests and the responses to them which his teacher, for his part, expressed in no uncertain terms. Later, in the 1840's, in the course of describing to me the skill with which Bakunin could cast aspersions on persons whom he suspected of mutiny against him, Belinsky added: "He would have it out with me, too. 'Have a look at this Cassius,' he would time and time again address my associates. 'No one has ever heard him sing a single song, not one melody has he been able to remember, not one note has passed his lips from birth, even by accident. He has no inner music in him, no harmonies of mind and soul, no urge to express the gentle, feminine side of human nature.' Those were the devious means by which he would worm his way into my soul in order to snatch it up unobtrusively and carry it off in his bosom." The two friends, as we know, quarreled incessantly straight up to 1840 and just as incessantly made peace with each other. But back in the summer of 1836 they were enjoying an intimately friendly, cloudless life.

The bond between the two friends was bound to grow even stronger when, in the course of 1836, Belinsky was made an intimate of the Bakunin household and found there, as acquaintances of his have related, a response of unusual warmth even on the part of its young female denizens. (Toward women Belinsky never could feel indifferent, convinced as he was that not a single creature of the opposite sex could be sympathetic to his unprepossessing exterior and uncouth manners.) Belinsky went to Tver and lived for awhile on the Bakunins' estate. The conversations he had under their roof, under the spell of his friendship with a member of the family and as object of the attention and solicitude of its bevy of young and cultured females, were bound, of course, to make a deeper impression on his mind than conversations in any other surroundings. The results soon made themselves known. When Belinsky once again returned to journalism and took over publication of the *Moscow Observer* (its previous editors having brought it to wrack and ruin) in 1838, the pages of the journal featured expositions no longer of Schellingian conceptions written in that lofty, lyrical tone they always assumed with Belinsky, but of rigorous Hegelian patterns of thought written with due severity of language and expression and often with a certain sacerdotal obscurity, though the fact was that the old conceptions and the new patterns had much affinity with one another. In addition, M. Bakunin was now one of the journal's collaborators, the one who was expected to bring about a revolution in the field of literature and thought. And he did indeed initiate a new phase of philosophism on Russian soil with his proclamation of the doctrine that all that *really* exists is sacred.

For a while, though a very short while, Bakunin, one could say, reigned over the circle of the philosophizers. He imbued it with his own attitude of mind, an attitude which can only be defined in terms of the result of *voluptuous* exercises in philosophy. For Bakunin at that time it was exclusively a matter of *intellectual pleasure;* and since the very versatility, deftness, and elasticity of his intellect required that it constantly be given fresh nourishment and stimulation, nothing could have been more apropos than the vast and boundless sea of Hegel's philosophy. It allowed free play for all Bakunin's powers and abilities—his passion for the intricately elaborate, his innate mental ingenuity incessantly seeking and finding occasions to score triumphs and victories and, finally, his grandiloquent speech, always somehow declamatory in form and stentorian, though also somewhat cold, unimaginative, and artificial. Yet, precisely this declamatory speech was what comprised Bakunin's power to subjugate his peers: its polish and brilliance captivated even those who were unaffected by the ideas it was meant to promulgate. And it was not only when expounding the essence of philosophical theses that Bakunin enjoyed rapt attention from his listeners, but also when he lectured dispassionately and with decorum on the necessity of errors, failures, profound misfortunes, and severe afflictions as ineluctable conditions of truly human existence.

Bakunin himself related the following story in later years. Once, after an evening devoted to the above topic, Bakunin's company, consisting largely of young men, broke up and went off to bed. One of them was lodged in the room where the master himself reposed. During the night, the latter was awakened by his young companion who, candle in hand and all the signs of despair written on his face, implored his help: "Teach me what I must do," he was saying, "I am a hopeless wretch. No matter how hard I think about it, I still cannot feel that I have in me any capacity for suffering." Indeed, to develop a fondness for suffering, especially in the years of one's youth, is no easy matter.

To be sure, so prolonged an intellectual, dialectical, philosophical carouse could have been staged only on the condition that thorough provision be made against protests on the part of people who were embittered by or indignant at life, on the condition that one could make reasonable, if not completely legitimate, everything to which their grievances and doubts pertained. It was essential, above all, to convince all who were extemely sensitive to *the issues of the day* that any personal, individual attempt to pass judgment on contemporary life or its mainstays was a crime against existing "Reality," i. e., a crime against the "Universal Idea" embodied in contemporary life at the given moment—in other words, against "Supreme Reason." Dispassion and a disposition of mind conducive to philosophizing could be purchased only at that price. And it was nothing more than overt or covert inculcations of this sort that occupied Bakunin during that period.

Bakunin was responsible for the introduction into print of the new pejorative Russian word *"prekrasnodushie,"* which caused such confusion in the minds of the public and on the pages of journals on account of its indeed awkward formation. A literal translation of the German *Schönseligkeit,* it was taken to denote in Russian high-minded but groundless relinquishments of one's own personal thinking and personal judgment about contemporary life. Bakunin was responsible for the dissemination in Russia of that extreme, that very pure, but at the same time contemptuous, idealism which turned away in horror from the hubbub of ordinary life, amalgamating under the one general term of *base phenomena of the subjective spirit* everything that disturbed its tranquil deliberations over questions concerning the fate and mission of mankind. It ignored the French Revolution of 1830; it discerned nothing in the movement which thereupon ensued in France (George Sand, Saint-Simon, Lamennais); it saw nothing in its own contemporary, the "Young Germany" in movement, which had already established its organ *Deutsche Jahrbücher* in 1838. It only stigmatized these phenomena by calling them unbridled pranks of the intellect having nothing to do with the philosophical mind. By estimation of this idealism even Schiller himself, on account of his youthful protests, his thirst for justice, truth, and humanity, was declared to be an infantile genius who could never ascend to the heights of cordial and generous feelings, the heights of dispassionate contemplation of ideas and laws governing human beings, the heights of an objective mode of apprehending things.

Father of Russian idealism though he was, Bakunin was at the same time extremely given to the pleasures of life, enjoying them without a qualm and pursuing them in a naive and ingenuous sort of way. Life and philosophy did not, in this instance, enter into conflict. However, I must repeat once again that nowhere, perhaps, had philosophical romanticism become incarnate in a representative so powerfully endowed with resources and talents as was Bakunin. Under cover of the mathematically rigorous formulas of Hegel's logic, his romanticism superficially appeared a very austere creed, whereas it was in fact merely a matter of gratification and justification for extremely subtle and refined lusts of a mentality which found its pleasures in itself.

For Belinsky, however, it was a different matter. Far from providing him amusement and distraction, philosophical studies were, quite the contrary, a grim and onerous ordeal which he underwent at the cost of pain and self-denial in hopes of finding truth and peace of mind and conscience once it was over. He had to habituate himself to the way the ideas disclosed by his new outlook were ordered and ruthlessly rid himself of any misgiving about it or any impulse to criticize. Philosophical optimism demanded a great deal. Proceeding by way of abstraction and metaphysical deduction, he attempted to make scientific axioms, philosophical truths and revelations of Spirit out of prevailing social principles, and with minor exceptions, out of almost the entire environment of contemporary life and a large share of all the practices, intellectual and otherwise, evoked and invoked by the current moment.

It was precisely this favorable interpretation of the present moment that was primarily responsible for the spell cast over everybody by the Bakunin of those days—the deeply conservative, religious-minded with even a mystical tinge, familial-virtuous, moral, *musical* Bakunin, such as people knew him until 1840 when he left Russia to go abroad. Since then he has profoundly changed direction, but his need to create systems and conceptions which deceive rather than satisfy man's needs has remained the same; and we hear the same romanticism, keyed to unusual conclusions and startling effects, in his call for the destruction of societies and the annihilation of civilization as we formerly heard in his appeals for the heroic feat of supreme understanding and fulfillment of morality and human dignity.

Even at the time, many people, including the late V. P. Botkin,[37] for example, and Belinsky himself, were now and again well aware of what underlay Bakunin's creed. In the course of describing Bakunin's personality to me in 1840, a time when it was a total unknown for me, Belinsky said: "The man's a prophet and thunder-hurler, but with roses in his cheeks and no fervor in his organism." Such was Belinsky's final impression of Bakunin, an impression derived from long contact and association with his teacher.

No one, however, has denied the social significance of Bakunin's philosophy; it did indeed constitute a step forward in the intellectual development of our society and did serve progress. The manner it adopted for conceptualizing the goals and missions of life did have much about it that was fantastic. Still, it stood immeasurably higher, of course, than the crude manner of apprehending life that predominated among the majority of his contemporaries. The meaning which Bakunin's system sought to discover not only in the political but also in the commonplace, ephemeral phenomena of the day was an arbitrary one, foisted on the phenomena forcibly; but it was, nevertheless, a meaning which required that much else be studied and much else be thought about before it could be mastered. The postulates of Bakunin's dogma did tend to legitimize far too much in existing institutions, it is true, but they did so in such a way that these institutions ceased resembling themselves: in comparison with what they had been in actual fact, they became ideals. Moral demands made on the individual personality bore the character of unlimited severity; the challenge to achieve heroic feats was the constant and favorite topic of all Bakunin's conversations. The Hegelian definition of personality as an arena within which the rite of self-affirmation and ultimate manifestation of the "Creative Idea" is performed was enough to warrant demands for the most strenuous efforts from each human being in the process of developing his consciousness and moral prowess. And demand these efforts is just what Bakunin did do, bringing to bear an inspiration and singlemindedness that had by then already become organic and automatic with him. Thus, even on the eve of the French Revolution of 1848 in Paris, when he himself had gone over to the arena of purely political activity and, strongly imbued with Polish propaganda, had entered upon secret talks, clandestine machinations and clubbist measures of a certain kind, Bakunin was always ready to exhort people to unsullied feats, to the immaculate life, to the idealistic conception of life's tasks. That was what prompted Herzen at that very time (1848) to dub him in jest "an old Joan of Arc," adding that Bakunin, too, was a "maid," though not *of* but *anti-*Orleans, inasmuch as he despised the king, Louis Philippe. . .of Orleans.

N. V. Stankevich, Bakunin's predecessor in the study of Hegel and the very one who, as we mentioned, initiated Bakunin himself in the science, never reached the point of complete and absolute optimism in philosophy. Stankevich could not rival his colleague in this if only because, while starting from the same bases as Bakunin and no less under the sway of romantic attitudes, his fastidious intellect and refined and poetic nature rendered him incapable of crude generalizing. For physiological reasons pure and simple, he became nonplussed and stopped short before an act of overt or covert injustice, as likewise before any excessive enthusiasm. He had a sense of measure which assessed overly presumptuous theses, and what is more, he was endowed with a sense of humor which enabled him to descry the reverse, shady side of things. Bakunin was utterly without this gift. It must be accounted a happy circumstance for Bakunin that during the most intense period of promulgating his creed, Stankevich and Granovsky were abroad (the former since the fall of 1837 and the latter a year before that) and Herzen was passing the time of his first banishment in Vyatka and later in Vladimir. Had they happened to be in Moscow then, Bakunin's role as a lawgiver and his decrees on speculative topics would have been considerably curbed and altered.

It now remains to take note of how all the properties and features of Bakunin's system of philosophy were then reflected in Belinsky's soul.

CHAPTER

[V]

INITIALLY, the influence of Bakunin's new system of philosophy did not work to the advantage of Belinsky's talents. At that time Belinsky set about first of all studying patterns, formulas, divisions—all the barely perceptible shades of the colossal world of abstraction called Hegel's Logic; and he set about it with a passion and a fanatical enthusiasm that were properties of his nature. Having taken an oath of discipleship to the system, he could not fail to abide by it to the very end. He kept his inquisitive mind and restless heart under strict control, drew up a plan, a program, virtually a set routine for his living and his thinking, and employed incredible efforts to ward off all the temptations his innate talent and critical and aesthetic aptitude offered. During all this time, he was haunted by doubt as to even so much as his right to devote himself to impressions of the world at large, to his own feelings and his own inclinations of soul. The notion, no less than the practice, of relating one's self to all that is real in one's own personal existence troubled him deeply. Far from being enjoyment of philosophy, as was the case during the period of Schellingian influence, this was drudgery and hard labor which he took upon himself in hope of resurrection in the near future and, from then on, a blissful existence on earth, free from doubts, vacillations, and agonizing questions.

The excruciating ordeal, voluntarily undergone by a personality of a kind least amenable to submissiveness, did not end even when Belinksy became acquainted with the doctrine on "Reality," although it was supposed, apparently, to relieve him of vain efforts to find ideally perfect precepts and bases for life. In any case, traces of this ordeal of initiation are in evidence in his articles of 1838. His style of writing, formerly exuberant and spontaneous, became, in the *Moscow Observer* of 1838, irresolute and nebulous, as if it were withering under the strain of its preoccupation with philosophical terms, their explication (the term *"konkretnost"* [concreteness] in particular cost him prolonged efforts and continual repetition in different phrasings of one and the same concept), their adaptation into Russian and interpretation of their meaning for the Russian reading public. At times, this weak and nondescript style of writing did attempt to take on a semblance of spontaneity, did attempt to conceal the scholastical bonds hampering its free movement and to make a show of being bold and free despite the chain with which it had consented to be bound. These were flashes corresponding to those momentary protests against theory about which we have already spoken. On the whole, however, the *Moscow Observer,* as Belinsky's organ, beginning in 1838, presented a woeful picture, over the course of several months, of that extraordinary and unique thinker in the humiliating position of an initiate suffering exhaustion and debilitation under the impact of a cruel intellectual discipline that, though it was draining his strength, he stubbornly persisted in imposing on himself and refused to regard as punishment. The journal wore out its editor and all who were then interested in it. Many of the editor's friends also felt very dissatisfied with him and did not hide their attitude. I shall in this connection take the opportunity to say a few words about my own impressions on this matter at the time.

CHAPTER

[VI]

THE *Moscow Observer* of 1838, as is well known, opened with its leading article, Roetscher's [38] "On Philosophical Criticism of a Work of Art." Though much was said about the article in our literature both then and later on, it behooves me to pause and say something about it again now. The article was one of those extremely dry and theoretical treatises in which concepts, under the practiced hand of the writer, automatically fall into intricate patterns, ignoring, as just so much encumbering nonsense, all considerations as to the pressing needs of the society in question, the conditions or requirements of its existence at the given moment. The article set the journal's subsequent trend. It divided criticism into four rigidly marked-off categories, giving preference, needless to say, to the first—the philosophical section—as the one which encompassed the only really valid and infallible laws of literary judgment. And the infallibility of these laws was proved by a process of investigation peculiar to philosophical criticism: once having diagnosed the idea of a work of art, philosophical criticism abstracts that idea from the work, elaborates it as an independent entity in its philosophical way, draws all the conclusions that can be drawn from it and then returns the idea once again to the work in order to observe whether everything that philosophical analysis of the work had brought to light was expressed in its images and details. If so, fine and good; if not, so much the worse for the work!

The three lesser branches of criticism—psychological, practical, and historical—did not, of course, enjoy Belinsky's sympathy. Not to speak of practical criticism, long scorned by him, he regarded both historical and psychological criticism as of extremely little value for their not being guided by the *absolute laws* of art and thought. In this connection it is extremely curious to give ear to what Belinsky had to say apropos of the latter type of criticism: "The details of a poet's life do not elucidate his creative works in the slightest. The laws of creativity are eternal, just as are the laws of reason. Of what interest is it for us to know how Aeschylus or Sophocles stood in relation to his government and fellow citizens or what happened in Greece during their lifetimes? In order to understand their tragedies, we must know the significance of the Greeks within the absolute life of mankind. . . . Political events and minor details do not concern us" and so on. Belinsky was simply unrecognizable here.

Meanwhile, in Roetscher's article, the humble manifestations of our press and literature were set before its rubrics of criticism; their measurement was taken and, on the basis of the feet and inches obtained, space was allotted them in some one of the sections. That is how Belinsky handled the works of Fonvizin, which he put on the agenda of historical criticism in the amazing company of—the works of Voltaire! The novel *Yury Miloslavsky* he made the business of psychological criticism, also providing it an extraordinary colleague and companion, namely, Schiller, that "strange half-artist, half-philosopher" (Belinsky's observation). But even Belinsky's talents and experience were insufficient to make the Russian authors named amenable to all the requirements of that section of criticism under whose jurisdiction they were placed or to find in them all the features which theory made absolutely requisite that they possess. He promised to substantiate this coincidence of theory and live example but did not fulfill his promise, and for quite understandable reasons. Had he accomplished that task, either theory would have had to burst its seams or examples would have had to break loose completely from theory

Belinsky brought about something else instead. The more he abrogated his own personal judgment, the more his mind became possessed with lifeless philosophical schemes and theses which did not merely divert his attention from the objects of art, but obtrusively and arrogantly took their place. When the actor Mochalov created the role of Hamlet in Moscow, Belinsky wrote a lengthy article about the tragedy and about the Moscow performer of its leading role. How did Belinsky, in fact, envision Hamlet? Exactly the same way Goethe had, of course—as a man suffering from paucity of will in the face of the enormous design to which he had committed himself. But, wondered Belinsky, whence comes this infirmity of will and its concomitant sufferings in a person quite capable of acting boldly and resolutely on occasion? The answer was formulated as a scheme. Hamlet, according to its definition, manifests in himself all the symptoms of that state of soul which obtains when a man, formerly living at peace with himself and by himself, is transposed into existence in Reality, in the outside world, a world so full of perplexities and absurdities at first sight. Hamlet is deprived of all the force of his will, of all the strength of his character by the struggle and by the sufferings inevitably entailed in this plunge into the chaos and seeming crudity of the real world. Force of will and strength of character return to Hamlet when, after a long and agonizing ordeal, he reaches a sense of humility before the laws governing that incomprehensible and portentous world of Reality, when he reaches the placid conviction that one must *always be prepared for everything*. Thus, Hamlet turned into a representative of a cherished philosophical concept, became the incarnation of a *certain* formula (what is real, is rational); and on that pedestal Belinsky fashioned his apotheosis of both the great creator of the drama and his remarkable interpreter on the Moscow stage.[39]

Incessant transformation of live images into abstractions became more and more a common feature with Belinsky. In his survey of journals for the year 1839, Belinsky included a commentary on Guber's article "Faust." What was Goethe's Faust? For the Belinsky of that period Faust was exactly the same kind of philosophical scheme as was Hamlet, even virtually indistingishable from the latter. Faust, as a man of profound and all-embracing character, was supposed to have broken away from natural harmony of Spirit, to have clashed with Reality, to which he had turned for consolation and knowledge, and after a series of bloody trials, after an agonizing struggle, after failures and temptations, to have returned to full harmony of spirit, but now a harmony sublimated by experience and consciousness. Toward the end, Faust's eyes were opened to Reason and the justification for all that exists. Faust dies in the bliss, and from the bliss, of this realization.

Troublesome though it may have been to take this procedure of defining works of art and apply it to anything homegrown, Belinsky was not to be deterred by the difficulty. I have mentioned that, when Pushkin's posthumous works began appearing in the 1838 *Contemporary*, Belinsky experienced a feeling of more than rapture, something even akin to *panic* in the presence of the majesty of the creative art revealed to his eyes. In the process of giving an account, in the "Literary Chronicle" section of the 1838 *Moscow Observer*, of the four volumes of the *Contemporary* which contained the great poet's unpublished works, Belinsky puzzled over the question: What is Pushkin? It turned out that the same scheme that had served as the yardstick for Hamlet's and Faust's inner quality was equally serviceable for defining Pushkin's last works. Here are Belinsky's own words: "Indeed," he said, "if one is to comprehend the whole profundity of these pictures of genius, if one is to decipher their entirely *mysterious* meaning and enter into their powerful life in all its fullness and luminosity, one must pass through an agonizing trial of inner life and from the struggle of lofty-heartedness [*prekrasnodushie*] emerge into a harmony of spirit sublimated and reconciled with reality. We repeat:

reconciliation by way of objective apprehension of life—that is the character of these last works of Pushkin's."

It would have been very odd if this philosophical thesis, which had so powerfully and despotically taken hold of Belinsky's mind, had been left without application to subjects of a political and social nature or had been replaced, in such instances, by some other, dissimilar outlook. The inconsistency of such disparity of definition would have been an outright repudiation of the very bases of his theory. And Belinsky was always consistent, both when it came to the truth and in his momentary lapses from truth. Thus, Belinsky came out also with a political theory by force of which a man, in order to establish proper relations to society and state, must resolve in himself exactly the same problem as Hamlet and Faust resolved through their persons and Pushkin through his works. The difference in this case consisted merely in that social and political grounds provided no possibility for making choices among phenomena, for preferring some to others, for grading and sorting them out, but made it essential to accord respect and recognition to them all equally and in toto. Belinsky therefore required that "a man unwilling to make do all his life with a phantom of existence instead of a genuine human existence must acknowledge the intellectual whims of his own person to be a sham and a delusion, must subordinate himself to the rules and regulations of the state, which is the only criterion of truth on earth, must delve down to the Idea lying at its depths, must convert all its mighty content into his own personal convictions and, by doing so, cease being a representative of fortuitous and private points of view and become an expression of the common life, of the national life, of, finally, the universal life or, in other words, become *Spirit in the flesh*." Belinsky continued further on: "Negation is an essential moment in a man's spiritual development, for he who has never quarreled with life cannot come to lasting terms with life. But this negation must be precisely only a moment and not an entire lifetime. The quarrel must not be a goal in itself but have reconciliation as its goal. Woe to those who quarrel with society that they may never reconcile themselves with it: society is the higher reality, and reality requires that man come finally to terms with it, that he accord it full recognition or else it crushes him under the leaden weight of its colossal hand."

This passage is found in his analysis of F. N. Glinka's book *Sketches of the Battle of Borodino*, which signalized, as we know, the full flowering of Hegelian optimism in Russian literature.

Such, in brief, is the story of the conception and development of Belinsky's Hegelian optimism, a story which, so to speak, unrolled before our very eyes.

[VII]

WE CANNOT BRING our discussion of this period in the critic's career to a close without repeating once more what was said about those frequent instances of his turning against his own dogmas: contrary to the whole tenor and all the conclusions of the doctrine which Belinsky had accepted and made his own, propositions smacking of heresy kept bursting forth from under his pen. Through these heretical outbursts, with their suggestion of rebellion against principles oppressive to his intellect, were expressed Belinsky's critical powers, powers temporarily held in check and kept in hiding, awaiting the end of the philosophical pogrom before coming out in the open once again in all their brilliance.

Wasn't it a surprise, for instance, in the very flush of Belinsky's Hegel-mindedness, when his veneration and relentless quest for the Idea were full-blown, to read the following passage in his analysis of Polevoy's [40] weak drama *Ugolino:* "In creative art the impact is lodged, not in idea, but in form, which, needless to say, necessarily presupposes and conditions idea. And form must be permeated with the gentle and devout glow of aesthetic beauty. Loftiness of subject matter (idea) is not only no guarantee of aesthetic beauty but often actually even makes it suspect. . . ." I well remember the confusion aroused in us by sudden changes of position of that sort (and there were not a few of them), which dealt more or less palpable blows at the bases and primary principles of his adopted philosophical system. I also remember that many of us would in such instances solicit the author for some explanation of these contradictions. But Belinsky's explanations, for the most part, expressed his annoyance at being put under examination and were given the way adults give answers to children who pester them with questions. "Do you really think," Belinsky would say, "that every time I express an opinion, I must check back on what I said some time in the past? Look here, right now I

35

hate you, but let a day go by and I'll be passionately fond of you."
There was much truth in these words.

At that time Belinsky was particularly apprehensive of contradictions that challenged the validity of his new system and he expressed
himself irritably and angrily in reaction to those who voiced them. But
it just so happened that it was precisely those people who were, more
than anything else, on his mind. Associated with this was another, no
less curious, feature. Belinsky would become indignant, morose, and
cross precisely at such times, rare as they were, when he encountered
unqualified agreement with his ideas; it was as if he felt deprived at
not having objections and confutations. Belinsky's inner life at that
period showed a truly tragic split and was fraught with suffering and
misgivings which he would from time to time make known to his
companions in some sudden, biting comment, in, one might say, an
outcry of his anguished soul. He desperately and convulsively held on
to his new beliefs, but with each passing day he felt more and more
that they were changing, fading away, and going up in smoke before
his very eyes.

However, it also happened during this same period that Belinsky
would bring to bear, in his struggle against oppressive conditions of
metaphysical despotism, not merely outbursts and sporadic activations
of his critical faculty but also whole carefully thought-out judgments
and verdicts that went against the grain of the theory and all its interpreters. And what pride Belinsky took in these demonstrations and exercises of his independence of mind! In a letter to I. I. Panaev dated
August 19, 1839, later published in the January 1860 issue of the Contemporary, he jocularly, but with a feeling of unconcealed elation,
recalled that back in the fall of the previous year, to the great indignation and astonishment of his Moscow philosopher friends, he had
pronounced the second part of Faust to be a set of dry and lifeless
symbols. These friends of his were virtually at a loss to express their
anger and contempt for the upstart who had dared lay hands on that
unique "philosophical Apocalypse." But now they were crestfallen,
having read an article in the Deutsche Jahrbücher by the young aesthetician Vischer, who, Belinsky declared, literally repeated everything
that he, that unknown and unacknowledged Belinsky, had brought
out only the year before. And there was reason to be proud!

As for us, Belinsky's heresies, Belinsky's contradictions, his deser-
tion of his own positions, his violations of philosophical dogmas were
something we craved, as if gifts. They seemed to return the old Belinsky to us, the Belinsky of 1834–35, who, despite Schelling, had his
own independent thought and his own orientation.[41] Not that our
circle of his Petersburg followers clearly perceived the unsoundness of

his system and of the conclusions that he derived from it—the circle was not philosophically sophisticated enough to do that. Rather, its members felt a sense of uneasiness as they observed their mentor developing. They became acutely perplexed when they were forbidden to grumble even about the most ordinary things in life, and they found themselves constantly harking back to the old Belinsky of 1835, the publisher of six issues of the *Telescope* with articles and analyses that are monuments of critical acumen still today, the verdicts of which outlived the generations that first read them.

It was possibly this supicious attitude of the circle, the unfailing readiness of its members to break away from philosophical theses and take the practical road of direct, prima facie evaluation of things without inquiry into their ideational aspect—it was possibly this attitude that made Belinsky grim, wary and restrained in his dealings with the circle. He was not confident of its commitment to abstract concepts, especially of its ability to steep itself in abstract concepts to the degree required. Once, a conversation struck up in his presence on the topic of the salutary, practical value of Petersburg, consisting in its cooling off ardent interests and its drying up all the sources of dreams and fantasies once they were exposed to its breath. Hearing this, Belinsky flared up and angrily retorted: "I see what you are driving at. You'll never be able to make of me what you desire!" He was still concerned for the fate of his idealism in Petersburg. And, indeed, for a long time afterward, even after his thinking took its sober turn in 1840, he held on to his idealism as if it were a mark of distinction which he must not lose in his new situation. Things, however, turned out otherwise.

[VIII]

My lengthy digression over, I now return to my story.

Once he settled in Petersburg, Belinsky began that toilsome and arduous life which he endured for eight straight years practically without letup and which undermined his very organism and sapped his strength. In the early days of his life there, after a fairly long stay at Panaev's apartment, Belinsky found lodging on Petersburg Island along Bolshoy Prospect in a small, handsome, wooden building, consisting of one rather spacious but damp and frigid room and a smallish study, which he kept swelteringly hot. It was there that I found him in the winter of 1840. The contrast in temperature between the two rooms did not seem to have any appreciable effect on the health of the tenant but did, on the other hand, constantly bestow upon his visitors the usual offerings of wintertime Petersburg—cold sores, influenza, and occasionally bronchitis.

Shut up in his torrid study, Belinsky devoted himself entirely to his thoughts and led a life of severe solitude, almost the life of an ascetic, from which he emerged now and again into the circle of his new acquaintances. There his grim appearance, combined more often than not with intermittent flashes of anger or satiric humor, made even more prominent the basic motif, the backdrop, so to speak, of his suffering soul. It was impossible to be mistaken: the least perceptive of his companions certainly felt, even if he did not understand, the fundamental trait of the man—his being a living embodiment of the images devised by poetry to convey the anguished strivings and agitations of a restless heart and seething mind. Only, this man was an ingenuous titan. In contrast to the character-type in its romantic version, which we generally find portrayed devoid of weak or kindly dispositions, Belinsky possessed both of these to a marked degree. One couldn't help but note his childlike trust in good words and honorable intentions expressed in his presence followed by his comical anger at himself when he discerned (as happened very soon thereafter) the not altogether untainted sources of these declarations. His naïveté and inexperience in social intercourse invariably misled him that way, though minutes after committing such blunders he would almost instantly come to his senses, and then he would discover aspects of people and things that persons of very inquisitive and wary cast of mind would have failed to notice.

However, generally speaking, Belinsky showed at that time no need for society, no need to circulate, to sound himself out on others or to sound out everybody else on one another. He would get along entirely without social life for whole weeks on end. Following the devastation of his new theory, he would spend his days and nights standing at his writing desk. His rather narrow, torrid study, with its two windows, between which stood his desk, also had in it, near its further wall and at a distance of some five or six steps away, a small couch and a small stand adjacent to it. Belinsky, as was the requirement for journal articles, almost always wrote on one side of a half-sheet and left off writing as soon as he reached the end of it. Thereupon, he would settle himself on his couch and take up a book, after which, changing the now dry page for another, he would again take up his pen. He experienced no difficulty in reading or writing from these pauses in the flow of his thoughts. It was in this manner that he composed his articles, both when pressed for time and when not, articles which tired him far more physically than mentally. His hand and his weak chest ailed him, but his head remained invariably fresh. This intensive work was, moreover, a moral need of his, something to circumvent and relieve the sense of loneliness he felt ever since he had left his Moscow circle of friends, exchanging it for another without having really found a substitute. . . . Also, for a long time he could not accustom himself to Petersburg, to its way of life—so methodical and circumspect; but he ended up by so fully recognizing its value and its advantages in providing guarantees of personal security by way of its civil code and police regulations that he became completely reconciled with it.

In place of society, however, Belinsky had at the time three constant and inseparable companions of whose words he could hardly ever have had his fill. I mean—Pushkin, Gogol, and Lermontov. About Pushkin we shall have nothing to say: the revelations of his lyric poetry, so fine of feeling and humane, and at the same time so robust and virile, had the effect of exciting Belinsky's wonder like a magic spell or some prodigy of nature. He did not shake off his fascination with Pushkin even when, dazzled by Lermontov's artistry, he turned all of his attention to the new luminary and looked to him to revolutionize the very concepts of the worth and aims of the literary profession. When I was about to leave for abroad in October of 1840, Belinsky asked me what books I was taking with me. "It would be an odd thing to cart books from Russia to Germany," I replied. "And what about Pushkin?" "I am not taking any Pushkin, either." "Speaking for myself," Belinsky observed, "I cannot conceive of the possibility of living, and in foreign lands to boot, without Pushkin."

About his second companion, Gogol, we shall presently say a few words of explanation. But as concerns the factors out of which developed a relationship between Belinsky and the third, the latest or, rather, the newest and youngest of his companions, Lermontov, since they constitute so capital a detail in the spiritual life of our critic, we shall have to speak about them separately.

Elsewhere [42] we have already pointed out the great importance of Belinsky in N. V. Gogol's own life and the enormous services he rendered the author of *Dead Souls*. We have already mentioned that Belinsky possessed a capacity to respond, in the throes of some philosophical or political preoccupation of his, to extraordinary literary events with the assurance and authoritativeness of a man sensible of his own real power and his own calling. During his Schellingian period, one such flash of wide-reaching illumination was his article "The Russian Tale and the Tales of Gogol," written following the publication of Gogol's *Mirgorod* and *Arabesques* (1835). It is this article which entitles us to assert that Gogol's real sponsor in Russian literature, the one who made his name for him, was Belinsky. This article was, moreover, an extremely timely one. It coincided with a bitter moment for Gogol when, as a consequence of professorial and scholarly ambitions to which he felt himself inspired, he was made to endure the most vile and virulent attacks not only on his work as a writer but also on his personal character. I knew Gogol intimately at that time and could plainly see how utterly alone he felt, not knowing where to turn or find support, nonplussed and abashed not so much by the outlandish ravings of Senkowski and Bulgarin as by the joint condemnation of the Petersburg public, his fellow academicians and even his friends. His Moscow acquaintances and sympathizers, for the time being, still confined their expression of appreciation for his creative talents in their organ (the *Moscow Observer*) to evasive and cautious terms, reserving themselves the privilege of expanding fully on their sentiments only privately, *in camera*, by letter, in a confidential-intimate manner. A helping hand, in the sense of a boost to his fallen morale, was extended Gogol by one from whom nothing was asked and nothing expected, who was a complete unknown to Gogol at the time—by Belinsky, coming out, as he did, with the above-mentioned article in the *Telescope* of 1835. And what an article!

In his article, he did not give advice to the author, did not sort out what in the author was worthy of praise and what deserving censure, did not criticize some feature on the grounds of doubtful accuracy or relevance for the work and approve another as contributing to the work's pleasure and profit. Instead, basing himself on the essence of Gogol's talent and the *worthiness of his view of life,* he simply announced that, in Gogol, Russian society had a *great writer* in the offing. I had the chance to witness the effect of this article on Gogol. He had at that time not yet become convinced that Moscow criticism, i.e., Belinsky's, had perversely misconstrued all his intentions and aims as a writer. He was gratified at the remark in the article to the effect that "a deep sadness, a sense of profound sympathy for Russian life and its ways makes itself felt in all Gogol's stories," and was pleased with the article, and even more than pleased—if the whole truth in my recollection of that time is to be told—he was bolstered by it.

Gogol's attention was particularly arrested by the article's definition of the criteria of genuine artistry, and once, when there was occasion to discuss the article, he read one of its passages out loud: "The artist's creation is still a mystery for everyone, he has still not taken pen in hand—but he already sees them (the images of the characters) clearly, he already can count the creases on their clothing, the lines on their passion- and sorrow-furrowed brows, he already knows them better than you know your own father, brother, friend, your own mother, sister, sweetheart; he knows, as well, what they will do and say, he sees in its entirety the thread that will wind around and bind the events together. . . ." "That is absolutely true," Gogol remarked, promptly adding with that half-shy, half-mocking smile of his, "Only, I don't understand what, after that, he finds so delightful in Polevoy's stories." A shrewd observation striking squarely on the critic's weak spot, but it must be stated that Belinsky had a reason, in addition to allegiance to romanticism, for evaluating Polevoy's stories favorably. He highly valued at that moment the services performed by the distinguished journalist and was deeply grieved by the compulsory cessation of his work as editor of the *Moscow Telegraph.*[43] All that influenced his judgment of Polevoy's career in belles lettres.

Still, the definitive, ecstatic word had been said, and said not straight out of the blue. To support and justify and reaffirm it in the public mind, Belinsky expended a great deal of energy, talent, and intelligence and broke many a lance, and, at that, in battle not only with the writer's enemies but with his friends as well. Thus, Belinsky argued against the critic of the *Moscow Observer* of 1836 when the latter, in some strange fit of enthusiasm, declared that supposedly for the sake of the single expression "I hear" which burst from the lips of Taras Bulba in answer to the exclamation of his son, his torturer and executioner, "Do you hear this, father?"—supposedly for that one single exclamation "I hear," Gogol had earned himself immortality. On another occasion, he argued against the same critic, and no less triumphantly, when the latter expressed the wish that no suggestion of "habit" be encountered in the story "Old-Fashioned Landowners," but that the relationship between the idyllic couple be explained solely as pure and tender, unadulterated feeling.

Let us also bring to mind the fact that Gogol's *Inspector General,* which had suffered a fiasco on first being performed in Petersburg and was virtually hounded off the stage through the efforts of the *Library for Reading* (inspired, it is said, from an outside quarter to attack the comedy as of a political nature alien to the Russian world)—Gogol's *Inspector General* returned to the stage, thanks to Belinsky, now with the epithet "work of genius." The boldness of the epithet even astonished Gogol's friends at that time, though they valued his first work for the stage very highly. Later on, bypassing the judicious remarks of prudent people, Belinsky wrote another sharp attack against all the detractors of *Inspector General* who were also patrons of Zagoskin's banal effort at comedy, *The Malcontents,* which they wished to oppose to *Inspector General.* This critical attack was entitled simply "From Belinsky" and proclaimed Gogol an unquestionably great European artist, thereby consolidating, once and for all, Gogol's position in Russian literature. Belinsky himself took a certain pride subsequently in recalling this feat of "straight-forward" criticism, as he called it, which anticipated the "devious" variety and showed it the way it did in fact later take. Such were Belinsky's services in regard to Gogol; the latter did not, however, remain long in debt to him, as we shall see.

Nikolai Vasilevich Gogol, at the time we are describing, was living abroad and had, two years before, taken up residence in Rome where he devoted himself entirely to completing the first part of *Dead Souls.* To be sure, he did spend some time in Petersburg during the winter of 1839 and read to us the first chapters of his illustrious epic at the home of N. Ya. Prokopovich,[44] but Belinsky did not attend that get-together (he happened to be in Moscow). It is unlikely that, at that time, Gogol considered Belinsky as a power to be relied on. At least, Belinsky was totally absent from the passing references to Russians of the period which I heard Gogol make somewhat later (in 1841 in Rome). The critic's services were forgotten, disrupted, and grateful recollections put aside. And understandably so: there had already come between them our critic's articles about the *Moscow Observer*, those bitter remarks of Belinsky's concerning certain people belonging to the circle which had made an appeal to Gogol to save Russian society from philosophical, political, and, in general, Western daydreams. N. V. Gogol was clearly disposed toward accepting this appeal and had begun to consider his real appreciators to be people of respectable cast of mind who valued the very kind of life which was being criticized and ridiculed. Nikolay Vasilevich thought again of Belinsky only in 1842 when the cooperation of the critic could have been of some use in assuring the success of *Dead Souls* with the reading public (the book was then in the hands of the censors). He arranged at that time one *secret* meeting with Belinsky in Moscow, where the latter happened to be, and another which, while not secret, was an entirely uncompromising one, in the company of Petersburg acquaintances of his who had nothing to do with literary factions. The secret of these meetings was in fact not divulged, but, as I learned later, the meetings did not allow time for the writers to strike up a personal relationship. All that I have just spoken of, however, was to come later on and occurred during my absence from Petersburg and Russia.

At the moment now in question, on the eve of my departure for abroad in 1840, Belinsky was particularly engrossed in a study and reconsideration of Gogol's works. He had also earlier so obsessed himself with the young writer that he was forever quoting those tersely comic lines with which Gogol's literary creations abound. Now, however, he concerned himself particularly and fervently with conclusions which could be drawn from those works and from Gogol's career in general. It can well be supposed that Belinsky was using Gogol to test the fundamental principles, distinctive features and elements of Russian life, and was anxious to clarify where the artist's works stood with respect to his, Belinsky's, own philosophical views and how they could be made compatible. We must here take note that it is extremely difficult to date the change and radical shift in Belinsky's outlook with any accuracy. It is an undeniable fact that an instantaneous shift on the part of the critic to new positions did occur the following year, 1841, but it was in preparation before that, even when the author had still not abandoned his old grounds and old theory. I remain convinced that among other factors bringing Belinsky to his senses—the lessons of life, the development of his own thought, the influences of his friends—Lermontov and Gogol figure not inconsiderably. Proof of this is furnished by the articles Belinsky wrote about them in the course of 1840. Under the effect of the poet of real life, such as Gogol was then, Belinsky's philosophical optimism was bound to disintegrate once he compared it with pictures of Russian reality. No logical strategies could have helped avoid disaster—he had either to concur with the artist from whom he could expect many more new works in the same spirit or to abandon him as a writer who failed to understand the life he was depicting. Moreover, Gogol's criticisms crowned a series of criticisms incited earlier by the very nature of life around him and Belinsky's own critical intelligence. Of course, Gogol was not at all responsible for giving Belinsky a truer conception of Hegel's famous formula about the identity of Reality and Reason which liberated his mind from a philosophical delusion, but Gogol did drive the point home. And it was in that way Gogol repaid the critic for all that he had received from him toward clarifying his true professional calling.

But the remarkable thing is this: Belinsky and Gogol were fated to exchange roles and to part company, taking exactly the same roads along which they had originally come together. While Belinsky, once set on the ground of realism, forged further and further ahead in one direction, the novelist who had helped him find that justly chosen road, returned himself, after prolonged wanderings, to the point of departure at which his critic stood in the very beginning. Having exchanged places, they, each in his own way, strove to reach the ultimate, the furthest possible conclusions of their positions. And both of them died equally martyrs and victims of their intense labor over ideas—ideas aimed in entirely different directions.

CHAPTER

[IX]

As for Lermontov, Belinsky took hold of him, so to speak, and entered into his view of things slowly, step by step, with firm control over himself. Upon the first appearance of Lermontov's famous ballad [*duma*] "With heavy heart I gaze on our generation," published in the first issue of the 1839 *Notes of the Fatherland*—that monologue over which the critic subsequently ruminated frequently and at length, of which he could never get his fill and about which, later on, never stop speaking—Belinsky, still living in Moscow, made a brief and clear-cut response: "This is a vigorous poem, mighty in its form," he said, "but *somewhat lofty-hearted* in its content." It is well known what this epithet "lofty-hearted" [*prekrasnodushny*] meant in our philosophical circle. However, Belinsky did not dismiss Lermontov with one definitive verdict. Despite the contradiction between the character of Lermontov's poetry and the critic's temporary attitude of mind, the young poet, on the strength of his talent and his boldness of expression, continued to excite, arouse, and provoke the critic. Lermontov had the effect of drawing Belinsky into a struggle with himself, a struggle which took place before our eyes.

Nothing could have been more foreign, at first, to all Belinsky's habits of mind and all his aesthetic standards than Lermontov's irony, than his scorn for warm and gracious feelings at the very moment they are conceived in a man, than his sardonic divulgence of his own emptiness and insignificance without any regret and even with a certain conceited pride. The novelty and originality of this course attracted Belinsky to the poet who could display such complete candor and such power.

It cannot be denied that Belinsky recognized in Lermontov a reflection of French Byronism as it was expressed in the literature of the Paris Revolt of 1830 and in the works of the "Young France" movement, and recognized also an admixture of the spirit of our Russian

45

high-society *frondeurs,* which had an even shakier foundation than did the Parisian skepticism and despair. But he sought other reasons and other bases for them than those stemming from the poet's own life. Lermontov's talent as an artist kept the poet's visage under cover and prevented one from recognizing him. Beside the extraordinary power of creativity he unfailingly displayed, he also distinguished himself by flashes of turbulent, probing, and independent thought. That was something new in poetry, and its source, according to Belinsky's theory, had to be sought in long and hard cerebration, in ardor of heart, in excruciating experiences, and the like, though to do so meant crediting them with a great deal that might not have been warranted. And so Belinsky took up Lermontov's defense—initially against Lermontov himself.

We remember the great to-do Belinsky made over each of the poet's verses appearing in *Notes of the Fatherland* (where they were regularly published from 1839 on) and how he descried in each one of them the depths of the poet's soul, his pained and sensitive heart. Later on, he made exactly the same to-do over *The Demon,* finding in the poem, beside a portrayal of passion, an ardent defense of man's right to freedom and the unlimited exercise of freedom. The drama of the poem, though it involved mythical beings, had a completely real content for Belinsky, like a biography or a theme taken from the life of an actual person.

Belinsky's superb analysis in 1840 of the novel *Hero of Our Time* remains the monument of his efforts at construing Lermontov's attitude of mind in the best sense. In it, saving Pechorin from being charged with the wild and erratic behavior, the cynical escapades of a relentlessly swaggering and self-justifying egotism, which would have made him an anti-aesthetic and so, according to Belinsky's theory, also immoral figure, Belinsky found an hypothesis able to supply a key to the rational explanation of the hero's most heinous acts. What Belinsky wrote, accordingly, was a consummately artful and eloquent, purely legalistic defense of Pechorin. The hypothesis he found consisted in the idea that Pechorin was not yet a complete man, that he was undergoing phases of his own development which he took to be the ultimate conclusion of his life, and that he himself misjudged himself, imagining that he was a dire creature born only to be the executioner of his fellow men and the polluter of any kind of human existence. This was his misapprehension and his self-calumny. Belinsky imagined a quite different kind of Pechorin when, in the future, he, Pechorin, would complete the full circle of his career. His exacting and unqualified self-criticism, devoid of hypocrisy, his frank examination of his inclinations, however perverted they might have been, and,

above all, the power of his spiritual nature—these things served as pledges that underneath the first was another, better man who was only going through his period of trial. Belinsky even prophesied for Pechorin that his reconciliation with people and the world, once he would have completed all the natural phases of his development, would come about through the creature degraded, crushed, and scorned by him now—woman. Like a kindly nanny, Belinsky kept careful watch over each and every impulse and notion of Pechorin's, intent on finding at any opportunity all extenuating circumstances such as might be used for a lenient verdict of him, of his insufferable ambition to play with human life at his caprice and to strew around himself the victims and corpses of his egotism. In one instance only did Belinsky stop short before an escapade of Pechorin's, completely abashed, unable to find words to make the hero's crude idea fit rationally and admitting that he did not understand him. This occurred at that point where Pechorin, imagining how the woman he seduced would spend the night in tears, is thrilled with an unspeakable rapture and says: "There are moments when I understand the vampire! . . . And here I am, reputed to be a nice fellow, and going after that appellation!" "What does this whole scene mean?" Belinsky finally exclaimed. "We understand it only as evidence of the degree of cruelty and immorality to which a man can be driven by perpetual self-contradiction, by an eternally unsatisfied craving for true life, true bliss, but *we utterly fail to understand its final detail.*"

Thus Belinsky struggled with Lermontov, who in the end, however, overcame him. The excerpt from Lermontov was a remarkable one: he never said a single word without its reflecting a feature of his personality in the process of its formation, a highly idiosyncratic formation owing to the confluence of circumstances. He forged straight ahead and showed no intention at all of changing his haughty, scornful, and, at times, cruel attitudes toward the phenomena of life in favor of some other, more just and humane conception of them. Prolonged observation of that personality, as well as of others akin to it in the West, cast into Belinsky's soul the first seeds of that later doctrine which recognized that the time of pure lyric poetry, of sheer pleasure over the images, spiritual revelations, and inventions of creative art, had passed and that the only poetry belonging to our age was the poetry reflecting its disjointedness, its spiritual ailments, the deplorable state of its conscience and its spirit. Lermontov was the first native Russian to alert Belinsky to that outlook, an outlook for which, be it said, his own inner state had already prepared him. In time to come that outlook sprouted profusely.

Thus, all the materials for obliterating Belinsky's abstract, phil-

osophical principles, all the necessary preparation for his emergence from a specious pseudo-Hegelian optimism were now at hand. Yet, Belinsky freed himself from his old conception of things, which he had so diligently inculcated in himself, slowly, as if from a love affair, although already in mid-1840 he could not help feeling horror and revulsion when recalling or speaking about his article on Menzel, the article with which he began that extraordinary year in his life, written in 1839 when he was still living in Moscow.

The aesthetic articles about which we have been speaking, the ones which followed the Menzel article, were the fruit of his Petersburg meditations. Glimmers of Belinsky's former orientation still adhered in many of their passages, but it was with these articles that the extraordinary critic reemerged into the literary arena in full possession of his thought and his engaging style. All his abilities, the whole force of his congenital literary perspicacity awoke. His articles were no mere periodical reviews—they were virtually events of the literary world of the time. All of them helped establish new points of view on things; they were read voraciously; they made a deep, indelible impression on the contemporary reading public, on all of us, despite whatever traces of former, not wholly relinquished, beliefs might have been found in them and despite the fact that the author himself subsequently renounced certain of their propositions and verdicts on account of their immoderate gusto and excessive loftiness. Belinsky the critic-artist was genuinely a man of power and authority who was able to bring others under his sway. We need do no more by way of explaining the captivating effect of all his 1840 reviews after the Menzel article than to mention that each of them conducted a sort of masterful dissection of the work considered—the work's whole inner structure was laid bare with a vividness and tangibleness that provided a pleasure sometimes equal to, and sometimes even exceeding, the pleasure one experienced reading the original work itself. It was a reproduction of the work, only a work now refracted, so to speak, through the soul and aesthetic sensibility of the critic and acquiring from this contact a new life, a greater freshness, and a profounder expression.

Thus, in his artistic-aesthetic criticism of 1840, Belinsky found a way out of the entanglement of his philosophical dogmatism. It was with this trend that I left him upon my departure for abroad.

CHAPTER

[X]

BEFORE LEAVING RUSSIA, however, I had occasion to spend some time again in Moscow. This time Belinsky supplied me with a letter to Vasily Petrovich Botkin whom I did not know at all but whom I had heard talked about frequently and at length. I hastened to call on him at the first opportunity. That was in mid-June of 1840.

I discovered V. P. Botkin in the summerhouse of the garden adjacent to the famous Botkin mansion on Moroseika. He had arranged himself a very elegant summer study there and spent his leisure hours surrounded by numerous editions of Shakespeare and volumes of Shakespeare commentaries by European scholars. He was in the midst of writing an article on Shakespeare. The Botkin I found then was a young man, wearing a handsome toupee, with extremely intelligent and expressive eyes the melancholy cast of which constantly gave way to sparks and flashes testifying to physical energies far from subdued by his intellectual occupations. He was pale, very gracefully built, and had hovering about his lips a kindly but somehow guarded smile—as if his innate skepticism, as far as people were concerned, were retaining its rights over him even in the sphere of boundless idealism in which he happened to be then.

It became clear later on that he was standing on the threshold of a radical change of moral attitude which even he himself did not as yet suspect. No one paid any attention to the sudden glimmers of passion that frequently broke out on his face and in his words, and it did not occur to anyone that there might be in him a person other than the one his close friends and companions knew and loved.

Naturally, we got to talking about Belinsky and his excruciating efforts to find a way out of his predicament, efforts very cogently derived from a certain thesis but very unsubstantial when it came to practical life. "He is paying now," Botkin remarked to me in a pensive and somehow grim tone, as if he were directing his remark to himself, "for an extremely important error in his life—his disdain for the French. He found no artistry among them, no pure creativity, and for that reason declared his implacable enmity for them. But in the meantime, without knowledge of their political propaganda there is no judging them. *Your Petersburg* will afford him a great advantage in this respect: he will certainly change his views about the French." Botkin did not, however, really think *our* Petersburg such a panacea for Belinsky's delusions as his remark made it appear. From the sizable correspondence Botkin carried on with Belinsky at the time, it is evident that the critic's friend was still very much afraid that, in his new locale, isolated from the Moscow circle natural for him, the critic might lose sight of the great principles of philosophical comprehension of things literary and moral.

The analysis of *Inspector General,* written at just that same time, served as Belinsky's answer to Botkin's needless apprehensions. Seeing that this article also constitutes a biographical landmark in the critic's life, I shall pause now to consider it.

Perhaps nowhere else did the most striking qualities of Belinsky's aesthetic criticism, the criticism about which we have been talking, find expression to so marked a degree as in this analysis of *Inspector General,* wherein Belinsky contrasted the play with *Woe from Wit.* In it, Khlestakov's every impulse and those of the mayor, his wife, his daughter, indeed of the comedy's cast of characters altogether, were perused with the perseverance of a theoretician-psychologist solving a knotty problem which someone has posed him. Each intimation of their personalities, often consisting in some single word or momentary feature, was seized upon with an inspiration equivalent, one might say, to the artist's own. The whole progression of the author's creative thinking was analyzed to the nth degree, and the reader of the article cannot help feeling that he is present in some laboratory of criticism where all the designs, devices, and pervasive schemes of the artist's craftsmanship are precipitated before his eyes. It was as if the secrets of another man's work did not exist for Belinsky.

Incidentally, a number of ideas were contained in the article, which, surprisingly enough, were later appropriated by Gogol himself and are to be found in his own defense of his comedy, an example of such ideas being the mayor's gross error in taking the whippersnapper Khlestakov for the inspector general as the result of an uneasy conscience. "Not dire reality but the apparition, the phantom or, rather, the shade of terror of a guilty conscience was bound to punish the man of apparitions (the mayor)," Belinsky said in one passage. Even the famous idea advanced by Gogol that the honest being in *Inspector*

General was laughter, even that had been said earlier by Belinsky. Having noted that the basis of tragedy arises in a struggle arousing pity and stimulating a feeling of pride in the dignity of human nature, Belinsky continued: "Similarly, the basis of comedy is in a comic struggle arousing laughter; but there is in this laughter not mirth alone but also *vengeance for injured human dignity, and thus, in a different way than tragedy, once again the triumph of Moral Law is revealed.*" Many other similar passages were included in the article. I forbear deriving any conclusions from this similarity, though it would be quite proper to suppose that Gogol had read Belinsky's article with, to say the least, utmost interest.

As for *Woe from Wit,* Belinsky regarded the comedy as a wonderful picture of mores and as a satire of genius, but he did not find in it a creation of truly artistic structure. Though he admired it, he regretted that he could not apply to it the philosophical-aesthetic procedures he had used in analyzing *Inspector General.* He was still bound by theoretical prohibitions and limitations; and somewhat later, in that period of attention to political and social questions that V. P. Botkin had predicted, Belinsky himself considered his verdict far from exhausting the entire meaning of Griboyedov's comedy.

Among other things, during this same period of time, Belinsky closed accounts and severed connections with a man of whom he had thought very highly only a little while before and whom he had deeply respected and loved—N. A. Polevoy. Under pressure of the onerous circumstances of his life, N. A. Polevoy, once having become editor of *Son of the Fatherland,* went over to the side of the enemies of the philosophical movement in Russia and of the very development of an independent, critical journalism of the era that, incidentally, he had in fact begun here himself. Now, by making disdainful and derisive remarks about youthful attempts to discover some special precepts for living and thinking without reference to experience and the conditions of the time, Polevoy thought to make himself an indispensable person in that entourage of people and ideas in which he had taken refuge after the demise of the *Moscow Telegraph.* But his plans did not succeed here, either. He was regarded by those people with suspicion even when he was defending them. However, it was enough to extinguish in Belinsky the embers of a heartfelt devotion for that former nimble-witted publicist and, more recently, romantic teller of tales. He expressed his attitude frankly in his analysis of N. A. Polevoy's *Essays in Russian Literature,* an analysis which can stand alongside his earlier analysis of S. P. Shevyrev's work in the vividness of its colors and the certitude of its conclusions. Both analyses averted any influence that authorities and reputations no longer meeting the needs of the time might have had on people of the new generation, and both analyses decided the fates of two important names in literature.

When I returned again to Petersburg after my summertime absence of three months, I found a great change in Belinsky. He had by then come out of the spiritual crisis he had been in when I left him. The reproaches he had made himself in private, in the depths of his heart, for his recent obsession he now expressed triumphantly, in no uncertain terms and for all to hear. The tone and cast of his conversations were permeated with self-criticism of the most blatant and merciless kind. He had already been through, and had forgotten, the pangs of mortifying confessions, and now made them publicly. Recipient of reproofs from all sides, he was now free to discuss, justify, and supplement them. Stankevich had written from Berlin, shocked about the *new* theories coming out in Petersburg; we have already mentioned above the indignation felt in Herzen's circle, which then included, beside Ogarev [45] and others, also Granovsky. Even the criticisms of outsiders, people much less likely to balk at hunting out unsavory sources to explain Belinsky's ultraconservatism, found an advocate in Belinsky. He adopted the position of his defamers, he himself enlarged on what they said, citing details which could strengthen the vitriol of their polemics, and only finding no justification for himself. Thus was his crisis resolved.

One suspected that Belinsky found something alleviating in those incessant scourgings of his reputation. Some feature of that kind of self-excoriation would crop up sometimes in Belinsky without any especially important reason for it, sometimes engendering hilarious and comical outbursts. We know that our critic, back in 1839, committed a five-act blunder—that psychologically flat and sentimental comedy of his, *Fifty-Year-Old Uncle,* about which he did not like to remember and of which he was ashamed. Once, several years after its appearance, at a time when Belinsky was a big name and a big influence in literature, he was introduced somewhere to the well-known professor of Slavic philology, I. Sreznevsky, who, before saying anything else, announced that he was not in sympathy with Belinsky's criticism but, on the other hand, thought his comedy a work of genius. Belinsky could never recall that remark afterward without an expression of utter perplexity, as if the matter in question were something totally impossible and contrary to nature.

Another circumstance worthy of mention is the fact that the conservative patriots of the period failed to discern the meaning of Belinsky's philosophical articles altogether, though the articles certainly should have appealed to them. Instead, they joined the crowd of the

critic's hecklers. Even highly educated people, people zealous on behalf of the inner as well as the outer dignity of Russian life, such as S.
Shevyrev, for instance, missed seeing the help Belinsky's articles were
providing their own cause through numerous highly intelligent and
apt observations about national psychology contained in them, observations which anticipated the science of the spiritual life of peoples
that has since emerged. Those educated men and professors dwelt
only on Belinsky's turbid language and went no further, well pleased
with the chance to direct extra gibes at an adversary. Thus, no important political meaning was discovered by either the one side or the
other. And how indeed could one have expected it then? The first
flashes of political meaning were engendered in our country only in
the heat of the great dispute between the Slavophiles and Westerners,
and it was there they grew strong, about all of which we shall speak
further on.

CHAPTER

[XI]

LATE IN THE FALL of the same year, 1840, the young M. Katkov,[46] translator of *Romeo and Juliet,* with an already established reputation as a highly knowledgeable philologist and impressively talented abstract thinker and critic of ideas, made his appearance in Petersburg from Moscow. His pursuits at that time included certain other, additional aims, for he endeavored to show himself not only a man of encyclopedic learning but also one with a lust for life, laboring no less at imbuing his physiognomy with a demonic cast than he did over philosophical matters, poetry, art, and creative efforts. The desire to be reputed a man capable of understanding and appreciating all aspects of existence put him up, at times, to outlandish endeavors, prompted in him actions and outbursts of a fantastic character, in part genuine, since he did indeed possess a passionate and enthusiastic nature, but in part consciously cultivated as an embellishment, a sign of distinction, a *beneficial* spiritual trait. All this fit together rather poorly with plans for study and a life of toil which he had made for himself, and the result was that he turned into an enigma for his associates, which was just what he wanted.

Katkov had already begun collaborating on Kraevsky's *Literary Supplements* and *Notes of the Fatherland* in 1839 and, when the editorial staff of the latter journal was reorganized, he, along with Belinsky, was among its chief directors. He, too, had stayed with I. I. Panaev—the instrument and agent of that reorganization—after arriving in Petersburg. He made but a brief appearance there, however, continuing his way from Petersburg to Berlin in order, first, to finish his philosophical and scientific education and, second, to acquit himself in an affair of honor. Some old and rather crude jibe of Bakunin's —a jibe not without Bakunin's usual moralizing—with reference to a certain happening in Moscow had caused quite an ugly scene in Belinsky's study between Katkov and Bakunin sometime after both had come to Petersburg. The matter was to have been decided by a duel in Berlin. To the satisfaction of friends gravely concerned about the adversaries, the duel never did take place.[47]

In Petersburg Katkov was preceded, as I said, by his reputation as a man of sensitive character and an original intelligence fostered especially by his acquaintance with the sources of then prevalent theories, and, finally, his reputation as a writer who had already distinguished himself for his skill in expressing aptly and vividly original aspects of philosophical ideas, historical periods, and topics in art generally. Katkov's critical articles did indeed betoken a very fresh, versatile, and powerful talent. Among his articles, one that remains memorable for me is his review of Zinovev's *The Fundamentals of Russian Stylistics*. The article justified the first emergence of rhetoric as a science by the tenor of the entire life and civilization of the ancient Greeks, and demonstrated the utter ridiculousness of rhetoric's claim to the appellation of a science in the life of modern society. This same quality of brilliant exposition and comprehension of the historical and social essence of problems was shared by many other articles of his in *Literary Supplements* and *Notes of the Fatherland* of 1839-40. Belinsky valued his collaboration on *Notes of the Fatherland* very highly and expected it to have momentous consequences for the journal, which, however, never did come about.

Katkov was then living through a phase of development one might well call the "wildness of youth" and which often finds issue in things which seem blatantly impossible and bizarre in connection with the person we know later on, when his character has assumed its definitive shape. His visage almost never relinquished an expression of a certain slight contempt for the *intelligentsia* in whose circle he moved, and his actions even more strongly expressed his conviction that he was privileged not to appreciate them. No exception was made for Belinsky. Katkov did not in the slightest conceal his lofty conception of himself and the great hopes he placed on his own future, and he was of the opinion that these could serve as adequate grounds for a tolerant attitude toward his flagrant antics and abuses of friends who, after all, were concerned only with supporting, encouraging, and reinforcing his career and influence.

During his brief sojourn in Petersburg, aside from certain bibliographical articles, he translated, together with others, Fenimore Cooper's *The Pathfinder* and composed the monograph "Sarah Tolstoy," which appeared in *Notes of the Fatherland* almost on the eve of his departure for abroad. Belinsky was very pleased with the article before its publication and even had a great deal to say about it. However, hardly two months later, he changed his opinion about it, a fact of which I became aware at a later time. Belinsky had felt a sudden revulsion for psychological probings in the domain of *Spirit*, for analysis of the elusive feelings and sensations of the inner life of man, in a word, for all that metaphysics of Mind and Will which was abundantly proffered in Katkov's essay but which had already begun to lose its meaning for Belinsky. There was still another consideration. It became more and more clear from the whole cast of Katkov's thought and work, once he had taken his very first steps abroad, that he was far more concerned with the idea of inculcating in his homeland new bases of positive contemplation and belief such as he had discerned in the latter-day philosophy of Schelling's "revelations" than with the mission of working for the enlightenment of the uncouth Russian social milieu directly and unequivocally, as the times demanded. Katkov himself soon confirmed all Belinsky's surmises.

While still in Hamburg, having barely, so to speak, taken his first steps on European soil, Katkov felt that the success of *Notes of the Fatherland* would provide Belinsky and himself the means for a secure existence for the rest of their lives, but less than a year later he had terminated all relations with the journal. It would be far too superficial and petty to interpret this as a matter of dubious financial dealings between the editorial staff and one of its members. The fact is that the matter is quite adequately explained by Katkov's aversion to following along the way of irrevocable negation that feared and shunned explanations. In 1842, on these grounds, he took a skeptical attitude even toward Gogol's *Dead Souls,* as I had the chance personally to corroborate, and not so much toward the epic itself as toward its future panegyrists whom he foresaw and of whom he was more apprehensive than of the conclusions of the work itself.

In mid-autumn, 1840 (October 5), Katkov and I boarded the *last* ship leaving from Petersburg for Lübeck. Belinsky, Koltsov, and Panaev accompanied us to Kronstadt.

I have mentioned the name of Koltsov.[48] This occasion was my first and last meeting with that extraordinary man. I see, as if this moment, the short and stocky poet with that purely Russian, high-cheek-boned face of his and his look of intense curiosity and alertness. During the whole time of our send-off he remained silent, as if nonplussed and cowed by the clever talk—and free and easy talk of literary authorities, at that—to which he listened with the docile attention of a neophyte. This was a sort of mask he felt obliged to put on in the company of literary people who had done so much to propagate his renown, for, after our dinner at Kronstadt, he even addressed me, a thoroughly obscure and totally uninfluential member of the circle, with the words: "Don't forget that you have a duty to teach us and enlighten us." There was much sincerity in the feeling which prompted him to say such things, but there was also much that was habit acquired from constant contact with a circle of writers. This habit did not, however, interfere with his ability to make judgments. According to Belinsky, there was never a man more observant, perceptive, and shrewd than Koltsov with his placid and docile appearance: he saw through people's accumulated layers of culture and civilization, and made quite apt and original judgments about them. This did not prevent him from surrendering himself irrevocably, from time to time, both in his personal life and in his poetic career, to the influence and control of some favorite personality, in which respect he also thoroughly expressed his Russian nature.

Belinsky, for one, had Koltsov's mind and soul absolutely in his power: aside from our critic's extirpating from Koltsov's folk song, with its stunning imagery, the poet's unfortunate penchant for moralizing rhetoric, he also, at one time, induced him to write his religious hymns and, at a later time, brought out in him rudiments of a poetic outlook on life and a craving for the delights of existence which such an outlook brings in its train. Koltsov, nevertheless, retained that same original form of his, that same turn and inimitable style of speech no matter with what topic it dealt. This feature should, I think, put a stop to recent aspersions cast at the poet to the effect that he appropriated other people's literary goods. There is a story, repeated time and time again by Belinsky, going back to the epoch about which we are now relating. Once, in the heyday of Moscow philosophic-mindedness, a group of friends, all students of the science of sciences, met at V. P. Botkin's, and met, moreover, in the happiest and gayest of moods. There still existed for the people of those days the *joy* of coming upon an idea in one's reading, the *joy* of discovering a new factor in spiritual life, the *joy* of attaining a new horizon for thought, etc. The circle was exulting at one such incorporeal and abstract joy that few people today are any longer able to appreciate. Koltsov happened on the circle at that moment, and without, of course, fully comprehending what the reason for his friends' ecstatic words was, fell under the captivating effect of the general mood. He himself became elated. Withdrawing to his host's study, he sat down at his desk, and a few minutes later returned to his friends with a piece of paper in hand. "And I have written a song," he said shyly and recited the poem "Song of the Outrider Kudryavich," it being his way of making a kind of response and contribution to the excited talk of the young Moscow enthusiasts.

It would not be amiss to mention in passing that a part of Koltsov's biography touching on his family ought, I believe, now to be taken with a certain amount of caution and qualification, and that this is essential especially if one is to corroborate surmises that no really deliberate, premeditated persecution on the part of members of his family did occur in Koltsov's life. The members of his family did not then, and for a long time afterward, consider themselves guilty before the deceased poet; and indeed they may well be, if not exonerated, at least pardoned in the tribunal of posterity. They lived according to the rules, usages, and views of an uncouth culture which they inherited from their forebears, and could not comprehend that merely by the mode of their brutish concepts and the life they lived according to those concepts, they were offending and ultimately destroying a fellow being. They wounded and tortured their victim without malice and without being conscious of doing so, and therein only does the tragedy of Koltsov's family situation lie, the tragedy of a man, so well-developed as he already was, doomed to life in a squalid milieu.

Thus we departed, leaving Belinsky at work devising principles of aesthetics, which he understood in no such narrow a way as one normally thinks applicable in aesthetic matters generally. Certain factors to which I have already referred make it possible to appreciate how enormously meaningful a content he imparted to those principles; and the further he went, the greater the scope of his aesthetic principles also became, encompassing not just conditions and problems of art but also questions of life and morality which were indissolubly bound up with them. Mention of morality is very apropos. On my departure, I took away with me the image of Belinsky as primarily a moralist, and I think a few words need to be said about that now.

It is common knowledge that the morality underlying all Belinsky's ideas and all his works was exactly the power of attraction that rallied ardent friends and supporters around him. His, so to speak, fanatic quest for truth and verity in life did not leave him even when, for a time, he departed from the truth. In the circle of his acquaintances his authority as a moralist never suffered from his delusions. The extraordinary integrity of his whole character and his ability to sway others and extricate them from pernicious trains of thought continued to have a captivating effect on his friends even when he went counter to their convictions. An account of his declaration of moral beliefs, an activity which lasted throughout his life, could also be considered his true biography.

By the end of 1840, Belinsky had ceased deriving moral good from the complete abrogation of one's own personality, of one's "I," and the transference of one's whole self into the expanse of infinite *love*, as was the case in his first (Schellingian) period of development; nor did it consist in the *understanding* of one's own self as the highest creative factor in the activity of Universal Reason and Supreme Idea, as was its Hegelian interpretation. Infinite *love* and absolute *understanding* of one's spiritual essence as principles out of which issued all the precepts of life were supplanted by a different and single agent. Now, moral good for Belinsky consisted in the aesthetic cultivation of one's own self, i.e., in acquiring a sensibility for the True, the Good, and the Beautiful, and developing an invincible, organic revulsion for ugliness of any shape or kind. I still vividly recall conversations in which Belinsky elaborated this postulation of his. It was his belief that study of the basic ideas in the creative works of true artists could serve as a good device for elevating one's self to the level of Rational Man and Purified Personality. For him, all these basic ideas were, at the same time, revelations of the moral world. From analysis and assimilation of them, society would experience little by little the emergence of a moral code, an unwritten code, without marble tablets or charters, but one better able than those others to take hold in the individual consciousness and better able to bring order to a man's inner way of life and, through the individual man, to the way of life of whole generations. To this informal code of moral precepts, each new artist of genius would contribute, so to speak, some new feature, some new detail, culled directly from observation and definition of elements of man's spiritual nature. Side by side with existing and functioning, written and unwritten, necessary and unnecessary laws of communal life and good order, another law would take shape, immeasurably more luminous, rational and serious, which people aesthetically developed would follow. A man cultivated on the world view of great artists, poets, philosophers, thinkers ultimately would become capable of creativity himself in the domain of moral ideas, would discover new principles of truth and promulgate them, submitting to them in his own behavior and making others do likewise. Belinsky came upon a great many profound ideas on this ground, abandoned by him in the final stage of his career for a different one which also provided him a great many conclusions of considerable importance and about which we shall speak further on.

And what a shock it gave him when, around this same time, a new journal, the *Lighthouse*,[49] was announced for publication, a journal primarily supposed, it was said, to promote the rehabilitation and development of the old, pre-Petrine, *tried and true Russian* morality neglected by our elite and literary society. Belinsky was the first to rush in and take up this gauntlet. He expressed his reaction to the imminent appearance of the journal in angry and belligerent terms. Just prior to my departure he even showed me, in an article he was preparing, a passage referring to the journal: "Our dormant literature has begun to be infiltrated by a Chinese spirit; the spirit has begun its inroad, not under its own proper, that is to say, Chinese, name *Tsun-Kin-Tsin,* but with a counterfeit passport, under an assumed name, calling itself *Moral Spirit.* It is said that the genial mandarins have conceived the honorable intention of publishing, in the Russian language, a journal whose aim is to diffuse that odoriferous Chinese spirit [50] in Russian literature" (from his "Analysis of *Olga,*" a novel by the author of *The Kholmsky Family*). The facetiously made-up Chinese word [51] greatly amused the author, but it did not come close to expressing adequately the magnitude of the indignation that seized him on learning of plans to found a journal for the defense of obsolete principles—their validity in the past for a very important historical epoch notwithstanding. All this was by way of premonition of that bitter struggle he was soon to carry on against exactly those principles in the hands of enemies far more efficient and numerous than the future editorial staff of the promised journal.[52]

Belinsky's attacks on moral sophistry led, however, to a misunderstanding that has continued practically to this very day. It is essential to bear in mind that Belinsky had completely adopted, for his own use, Hegel's division of moral principles into two realms: the *ethical* (*Moralität*), to which he relegated more or less well-conceived rules of communal life, and *morals* proper (*Sittlichkeit*), which, in his conception, embraced the very laws governing man's spiritual world and engendered ethical needs and notions. Having become the sponsor of those ideas in Russian life, Belinsky began his long and noble campaign of assailing what he called moralizing or moral sophistry in literature and in the various manifestations of our society generally. When his graphic and straightforward style of writing returned to him after something of an hiatus, he pursued incessantly his vigilant campaign of running down moral sophistry, which had then assumed a position of dominance with us in the theater, in all branches of literature and in life, seeing that it served people as a means whereby they could hide their spiritual nakedness and attempt to delude themselves and others on the matter of their moral vacuity. Everything smacking of seemly but, in fact, dastardly moralizing rhetoric, with its desire to supplant obvious facts with a specious interpretation of them; everything bearing the stamp of wishy-washy, vacuous sententiousness calculated to obtain by cheap means, without trouble or effort, a reputation for honesty and decency; everything, finally, smacking of Chinese kow-towing to the good old days and fanatic loathing for the efforts of the new age—all these things were stigmatized by Belinsky with the tag "moralizing" or "moral sophistry," and were assailed by him with a courage truly extraordinary for those days.

Belinsky's merciless exposé of this monster "moralizing" is to be found spread practically throughout all his articles dating from that time. To get an idea of how energetic a tongue was used usually to carry this out, those interested can read any review of his (see, for instance, his review of R. Zotov's *Tsin-kiu-Tong*) or any theatrical notice. (See his notice on S. Navrotsky's comedy *The New Minor*— Belinsky also composed theatrical feuilletons when writing for *Notes of the Fatherland*.) He went so far as to make "moralizing" a bad word in our vocabulary, but this work of his did not leave him unscathed. It gave his enemies the opportunity to contrive, using misinterpretation and play on words, and to foist on him, a reputation as an immoral creature who repudiated the laws without which no society could sustain itself. They succeeded in declaring immoral a man who throughout his life sought the basic principles of an ideally virtuous existence on earth, who, in spite of his own ridicule of moralizing, was one of the most remarkable *moralists of his age*, and who professed and sanctioned in his milieu a salutary hatred for all that was banal, hypocritical, degrading.

I spent three years abroad, receiving exceedingly little news from home. During that interval of time, an extremely important change ensued in Belinsky's state of mind and spirit and in the trend of his whole career, which means also in his notions about morality, as we shall soon see.

CHAPTER

[XII]

WE LEFT PETERSBURG engaged in an occupation unusual for it. Petersburg had taken up the reading of foreign newspapers: it was unexpectedly in a stir over the *Egyptian* question. Ten years previously, in the early 1830's, our public had been very little interested even in such an event as the French Revolution of 1830, and made no effort to apprise itself of the causes that engendered it. Now the situation was somewhat different: at the first rumor of the possibility of clashes in Europe, curiosity siezed even the lazy-minded. Foreign newspapers and pamphlets, as many as could be obtained, turned up even in the hands of people least used to bearing a like burden. The habit of keeping informed about the course of events in Europe remained, however, even after the threatened danger had passed. What had previously constituted, so to speak, a privilege of the highest aristocratic and governmental spheres now became a common practice.

The influence that Europe and its affairs began to exert on our intelligentsia, from 1840 on, obliges me to turn reluctantly to my travel recollections and to say a few words about what Russians generally found in contemporary Europe and, most particularly, in France, which had succeeded Germany in their favor as regards Western cultures.

To begin then, in Western Europe, where we arrived after four days of rather rough sailing, momentous preparations were going on. Germany was on the point of going to war with France over the principle of *legitimacy* violated by the Egyptian pasha, who had conceived the idea of exchanging his vassalage to the Porte for status as a French protectorate, with France supporting him in that intention. England, little concerned with principles of legitimacy when appealed to by European councils, was the first to rise in defense of their sanctity once the matter involved Turkey. The governments on the continent were overjoyed at England's support: it provided them the opportunity to display without risk their pent-up hatred for revolutionary, *unprincipled* France; their peoples, still denied representation, were ready to do battle with the enemy for the sake of their honor, which had been injured by the bluster of Parisian journalists and the bravado of the republicans and left side of the French Chamber of Deputies. This imbroglio was beginning to reach fever pitch when we disembarked at Travemünde. At one of the stops on the way from Lübeck to Hamburg, M. Katkov, while breakfast was being prepared for us, showed me a page of a German newspaper featuring something new, Becker's famous patriotic song *"Sie sollen ihn* (the Rhine) *nicht haben,"* which subsequently made all the rounds of Germany from one end to the other.

The militant activity caused by the wild, raving, and, despite all his slyness, paltry Egyptian exploiter did not, fortunately, last long, a circumstance that relieved Europe of the pleasure of seeing Phrygian caps behind the French *contingents* and behind the German *Landsturm,* our own commisariat officials. Louis Philippe wearied of hearing the "Marseillaise" played under his windows at Tuileries every day and of receiving one report after another about military-revolutionary attitudes of mind. Sensible England, having signed a treaty guaranteeing Turkey's rights with practically all of Europe, left the treaty open, should France at some future time wish to join it. Everything was saved thereby, and the Neptunes from the banks of the Seine and the Thames could, without disgrace, turn back the storm they had unleashed and retire to peace and quiet.

When everything had calmed down in the North German world, it turned out that France had not only not lost credit there but that its credit had all but actually grown. At least it was possible to think so in Berlin, judging by the combined efforts of its police, church, scholarship, theater, and even ballet to deflect the public's aroused attention away from Paris and its goings on. Whole bureaus and corporate bodies in Berlin seemed concerned only with the question of how to combat Paris, counter its influence, and protect people from its blandishments, both in the world of ideas and in the pragmatic world, for which purpose they devised, to replace the Parisian ones, their own blandishments, but of a less emphatic and lurid character.

Not to speak of efforts to endow the then meager town on the River Spree with the false semblance of a large capital and important political center, up to 1848 it was the site where sermons were composed, scientific treatises published, and a philosophy and art created —all for the struggle against French *impiety* and for the purpose of putting it to shame. One question was posed in an endless number of different ways and was heard, one might say, in every quarter: Will

the staunch German mind and German devotion to historical traditions, the attachment of Germans to their hearth and home and their
indigenous ways, and, finally, the German compulsion to penetrate to
the core of every idea—will all this allow itself to be overruled by the
frivolity and impiety of a certain Romanic tribe that had lost touch
with the fundamental bases of human and political existence? This
question was openly posed by representatives of the regime, by min-
isters, by orators, from the church pulpits, by many professors, journalists, men of letters, and artists. The subdued and discreet France of
Louis Philippe engendered in certain official and conservative circles
such a store of secret resentment and anger as those circles could not
find in themselves when, fifteen years later, that same France hung
heavy over practically all the councils of Europe.[53] There is a simple
explanation for this: the July 1830 Revolution dealt the first severe
blow to the treaties of 1815 and to the moral and political foundations
established by the "Holy Alliance." The wound which, in 1830, France
had inflicted on the customary order of things and trend of ideas in
Europe was far from fatal, but the wound, nevertheless, ached and
provoked grim thoughts about the eventual outcome of the malady.
Hence—the hue and cry, the summoning of endless numbers of doctors, and the search for possible means of an immediate cure.

For the time being, however, all attempts to screen Paris and
France from people's eyes fell short of the success desired. Significant
interference came from the so-called Young Germany, which instantly
aroused attention in Russia. Defeated on the streets and squares ten
years before, it had since succeeded in taking over a sector of publicistics, the philosophical polemics, and, primarily, the adverse criticism of German science, life, and art; it followed openly the banner
and fortune of a foreign nation skilled in posing to itself great quan-
tities of political and social questions. It was not that this party possessed any fruitful political idea or any doctrine able to respond to all
demands. It had undertaken to shake up the German world, and it
numbered among its supporters even a certain rather significant mi-
nority of prudent and dispassionate minds who were unhappy with
the long delay in the fulfillment of certain solemn promises made to
the people in 1813 and with recent attempts to change, wherever possible, the meaning and essence of Protestantism. The majority, however, resisted the disintegrating effect of Young Germany as staunchly
as possible.

German society of the time, with the government administration
at its head, applied a very simple system of dividing people into two
categories: those whose sympathy was with France, having forgotten
all her numerous sins against Germany, and those whose trust lay in

the German genius, notwithstanding its failure as yet to display all its powers and resources. The latter, who enjoyed protection and support from the highest official circles, also professed a doctrine holding that any free political activity by the people must always be preceded by rigorous preparations in the imperturbable realm of thought, science, and theory. The University of Berlin, thanks to the combined efforts of the government administration and men of science, grew into just such a ready-made realm. German scholarship flourished there as it had nowhere else. Taking advantage of the privilege of familiarizing oneself with courses before registering for them, we went from auditorium to auditorium every evening, listening to the lectures of the University's most distinguished professors. I found, still at the University, the esteemed Werder, friend and teacher of Stankevich, Granovsky, Turgenev, Frolov,[54] and many other Russians. He was expatiating on Hegel's Logic and continued to quote Goethe's verses and aphorisms for the sake of infusing the master's abstract formulas with tints of life and poetry. Ritter [55] and Schelling had also begun their courses. My interest was aroused by a lecture given by Stahl, the philosopher-pietist and one of the future founders of the newspaper *Kreuz-Zeitung*, who was expounding the fundamental bases essential for the realization of a truly Christian state, the genuine type of which had not as yet been achieved anywhere in the world, etc.

However, the liberal, political commotion of minds, begun in 1830, was not drowned out by the University of Berlin programs, but, on the contrary, continued to grow in the shadow of the University. To support it, there still existed Ruge's still very vocal *Jahrbücher*,[56] a purely revolutionary organ which had also not abandoned philosophism, having made it serve as a weapon in the campaign against German institutions and, in general, the modesty and narrowness of German outlook on life. As if in refutation of this reproach to native science, Germany had produced somewhat earlier a book replete with theological erudition, and arousing, at the start, universal horror, not only in government councils and offices but also among outright liberals—the famous book by Strauss.[57] Free investigation was beginning to outgrow the requirements of those who had brought it to life and defended it. The time was not far off when German erudition and theory would develop, especially in the area of theology and political economy, so great a daring in its conclusions and propositions that it would provoke our newspaper and clubroom sage of the day, N. I. Grech, into making his ubiquitously known and momentously meaningful observation. About 1848, in public hearing, he declared: "Not France, but Germany has now become the stuffer of heads with perverted ideas and anarchy. Our young people ought to be forbidden to travel, not to France, but to Germany, a place where they are still expressly sent to study. The French journalists and various revolutionary fantasizers are innocent babes in comparison with German scholars, their books and pamphlets." He was right in the last instance, but for the time being it was possible to remain in Berlin without detriment to one's morality and to select freely among the disputing factions a point of view and a tendency to suit oneself. Each newly arrived Russian was asked jokingly by his fellow countrymen who had already spent a number of years in the center of German erudition, if the former expressed any desire to remain there, what, first of all, he intended to become: a *true*, noble German (*der treue, edle Deutsche*) or a silly, foppish Frenchman (*der eitle, alberne Franzose*)? There was never any question about whether he would want to stay a Russian; and indeed, there could be no such question. Real Russian Russians did not even exist then: there were registrars, assessors, councillors of all possible appellations, and finally, landowners, officers, and students speaking Russian, but a Russian type in the positive sense of the word and of the sort who could pass muster as a sound and independent person—that kind of Russian had not yet come on the scene.

One evening at a certain Berlin coffeehouse (Spargniapani's *Unter den Linden*) which was noted for its huge collection of German and foreign newspapers and journals, I met two Russians of tall stature, with remarkably handsome and expressive faces—Turgenev and Bakunin, who at that time were inseparable. No exchange of greetings ensued: I was not yet acquainted with either one of them and had no inkling of my future close relationship with the former. In Berlin, I also said goodbye to M. Katkov. He had registered as auditor at the University, whereas I was headed for the south, close enough to Italy to be able, with the coming of the first days of spring, to set foot on its classic ground.

CHAPTER

[XIII]

I HAPPENED TO SPEND the winter of 1840–41 in Metternich's Vienna. It is virtually impossible now even to imagine the magnitude of the deaf and dumb decorum which the famed chancellor of Austria had succeeded in establishing, thanks to his unflagging surveillance of every manifestation of social life and his boundless suspicion of anything new throughout the whole extent of the territory from the mountains of Bohemia to the Bay of Baia and even beyond. It would happen that you would travel through that magnificently appointed wasteland, as if through the mausoleum streets of Pompey, amid the appalling decorum of death, met and escorted by phantoms in the shape of customs officials, passport officials, gendarmes, porters, and inspectors of passengers' pockets. You would not encounter a single thought or word or piece of news or opinion, but only their semblances supplied from the official factories that manufactured them for mass consumption by the inhabitants and put them into circulation under their official stamp. For contemplative persons this silence and tranquillity was a windfall: they could lose themselves completely in self-study or study of subjects of their own choosing without being distracted by the hubbub of the crowd or the clashes of factions. Gogol, Ivanov,[58] Iordan,[59] and many others lived fully and happily in that environment, thus realizing in themselves considerably before Carlyle certain features of his ideal man of wisdom, devoutly paying homage to the geniuses of art and literature, keeping the sanctum of their souls for themselves, devoting the whole of their beings to their chosen tasks, and not chatting idly with everyone about everything on the occasion of the latest issue of a journal.

However, behind the wise men and the contemplatives could also be seen the noisy, thousand-eyed crowd which could not abide the long silence around them, especially where there was an admixture of southern temperament, as was the case in Italy. To find ways of amusing that crowd became, in fact, the chief concern and undertaking of the government. Who has not heard about the pleasures of Vienna and about the perpetual, if sedate, properly policed and decorous, orgy that prevailed in it? Who does not also know about the festivities of Italy, about the magnificent orchestras which daily boomed out on each of the plazas of its big cities, about its religious processions and about its impresarios who staged operas in its theaters (on which occasions the noisy Italian public was permitted, notwithstanding two white-uniformed soldiers flanking the orchestra with rifles in their hands, to have its fling howsoever and as much as its heart desired)? To amuse the crowd was considered serious government business— but in the wake of so many eyewitnesses, there is no real necessity, of course, to reproduce that scene here.

Only one feature in that so well-ordered world continually struck and amazed me. Despite all the magnificence and all the trappings of public life and despite the strictest possible ban on foreign books (in the duchy of Modena possession of a book without the censor's stamp was punishable no more, no less than by a sentence to hard labor), a turbulent French undercurrent kept seeping through under the ground of the entire political edifice of Italy and kept eroding it away. Its underground existence was a matter about which even the least inquisitive and attentive minds were left in no doubt. It was no secret either for the Austrian government, whose attention it constantly drew to the melancholy necessity of considering itself, treaties notwithstanding, a temporary and fortuitous government in the provinces under its keeping and of increasing, for its own protection, its army, budget, surveillance, official measures, etc.

In March 1841, I was already in Rome, had taken up residence near Gogol and saw Pope Gregory XVI officiating at all the numerous spectacles of Roman Holy Week, and officiating, moreover, in a rather half-hearted and lackadaisical manner, just as if attending to some habitual, domestic piece of work. In the intervals during the donning of vestments and, later, the services, he seemed concerned more about himself than anything else, blowing his nose, coughing, and gazing glumly about at the surrounding crowd of co-worshippers and curious bystanders. In just exactly the same way as he did the church service, this aged monk administered the state that fell into his hands: lethargically and dispassionately, he filled the jails of the papal realm to overflowing, not with criminal offenders, who were free at large in his territories, but with offenders who could not accustom themselves to monastic discipline, to his despotic and hypocritically benign system of rule.

On the other hand, Rome had now turned itself into a city of archaeologists, numismatists, and historians of all calibres. Anyone who managed to work his way to it through the network of scoundrels and rogues surrounding it and, finally, to find himself a quiet corner in it, immediately turned into an artist, bibliophile, curiosity seeker. I saw our own holidaying merchant-barons, respectable old landowners and officer-habitués of Dussot's, who had caught the archaeology bug, expatiating on monuments, cameos, Raphaels, interspersing their raptures with exclamations on the wondrously deep Italian sky and the boredom which held limitless sway below it—a cause of great amusement for Gogol and Ivanov, who would frequently hold forth of an evening with curious tales from their long years of experience with Russian tourists. Astonishingly enough, I noticed that the French question was far from an indifferent matter for even Gogol and Ivanov, who had succeeded, to all appearances, in liberating themselves from the feckless cares of their epoch and in concerning themselves with tasks that were in advance of that epoch. The insinuation that European civilization could still expect important services from France had the effect on more than one occasion of setting the imperturbable Gogol's teeth on edge. His negative attitude toward France was so inveterate and decisive that he would lose his customary presence of mind and discretion in arguments on the subject and plainly display a not altogether accurate knowledge of the facts and ideas to which he referred.

Ivanov's convictions about the inconsequentialness of French life were of no lesser magnitude, but as often happens with men of profoundly ascetic natures, temptations and doubts lived side by side with all his beliefs. He never could overcome the anxieties of his conscience. It can even be said of this remarkable man that all his most fervent attempts to actualize his beliefs and his convictions in creative work were born in him, no less than anything else, out of a tormenting need to quell, at whatever cost, the doubts agitating him. And in this he did not always succeed. Moreover, contrary to Gogol, he nurtured a secret lack of confidence in himself, in his judgment, in his qualifications to reach decisions about questions that occupied him, and, therefore, he was happy and grateful to rely on Gogol in those incessantly recurring perplexities of his own thought, though he was never able to placate his thought completely even with that support. That is the reason why, when a dispute arose suddenly between Gogol and myself, over dinner at Falconet's, on the subject of France (and disputes about France arose then by the minute in every city, every family, every circle of friends), Ivanov listened to the arguments on both sides with rapt attention but did not say a word. I do not know how our debate was reflected in his mind or whose side he secretly favored then. Two days later he met me on Monte Pincio and, grinning, repeated to me a not very ingenious mot I had uttered in the heat of the conversation: "And so, old man, France is the fire placed under Europe to keep it from growing cold or moldy." He still had the conversation on his mind, whereas Gogol, good-heartedly making up with his hot-headed opponent that very evening (he made him the offering of an orange, painstakingly selected at a shop on the way from Falconet's, as a pledge of reconciliation)—Gogol did not even give a thought to what had been spoken about an hour before.

It should be mentioned that disputes over France and its future fortunes raged in every corner of Europe at that time and even considerably later on, straight up to 1848. Very likely, they occurred at the same time in our far and distant fatherland because from that moment sympathy toward the land of Voltaire and Pascal came into prominence in our country, breaking through the crust of a German cultural overlay and emerging into the light. But, all the same, one should take note that the Russian intelligentsia grew fond, not of the real, contemporary France, but of some other one, a France of the past with an admixture of the future, i.e., an idealized, imaginary, fanciful France, about which I shall speak further on.

CHAPTER

[XIV]

THE MORE I HAPPENED to get to know of Paris, which I finally reached in November 1841, the more strongly I became convinced that there was indeed much about her to give her neighbors cause for envy, thanks to her extremely well-developed social life, her literature, and the like, but exceedingly little reason for superstitious terror of her very name. I found Paris willy-nilly under the control of a strictly constitutional order. It is true that no one was willing to see this, but saw instead only the perils that the French national character presented, forgetting, in the meantime, the fundamental feature of a constitutional regime—its ability to inhibit the development of pernicious national traits and inclinations. There were still many people who considered even that means of saving nations from delusions and obsessions more dangerous than the very evil it was meant to cure.

After the popular and militant Thiers, the government of France was taken over by Guizot, an *anglomane* in his convictions, who concurred completely with the king in the matter of hatred and scorn for the self-initiative and excogitations of the masses of the people and their leaders, though both of them owed exactly those masses and their leaders the positions of eminence they occupied. Also, they were both extraordinary thinkers of different kinds: the king—a skeptic who had gone through a great deal in his lifetime and, therefore, put no store in the power of principles alone without a corresponding reinforcement of them via various other, undercover means; his minister —a former professor accustomed to put principles of his own discovery into effect and to believe in their infallibility. From this combination of two doctrinaires of opposite kinds emerged a unique system of constitutional rule which endeavored to institute in that land of revolutions a sagacious, cogitative, and self-regulating freedom. The system held a great many attractions for energetic people out to make themselves a name, a fortune, a career, but was ruthless in its treatment of those who refused to recognize its mission of instituting intellectual order and its doctrine on the importance of governmental spheres and strict hierarchical subordination.

To a good many Frenchmen, however, the system was unspeakable banality incarnate. To live without hope of success for some sudden political improvisation, some desperate and felicitous act of subversion (*coup de tête*)—and such attempts, incidentally, were crushed with particular swiftness and energy by Guizot's administration over the course of its eight years—to live that way meant, in the words of the partisans of direct popular initiative themselves, to doom oneself to ignominy in the face of posterity. The parties wore themselves out in efforts to undermine his administration, and in 1848, by sheerest chance, they did overthrow it but, by then, the constitutional monarchy together with it, as well.

Truthfully speaking, there was no reason indeed why they should have liked that administration. Its "middle-class" probity and squeamishness kept it from gratifying France with pronouncements on her mission to conquer nations for their own greater weal, and also prohibited its sharing the crowd's raptures over the country's still quite recent past, a time invariably referred to as the time of gallantry and glory. In addition, Guizot's administration never ceased exposing the vacuity and paltriness of national ideals, of projects for a revolutionary renovation of the state and of various deep-seated dogmas of national pride and vanity. All this integrity of behavior could not, of course, make Guizot's government popular in his homeland. Nor did he pursue popularity—he scorned it just as much as he scorned the enthroned champions of the clubs and parties, relying entirely on the support of the businesslike, temperate part of the population, who, the moment he needed them, shamefully betrayed him, as is well known. Instead of popularity, Guizot aspired to an honorable name in history and thought to find it in the company of his old king, once having made of France a free and orderly state, and, so, went about inculcating constitutional *habits*, working indefatigably at curbing extreme political passions—all this under the cross fire of the press, which, despite the renowned September laws, enjoyed a freedom during his regime that was unmatched anywhere on the continent with the exception of little Belgium and a few Swiss cantons. Guizot, moreover, daily brought his system up to public discussion at the stormy (as they almost invariably were then) sessions of the Chamber of Deputies, where he often attained the heights of heroism in his candor and the depths of cynicism in his replies to foes. Subsequently, all this seething life, doggedly working out the constitutional foundation of the country, was brazenly declared, with the advent of the Second Empire, a contemptible game of parliamentarianism and was supplanted by a game of police spies in the streets, scandalous journalism in the press, and a legislature confined within four deaf walls, with no rights to speak out and no publicity.

Out of fear of being reputed an egotistical "bourgeois" bereft of the faculty for understanding popular aspirations and the hidden miseries of the working classes, few people could bring themselves to give full voice to all they felt about the Paris of the 1840's. It is an undeniable fact, however, that travelers to Paris at the time came in contact with a city of irreproachable manners and customs, distinguished, as a natural outcome of constitutional order, by an ease of social intercourse, by the possibility for any foreigner of finding appreciation and sympathetic response for any serious opinion or initiative, and, finally, an integrity, relatively speaking, in all transactions between private parties. All this, as we know, immediately vanished with the advent of the Second Empire. To verify this brief sketch, it is sufficient to draw a comparison between it and what the city of Paris became after the loss of the July Constitution.

There are, of course, some black marks on Guizot's conscience and reputation. For example, he has been rebuked for utilizing dishonorable means to provide his system support, for securing electors by inducements and, especially, for keeping the number of electors limited to the figure at which it had been when he assumed office, in order the more easily to control them. All of this is true and cannot be refuted, but it is also true, as experience later proved, that he could make a constitutional system secure in France only and exclusively in league with that like-minded band of men whom he held in his hands. Experts in English history as they were, King Louis Philippe and Guizot could not have been ignorant of the fact that only a *secure* constitutional system was capable of rebuilding itself completely anew without loss of its strength or its fundamental bases. The example of the English constitution was plain enough: it, too, had had its periods of *"obliging,"* induced parliaments, but not only emerged victoriously from all dangers and difficulties but changed the whole code for election to the House of Commons, restored to slighted locales and strata of the population their rights to send representatives to Parliament and reformed the whole structure of its representational system, without losing so much as a hairsbreadth of its fundamental meaning for, and influence on, the country in doing so. Thus, for Guizot and his administration, the whole matter came down to making the constitution *secure*, and it cannot be said that he blindly, self-indulgently, and unthinkingly defended existing electoral laws. In the heat of debates on the extension of those laws, he more than once made public his opinion that in such a country as France change in those laws could not stop with merely adding the *capacités* to the electorate. Beyond this *adjonction des capacités* he already foresaw new concessions and national universal suffrage—that uncouth and fatuous echoing tumult of the crowd, who invariably return the questioner only the words he himself has cast into their midst, which is just what did keep on happening during the reign of Napoleon III.

Be that as it may, still one may be allowed the supposition that the parliamentarianism of Guizot and Louis Philippe, a doctrine so maligned and defamed in later time by their foes, would have advanced the welfare of France and her working classes, in a gradual, progressive development, no less than did the subsequent *decrees* of the Second Empire on national workshops, on the whole new rebuilding of Paris, on the creation of workmen's "towns" (*cités ouvrières*), and the like.

CHAPTER

[XV]

NEED IT BE SAID that the France enjoying the sympathy of eager and impetuous minds in Europe was not at all the France of Guizot, but the one standing behind it and protesting against its constitutional schemes as being, to its way of thinking, not what the spirit of the country required? Indeed, what need had Germany's progressives and, after them, other political circles for some new kind of France, one endeavoring to keep within the limits of its charter—a decent, upright France and, for that very reason, spoiler of all the old conceptions about the country that had been built up among European peoples since the end of the last century? For them this was an entirely un-known France and one that they had no desire to study. Instead, they sought out the earlier, still quite recent, universally well-known, typical France, the France that had had categorical solutions for all questions of a social, political, or moral character, the one that, when those solutions were slow in coming, had taken measures to produce them by force. It was this latter, older France which for many people in Europe was then still the immemorial, the eternal France, whereas the other France, only just beginning to loom on the political horizon, was a fraud, a deception of the Evil Spirit, in short, an apparition which, by usurpation, had substituted for the indigenous physiognomy of the country some sort of disgustingly slick and silly mask. Not knowing how to explain that transformation, foreign parties tried ex-plaining it as nothing more or less than an outrage unparalleled in the annals of history. The mild citizen-king Louis Philippe was treated, both in his homeland and outside it, to the nickname *"le tyran";* Guizot was known abroad, in England, for instance, by the name of the constitutional "duke of Alba" and by other, similar names, etc.

Russian circles' views on France differed little from the general conceptions of France's activities such as had formed among extreme European liberals: in our country, too, it was the hidden France, and not the France in plain view, which was the object of interest, and it was expected that the former France, sooner or later, would replace the latter. And this actually happened sooner than expected, producing wholly unforeseen results. What it did was to clear the way for the magnificent French Empire which took so thoroughgoing a revenge for all preceding governments, scattering and crushing both their and its own enemies. Its whole historical mission consisted, it would seem, in that role of Nemesis. In Russia there was only one person, T. N. Granovsky, who, owing to the keen feeling for history with which he was endowed and his innate sense of truth, endeavored to echo as little as possible the chorus of revilers of Louis Philippe's monarchy, revilers included among whom were some very high governmental figures in Russia. I remember how, in the summer of 1845, while at a country house in Sokolovo (near Moscow), some words of mine spoken in defense of Guizot caused a general scoffing protest on the part of my friends. Granovsky, however, when the argument was most intense, took me by the arm and, as he led me off to a nearby garden lane, declared to them with a kind of humor and intonation impossible to communicate on paper: "Let me have a few words with him in private, gentlemen, and don't you worry about us. We shall rejoin you as decent, upright men." And thereupon he expressed his opinion to me that Guizot's political ideals were intentionally narrow and modest in conformity with a rather low estimation of Frenchmen's political abilities which the minister never concealed. "But disregard for the national spirit," Granovsky added, "cannot come off scot-free in France. France knows that it is to this national spirit it owes its place and role in the history of Europe. One way or another, sooner or later, Guizot and Louis Philippe's system will collapse. They are intelligent and make un-Gallic mistakes, and *that* they will not be forgiven." I did not suspect then that Granosvky's words were—a prophecy.

One also ought to take note that revolutionary France, the embattled France in the background holding everyone's attention, produced its attacks on the constitutional mode of life and the constitutional regimen it set in motion, attacks carried out with considerable skill, energy, and extraordinary talent and that France consisted almost entirely of the most gifted men of the age. The group of writers who heckled Louis Philippe's system made an irresistible impression on people of literary culture and also possessed another engaging quality: they raised, aside from current questions of the day in the face of which we were always sensible of the inadequacy of our practical experience and judgment, also, and above all, broad, abstract questions of the future, topics of the new social structure of Europe, daring designs of new forms for science, life, moral and religious beliefs, and, finally, criticism of the whole trend of European civilization. In this instance we were already, as the term goes, free at large, versed from youth onward in grandiose hypotheses, in sweeping, breathtaking generalizations and deductions.

Thus, it happened, when I arrived back in Petersburg in the fall of 1843, that I was far from done with Paris but, instead, found at home reflections of many aspects of her intellectual life of the time.

Proudhon's book, *De la propriété,* by then almost out of date, Cabet's *Icarie,* little read in France itself except by a small circle of poor worker-dreamers, the far more widespread and popular system of Fourier—all these things served as objects of study, of impassioned discussions, of questions and expectations of every sort,[60] and understandably so. In the vast majority of cases, these treatises were the familiar metaphysical maneuvers, maneuvers transferred to social and political territory. Whole phalanxes of Russians followed them there, overjoyed at the chance to change over from abstract, speculative thought without real content to just the same kind of abstract thought but now with a seemingly real content.

The portion of valid and mature practical recommendations contained in these treatises, which the European world did not hesitate to make use of, attracted our attention least of all, and it was not there by any means that the mission of the treatises on Russian soil lay. In the interval of the years 1840–43, treatises of this sort were supposed to bring about a decisive and severe change in the philosophical pursuits of the Russian intelligentsia, and they did finally accomplish that task. The books of the authors already named were in everybody's hands those days; they were subjected to thoroughgoing study and discussion; they produced, as Schelling and Hegel had done earlier, their spokesmen, commentators, interpreters, and even, somewhat later—something which had not occurred in connection with earlier theories—their martyrs, too. The theories of Proudhon, Fourier, and —a later addition—Louis Blanc, with his famous treatise, *Organisation du travail,* brought about in Russia the formation of a special school where all these doctrines lived, jumbled together and professed at practically one and the same time by the school's disciples. Some fifteen years later, these theories made their appearance in the Russian press in just such a none too cohesive and solid amalgam.

Belinsky attached himself to the general trend as soon as the first rays of the social metaphysics reached him, but here, too, just as in his philosophical period, he began from the beginning. Belinsky himself did not correspond with anyone abroad, but rumor reached us via newcomers that he had engrossed himself in reading Thiers' voluminous *History of the Revolution of 1789*. That renowned composition of Thiers', whose understanding of the epoch was not very deep, but who exposited its most obvious features very effectively, introduced Belinsky into a new world, a world with which he was, until then, little acquainted, and forced him to go further in his study of it. When I was already back in Petersburg, he took up the reading of another history of the same event, one remarkable for its total lack of any verification of things and people dealt with, I mean—Cabet's work, *Le Peuple*, which discovered signs of a vast collective intelligence in all instances where the masses of the people entered into the action and which explained, in the end, even the fall of the Republic in terms of the moving and blessed unselfishness of these same masses who had sustained a victory over their foes, not for themselves, not for any immediate benefit to be derived from the event, but for the glorification of their principles—liberty, equality, and fraternity. What these works, and other works completely opposite them in spirit, did for Belinsky, however, was to serve him simply as a means of discovering the first seeds of socialism which the Revolution of 1789 had cast on European soil: he had to see its inception with the Convention, the Paris Commune, the heroes of the old communism, Babeuf and Buonarotti, in order to perceive its contemporary aspect and to gain a sound understanding of certain of its inroads into our epoch. He had no explanation for all these phenomena and was dissatisfied with all the explanations proposed at the time. Only Louis Blanc's *Histoire des dix ans* made an exceptional impression on him for the very reason that it showed what manner of interest, what mass of instruction and even of artistic merits could be contained in a history of our days, of the very instant, so to speak, being experienced, under the hand of a powerful talent, even though a history of that sort did incorporate sometimes materials of unproven trustworthiness and sometimes even mere talk of the town.

On my return to Petersburg in 1843, virtually the first word I heard from Belinsky was his ecstatic exclamation about Louis Blanc's book: "What a book Louis Blanc has written! Here's a man the same age as we are but, meanwhile, what am I compared to him, for instance! I'm simply ashamed to think of all my scribblings compared with such a work. Where do they get their power, these people? Where do they derive such vividness, such perspicacity and certitude, and such skillful writing besides! A life of statesmanship and public affairs certainly seems to give far more substance to thought and talent than do literature and philosophy." Obviously, his aesthetic and publicistic orientation had already lost its attractions for him and had retreated to the background in his mind, but he remained with it, nevertheless, having really no choice because it was only with its help that he could raise the most elementary questions of social morality and touch upon, however indirectly, topics in contemporary Russian social life and development. Just as peasants then used to buy the lands they needed in the name of a landowner bribed by them for that purpose, so, in literature, the right to speak about the most innocuous but, nevertheless, public matter and about the significance of this or that thoroughly well-known social phenomenon was purchased at the price of calling upon the help, and making a front, of grammar, mathematics, good or bad verses, even the vaudevilles of the Alexandrine Theater, Moscow novels, etc.

Such was the effect of French culture on a good half of our Russian world. But here's what is really remarkable: though they changed their manner of viewing the vocation of a writer and now fit problems of literature into the context of social questions, neither Belinsky nor the circle of Westerners of the time thought to throw their former conceptions overboard as useless ballast, nor did they offer up any cannibalistic sacrifices from among the fundamental bases of their former outlook. However different their understanding of the essence of certain political-economic topics, however impassioned their arguments over particularities and methods of applying the newly obtained ideas, the whole circle unconditionally concurred, nevertheless, in certain principles: all took the moral factor as the starting point for any activity, whether in life or in literature, all acknowledged the importance of aesthetic demands on themselves and on works of the intelligence and the imagination, and not a single member of the circle held any such notion that one could do without, for instance, art, poetry, and creative work generally in the political education of people any more than in life.

Let us take note, in this connection, of the suspicions later expressed in our literature, in view of the frequent quarrels among the friends, that the circle also maintained a division between "blue-bloods," who were only amusing themselves with ideas, and democratic natures, who took all philosophical propositions closely to heart and made them the task of their lives. This opinion may be relegated to the category of suppositions utilized to facilitate avoiding the difficulties of defining things exactly. In the circle in question it was not always only "blue-bloods" who endeavored to forego rigorous conclusions and deductions such as necessarily result from theoretical propositions, and it was not always only the "democrats" who understood the essence of principles more clearly than their comrades and who more conscientiously pursued philosophical problems to their ultimate expression. Very often the roles were reversed, and the people one would have thought least likely to do so became the enemies of abstract preoccupations and the defenders of extreme points of view—a fact which can be corroborated by innumerable examples. The point is that the distinguishing characteristic of the whole circle must be sought elsewhere, above all in the vigor of its philosophical enthusiasm, which did away not only with the differences in social standing of those involved but also differences in their educations, thinking habits, unconscious predilections and predispositions, thereby turning the whole circle into a community of thinkers who subordinated their own tastes and feelings to the principles brought up and discussed. Of course, individual temperaments in the circle did not fade away, people's spiritual and philosophical distinctions were exhibited freely, a range of greater or lesser power in understanding and expressing thoughts existed, but all these energies were aimed toward, and were meant to serve, the idea prevailing at the given moment, an idea which joined and bound the members of the circle together into one indissoluble unit and which, if one may so express it, shone alike on all their faces. Persistent controversies did occur in the circle's very midst—on more than one occasion some furious battle shook the circle to its foundations, as we have already reported and as we shall see again further on, but these instances of internal strife came about exclusively over the rights of some principle or other to preeminence in the circle, over efforts to inculcate some philosophical or political scheme and secure its rights to sympathy and allegiance. No other sort of excitement, no other matter was known to the circle. And thus it went until 1845, when, under the weight of its own overly abstract concerns and the pressure of new social and societal questions, the circle began to disintegrate, completing the process of disintegration by 1848 and leaving behind it memories which will still from time to time, we believe, claim the attention of thinking Russian people.

CHAPTER

[XVI]

On my way through Moscow in the fall of 1843, I made the acquaintance of Herzen and, also, of T. N. Granovsky and the whole circle of Belinsky's Moscow friends whom, until then, I had only heard about. I found a scholarly and, so to speak, joint-class elation going on in Moscow on the occasion of the first public lectures of Granovsky, who had gathered around himself not only the scholars, the literary parties, and his usual ecstatic auditors—the young people of the University —but also the whole *educated* class of the city, from old men straight from the card tables to young misses still breathless with their success on the dance floor, and from governor's aides to private noblemen. The unanimity with which the amiable professor was greeted by all these people, so unalike in the kind of life they led, their occupations, and their goals, was regarded then as a very significant fact; and that fact did indeed have a certain meaning in revealing the existence of objects of respect for the mass of the public, aside from the ones long since sanctioned officially and by general consensus.

From that point of view, Granovsky's lectures could perhaps have been accounted a political event, although the eminent professor, devoting his discourse to compressed, but eloquent, studies of a few historical personages, undeviatingly confined himself, with a tact and sense of dignity which never left him, to the narrow terrain assigned to him for teaching. Out of that terrain he made, as best he could under the circumstances, a flowering oasis of knowledge. In his masterful hands, the narrow terrain under investigation assumed quite large dimensions, and the way was opened in it for making the experiment of applying science to the life, morality, and ideas of the time. The professor's lectures were especially distinguished by their making one sensible of his adroit arrangement designed to skirt areas still not open to free investigation. On that subdued, neutralized tiny plot of hard ground, a plot of his own making and cultivation, Granovsky felt himself in full control: he said everything that could and should have been said in the name of science and *sketched in* everything that could not yet be said in the simple form of an idea. The majority of his audience understood him quite well, including the lecture on Charlemagne to which I had the chance to listen.[61] The picture of the restorer of civilization in Europe was, at one and the same time, a work of art by the brush of a master, reinforced by a vast and refined erudition, and also an exemplification of what the real role of any power, any majesty on earth should be. When, at the conclusion of his lectures, the professor turned directly in his own name to the audience, reminding it how huge a debt of gratitude we owed Europe wherefrom we had received, without paying any price, the blessings of civilization and truly human existence, which it had achieved through bloody toil and bitter experience, his voice was drowned out by a burst of applause resounding from every nook and cranny of the auditorium.

This unanimity of praise for the professor's daring (at the time a public declaration of sympathy toward Europe could constitute an act of daring) engendered the thought in certain friends of his that the real moment had come for a reconciliation between the two big literary parties—the Slavophiles and the Westerners—whose quarrel had already reached fever pitch between 1840–43. The following year, 1844, for the purpose of bringing the adversaries together and laying the groundwork for a meeting of minds, it was contrived to hold a friendly banquet, which was attended by almost all the coryphaei of the two opposed doctrines who were then in Moscow. At the banquet they shook hands with one another and announced that they were mutually bound by service to science and mutually respected all impartial convictions engendered by it. But a *diplomatic* truce, when the battle has not been fully played out, rarely affords firm grounds for peace among people. Reasons for dissension among those who attended the banquet still existed in such abundance, owing to a conglomeration of circumstances (Belinsky's activity among them), that, as it might be put, with the end of the last toast proposed at the banquet, all of them were back again in their old positions and in full armament.

What had happened during the interval of those last three years? Nothing actually new had happened, only a repetition, in renovated form and on different, considerably more complex and more reasoned grounds, of the old manifestation of Moscow's resistance to Petersburg's presumptuousness as civilizer. Moscow made up, on the basis of old principles of Russian culture, the conservative opposition to Petersburg, which had proclaimed the insubstantiality of almost all

old Russian principles in the face of the principles of universal mankind, i.e., in the face of European development. Our two capitals had
already had occasion more than once to engage in battle on these
grounds, but never before, perhaps, had this quarrel embraced so
many questions of a scientific character and displayed so many talents,
so well-rounded a culturedness, although it was forced, as usual, to
keep within the bounds of literary, aesthetic, philosophical, and also,
partly, archaeological arenas, and to pretend, without deceiving anybody, by the way, to be an innocent quarrel of two distinct branches
of one and the same Russian patriotism, and even sometimes the trivial disagreement of two pedantic factions.

In fact, the matter here concerned was one of defining tenets for
morality and for the beliefs of society, and also of creating a political
program for the future development of the state. The names with
which the two parties mutually tagged one another—the *Moscow*
party and the *Petersburg* party or *Slavophiles* and *Westerners*—were
not very precise, but we shall still retain them because they have become the ones generally used, and for lack of better ones. Inaccuracies
of this sort are inevitable in all instances where a controversy is not
located on its own proper ground and is not conducted in the
manner or in the terms and arguments really required. The Westerners, whatever else may be said about them, never argued against
historical conditions giving special character to the civilization of individual nations; and the Slavophiles were exposed to entirely uncalled-
for criticism when reproached for inclining toward the establishment
of static forms for mentality, science, and art. One can admit somewhat more easily the division into *Moscow* and *Petersburg* parties, a
division understandable in view of the mass of the audience adhering
to each of the opposed doctrines in those respective locales, but it is one
which does not withstand rigorous examination: some of the most influential Westerners, such as Chaadayev,[62] Granovsky, Herzen, and
others, belonged, as a matter of fact, to Moscow society, whereas
Petersburg was the place of publication of the journal *Lighthouse,*
which reminded one, in its manner of defending old authorities, of
that renowned contemporary of ours, Veuillot, and could have been
called the *Père Duchêne* of conservatism, of the traditions and ideals
of bygone days.[63] In Petersburg, moreover, one could hear sympathy
toward Slavophilism repeatedly and clearly expressed in the upper
strata of society. We shall even see that the antagonists had, for the
time being, an extraordinary number of points of contact, which they
lost afterward, and that amidst them existed ideas, topics, and beliefs
before which differences of opinion fell silent.

Herzen, when I made his acquaintance, read us the famous, witty comparison of his between Moscow and Petersburg that he had then just finished writing. Contrasting Moscow's tenacity in preserving all its various distinguished and undistinguished characteristic features with the frivolity of Petersburg for which nothing in the world was of any importance whatsoever, with the possible exception of an *order* handed down from proper authorities, Herzen, despite all the humorous and sarcastic sallies he visited upon both our capitals in equal measure, could not conceal, nevertheless, his covert partiality for one of them—the older of the two—a partiality which he did not discard even during the period of his emigration abroad. And what is more, he made no effort to do so, but, on the contrary, seemed to cherish that feeling. And who, if not he, was a Westerner! Many such examples of a manly inconsistency of conviction are to be found in other persons of both parties.

All the same, the struggle between the parties went on with might and main, especially a little later on, after it had had time enough to set specific goals for itself. And there was, indeed, reason to fight. By the 1830's, the educated Russian world had awakened, as it were, for the first time and seemed all of a sudden to sense the impossibility of living in the situation of intellectual and moral consternation which had obtained until then. Society no longer heeded invitations to let itself simply go along with the current of events in silence, without inquiring which way the wind was carrying it. Everybody with even the slightest inclination to think began about that time to search eagerly, and with the ravenousness of famished minds, for bases of a fully conscious, rational existence on Russian soil. Needless to say, their very first steps led them to the necessity, above all, of delving into the inner meaning of Russian history, of arriving at clear conceptions of the old institutions which once regulated the political and private lives of the people, and arriving at a proper understanding of the new institutions which had replaced the earlier ones. Only with the help of convictions procured through such an analysis could some idea be formed of the position we occupied among European nations and of the means of self-education and self-definition we needed to choose in order to make that position a worthy one in all respects. Everything sprang into motion: the search began, as we know, from two opposed points and was bound, sooner or later, to bring the investigators into conflict. The clamor of their first mistakes is what made up the content of that whole period in our development going under the general title of the epoch of the 1840's.

The people of that epoch have been repeatedly denounced, even in their own lifetimes, as impotent idealists incapable of effecting the least reform or making any change whatsoever in the structure of life

around them. It is remarkable that the idealists of the 1840's themselves were close to agreeing with their judges, and constantly re-
iterated, even in print, that their generation, as a transitional one, was
destined only to prepare the materials for reforms and changes. Their
whole quarrel was nothing but an argument about the quality and
serviceability of those materials. And that the argument was not entirely fruitless is proved by the seeds of progress which it sowed
throughout all the strata of the educated society of the time and
which came up, even after a systematic uprooting in 1848, still full of
energy and life in the two great reforms of the present reign. No one,
we may assume, will take issue with the assertion that the basic principles of Russian national culture evident in the peasant reform and
the principles of European law discernible in the judicial reform were
prepared long ago by the very argument about which we have been
speaking. One might well wish all present-day subjects of dispute so
enviable an historical fate.

[XVII]

ONE OF THE CHIEF COMBATANTS in the fruitful debate then set in motion on Russian soil was Herzen. In the early days of my acquaintance with him, I must admit, I was stunned and nonplussed by that extraordinarily mobile intellect which ranged from one subject to another with inexhaustible wit, brilliance, and incomprehensible rapidity, and which was able to grasp, be it in the case of someone's speech or some simple happening from current life or any abstract idea, the one telling detail that gave it its distinctive shape and vital expression. Herzen had an unusually well-developed talent for making, on the spur of the moment, and one after another, parallels between heterogeneous things, a talent which was sustained, first, by his power of subtle observation and, second, by the formidable capital of his encyclopedic knowledge, and which was so well-developed that it ended up by wearying his listeners. The inextinguishable fireworks of his speech, his inexhaustible imagination and inventiveness, a sort of reckless intellectual prodigality—these things constantly aroused his conversation partners' astonishment. After the always impassioned, but not always strictly consecutive, speech of Belinsky, Herzen's tortuous, endlessly mutating, often paradoxical and irritating, but invariably intelligent talk required of his conversation partners, aside from strenuous attention, also the necessity of always being on guard and armed with an answer. For all that, however, no banality, no flabby thinking could withstand even a half-hour's confrontation with him, and pretentiousness, pomposity, and pedantic conceit simply fled from him or melted before him like wax before a fire. I knew people, people predominantly from among those called serious and competent, who could not abide Herzen's presence. On the other hand, there were people, even foreigners during the period of his life abroad, for whom he quickly became not only an object of wonder but of passionate and blind devotion.

His literary and publicistic activity produced practically the same results. Herzen very early—from his first appearance in the social world—revealed the qualities of a first-class Russian writer and thinker, and he retained these qualities throughout the course of his life, even when he suffered from delusions. Generally speaking, few are the people to be encountered in the world who could maintain, as he did, their rights to attention, respect, and study at the very same time as being in the throes of some obsession. His mistakes and delusions bore the imprint of thought of the kind impossible to dismiss merely with an expression of scorn or rejection. In this aspect of his career, he resembled Belinsky, but Belinsky, constantly soaring in the region of ideas, had none of that ability to discern people's characters on first meeting and possessed none of that wicked humor of a psychologist and observer of life. Herzen, on the contrary, seemed to have been born with a critical bent of mind, with aptitudes for exposing and hounding out unwholesome aspects of existence. This became evident in him from the very earliest times, from as far back as the Moscow period of his life about which we are now talking. Even then Herzen's was an indomitable and uncompromising intellect with innate, organic abhorrence for everything made to appear the established rule, glossed over with general silence, concerning some unverified truth. In such instances, all the, so to speak, predatory aptitudes of his mind arose and issued forth en masse, astounding people with their acerbity, cunning, and resourcefulness. A resident of Sivtsev-Vrazhek in Moscow and still a figure unknown to the public, he had already acquired a reputation in his own circle as a clever and dangerous observer of the surrounding milieu. Of course, he did not always manage to keep secret those dossiers, those service records about people near and far which he kept in his head and to himself. People who took their friendship with him for granted could not help being astonished and, at times, becoming angry when some portion or other of this automatic activity of his temperament came out in the open. Surprisingly enough, this existed side by side in him with the most tender, almost loving, regard for special friends, who were not exempt from his analysis. But for an explanation of this matter, we must go to another side of his character.

As if to restore some equilibrium to his moral makeup, Nature had taken measures to implant in his soul one indomitable belief, one invincible proclivity: Herzen believed in the noble *instincts* of the human heart; his analysis would fade away and stand in awe before the instinctive promptings of the moral organism, as before the single, indubitable truth of existence. He had a high regard for noble-minded, deeply felt obsessions in people no matter how out of place

they may have been, and never made fun of them. This dualistic, contradictory play of his nature—suspicious negativism, on the one hand,
and blind belief, on the other—caused frequent difficulties between
himself and his companions, and led to quarrels and confrontations;
but it was in the fire of just these altercations that, until the very
moment of his departure for abroad, people's devotion to him, instead
of disintegrating, was tempered even harder than before. The reason
why is clear: in everything Herzen did and thought then, there was
not the slightest trace of falsehood, secretly nurtured bad feeling, or
self-minded calculation; on the contrary, he was always his whole self
in every single word and act. And there was still another reason that
made people forgive him, even his insults, sometimes—a reason that
may seem incredible to people who did not know him.

For all his staunch, proud, and energetic intellect, his was an utterly soft, kindly, almost feminine character. Under the severe exterior
of skeptic and epigrammatist, under the camouflage of a humor virtually without scruple and anything but timid, there lived within him
a child's heart. He had the ability to be somehow ungainly tender and
delicate, and should he deal an opponent too harsh a blow, he had a
way of instantly making obvious, though only implicit, apologies. Particularly beginners, people still searching for their way and still sounding themselves out, found sources of encouragement and strength in
his advice: he would bring them directly into full communion with
himself, with his thought, which did not prevent his anatomizing
analysis from conducting, at times, very painful psychological experiments and operations on them. Should one speak of some peculiar
anomaly? He himself was sensible of this note of kindliness in him,
and he took measures to keep it from ringing out too clearly. It was as
if his pride was offended at the thought that people might also notice,
aside from his intelligence and talents, that he had kindness of heart.
On occasion he would do deliberate violence to his natural character
in order to appear for a time, not the man he was created, but one of
truculent mold. But these caprices did not last long. Matters changed
when he arrived abroad and secured his position in the party movements: he undertook a very serious overhaul of his character then. It
was not possible to remain in the midst and at the head of European
democrats and keep the same candor in his ways of living and conducting himself as in Moscow. That in itself could have ruined a man
in the eyes of the clubbist and socialist assembly, who willingly made
use of good-naturedness but valued it very cheaply. Herzen began to
groom himself for his new public as a man bearing on his shoulders
the weight of an enormous political mandate and mission, whereas
what occupied his interest were all the extremely diverse ideas of sci-

ence, art, European culture, and poetry, for Herzen was also, in his way, a poet. Indications of this unseemly operation on himself came to the fore especially after his first attempts to aid Russian society in its task of divesting itself of the garb of *archaic* man met with general sympathy: he contrived to make himself over into an unrecognizable type of person. What readiness to trample on all old ties and remembrances, all old sympathies, in the interests of abstract liberalism! What arrogant credulity in accepting reports flattering to his personal outlook and merely echoing him! And what a perpetual standing on guard lest any feeling of his own, any personal or national trait, distort the majestic image of the impassive man incarnating the fate of nations! However, it must be added that Herzen never did fully attain the goal of his strivings. He did not succeed in turning himself inside out; he only succeeded in ruining himself. He succeeded also in one other thing—in bringing down misery on himself from which there was no escape; and if anyone's fate can be called tragic, then it is, of course, his fate toward the end of his life.

With his unusually inquiring and penetrating mind, he discerned down to the last speck the paltriness, the banal and comic side of the majority of the coryphaei of European propaganda, and, nevertheless, he followed them.[64] With that vital moral sense which he shared in common with Belinsky, Granovsky and the whole Russian epoch of the 1840's, he felt indignation at the shamelessness, the cynicism of thought, and action among the *free* people who banded together under the same banner with him, and he carefully concealed his revulsion. For all his efforts, his comrades, governed by a sense of self-preservation, descried in him an enemy and turned on him their usual weapons—calumny, libel, defamation, lampoon. Herzen remained alone.[65] But all of this was still far away. When I got to know him, Herzen was in the full bloom of youth, filled with high hopes for himself, and was the pride and consolation of his circle. During the period of Granovsky's first public lectures, he was in a state of excitement, wrote articles about the lectures, and celebrated his friend's success so resoundingly that it seemed as if he were commemorating his own jubilee.[66]

Meanwhile, Herzen's ties with T. N. Granovsky began far from under auspicious portents. It is a remarkable circumstance that the germs of various trends and their first sprouts appeared in Russia virtually all at the same time, at the end of the 1830's and beginning of the 1840's. Hardly had impassioned study of German philosophy— from the positive aspect of it, about which we have spoken—gotten underway, when a circle of young people at the University of Moscow was already forming and directing attention to social, not philosoph-

ical, questions and revering, not Hegel, but Saint-Simon (1834). At
the head of the circle stood a youth, a student of the Faculty of Natural and Mathematical Sciences, and a future doctoral candidate of
that faculty—I mean, this very same Herzen. At a later time, he told
me that both he and his young party regarded Stankevich and
Granovsky with great suspicion and made hostile and derisive remarks about their concerns, as if about an amusing pastime adopted
by people of leisure. Herzen, in the early stages, virtually made a
Koran of his Saint-Simon: he relates in his memoirs that during a conference once with N. A. Polevoy, he called the latter *backward* because of his expression of disinterest in that reformer. In sadness and
anger N. A. Polevoy remarked: "You work and slave your whole life
so that the first youngster that comes along can call you a good-for-
nothing! Just wait," he added prophetically, "the same thing will
happen to you!"

For the time being, the young socialist's mind was host to utter
scorn for pure thought and its exponents on Russian soil, so much so
that when Herzen returned to Moscow from his first stay in Vyatsko-
Vladimir (1839), the circle of our philosophizers received him rather
coldly and did not conceal their opinion of him as a person of undeveloped and backward mentality. It was this circumstance that made
Herzen turn to the source of grace—the study of Hegel—which he
had neglected until then. The discovery which he made thereupon
had important consequences. He discerned in the master's system
something quite different from what his new friends saw. He acknowledged the concurrence of history and human progress with the movement of an idea, dialectically evolving in Hegel's logic, but he held
that the moments of change in the idea corresponded only to the social and religious upheavals of history. According to this interpretation, mankind's steps forward make their appearance when some one
or another historical people begins to change the old bases of its life.
Then and only then do instants come about of real incorporation into
history of progressive ideas. These, so to speak, perpetual but, also,
spontaneous chance protests of mankind are what supply the substance enabling one to recognize the unity of evolution between logical idea and historical phenomena, and not the immanent, fated, and
inevitably progressive march of human development. Hegel's system
equally allowed of that way of conceiving things as it did others: it
was solely a matter of transferring the master's ideas from one category of facts to another. Herzen even attracted the old-believers of philosophy to his way of understanding things. The result was that,
though entering the arena of life and literature with a hostile attitude
toward the best circle of people then existent, Herzen not only came

to terms and united with that circle but even assumed a position in its vanguard as an authority on questions of abstract thought. Philosophy in his hands became an extremely trenchant and far-reaching weapon, but the Slavic party brought up against it a different, but also tried and true, weapon.

Thus, at the start of the 1840's, after a brief difference of opinion, Belinsky, Granovsky, Herzen, and the others were united together by the singleness of their aspirations, and although internal quarrels continued to break out from time to time, with their common set of principles and, especially, in the face of a dangerous foe, the Slavophile party, they never went so far apart as not to hear one another's voices or fail to respond to a comrade's call.

CHAPTER

[XVIII]

NOT BEING A PERMANENT RESIDENT of Moscow and my visits there being chance occurrences with fairly long intervals of time between them, I was not fortunate enough to become acquainted with the Elagin household. Consisting of the mistress of the house, A. P. Elagin (a niece of V. A. Zhukovsky), of the well-known brothers P. V. and I. V. Kireevsky,[67] her sons by her first husband, and of the family acquired in her later marriage, the Elagin household was the favorite meeting place of the celebrities of the learned and literary world of Moscow; its reigning tone of temperateness, decency, and kind attention made it into something like a neutral territory where conflicting opinions could be expressed freely without fear of ambushes, sallies, or personal insults. This venerable house had a very marked influence on Granovsky, Herzen, and many other Westerners who were its assiduous visitors; and they spoke of it with great respect. Perhaps it is to that house they owed a certain moderation in their judgments on questions of folkways and folk beliefs, a moderation which Belinsky, who stood and acted in seclusion, did not know and which he curtly called tea-table affability. That the Westerners, in turn, had an effect on the Moscow Slavophiles, who made up the majority of the company at the Elagin house, is also beyond any doubt. All this taken together gives the house the right to an honorary page in the history of Russian literature equally with other, similar oases where Russian thought remained in sequester during those periods when organs for its expression were still lacking.[68]

I myself had a chance to see an example of the effect on Herzen of conversations with people whose attitudes differed from his own, albeit the example I wish to cite also has overtones of his former involvement with social questions. On one of my morning visits to Herzen in the garret of his house in Sivtsev-Vrazhek, where his study was located, he began talking of the scorn Belinsky had expressed for peasant life in general, calling it *"bast-shoe and sackcloth reality."* The term was used in an analysis of some silly book of stories taken from folk life, which the author had crudely and comically idealized. "The book is one thing," said Herzen, "but the review is irresponsible both in itself and for the fact that it eggs the journal on to consider itself a great lord before the people. Why despise bast-shoes and sackcloth? They are, after all, nothing more than a sign of extreme poverty and crying need. Should one really make shameful epithets of these words? And besides, such epithets are beginning to appear in the journal by the score. It is sometimes difficult for me to defend it. For instance, I could find nothing to say in answer to Khomyakov [69] when, making a point of these false notes, he observed: 'If only you could make the editor realize that he is wearing leather shoes only because he has subscribers to his *Notes of the Fatherland,* and if he did not have subscribers to his *Notes of the Fatherland,* he would himself be not much better off than a bast-shoe wearer.'"

T. N. Granovsky, also, occasionally regarded certain polemical sallies of Belinsky's, particularly those touching on writers' personalities, with something less than approval, but neither he nor Herzen so much as thought to connive with the Slavic nationalist party in its complaints about the critic's outspokenness, complaints which had constant reference to his analysis of past and present literary *"glories"* of Russia. In their opinions about these so-called *glories,* Granovsky and Herzen invariably agreed with the critic. No later than 1842, indignant over the fact that one of the Moscow professors could not regard his investigations in the field of literature anywise other than as crimes against the majesty of the Russian people (*lèse-nation*), Belinsky wrote a rather wicked and witty pamphlet entitled "The Pedant," in which he ridiculed the weak aspects of his over-choleric opponent's views and arguments. The pamphlet had considerable success and, needless to say, utterly mortified the person who had served as the original. The injured party, apparently assuming it possible to ask substantial concessions from Granovsky on the grounds of their acquaintance through the University and the Elagin house, presented him, in the presence of a great many witnesses, with the following rather arrogant question: "Could he, Granovsky, after such an article, possibly still dare to shake hands with Belinsky in public, should he meet him?" "What? Shake hands?" retorted Granovsky. "I'll throw my arms around him in the city square." [70]

Generally speaking, Belinsky was, if the expression can be used, the disturber of the peace of Moscow life: were it not for his provoking words, Moscow could, perhaps, have kept for a longer time the mien of refined difference of opinion, not unconducive to easy and genial relations between disputants, which comprised its distinctive feature during the first period of the great literary debate that had begun in Russia. With his peremptory aphorisms and the progressively greater boldness of his conclusions, Belinsky kept sending his Moscow friends every minute to the barricades, so to speak, against his enemies in Moscow.

The first person to sense the absurdity of this situation where people went out of their way to be as polite and considerate as possible in inflicting on one another, if not fatal, in any case very serious wounds, was the exceedingly decent and exceedingly consistent Konstantin Sergeevich Aksakov. It is quite true that Slavism and Russian national life constituted for him something more than a doctrine or set of ideas that one was honor-bound to defend: Slavism and the Russian national mode of life became the vital basic motive of his existence and his very life's blood. In his memoirs, Herzen relates the story of how K. S. Aksakov, meeting him on the street, movingly bid him farewell forever since he could no longer consider him a companion on the road of life. This was even more impressive in Granovsky's case. K. S. Aksakov came to him late at night, woke him up, threw his arms about his neck, and, pressing him tightly in his embrace, announced that he had come to him to perform one of the most grievous and onerous duties of his life—to break off relations with him and to bid him a last adieu, as one does a lost friend, despite the deep respect and love he felt for his person and personality. Granovsky urged him to look on their differences of opinion with greater dispassion, but to no avail; he said that, apart from ideas of Slavdom and nationality, they had other ties and moral beliefs between them which were not subject to the peril of a rupture, but K. S. Aksakov remained unwavering and departed from him very upset and in tears.[71] That was a time in Russia when doctrine and opinions could still cause inner, intimate dramas.

Also at Madame Elagin's house, Herzen would meet his perpetual opponent, A. S. Khomyakov, in whom he regarded with extreme respect his very own ability to discern the inherent negative side, the diseases and distempers, in ideas and facts, and for that reason would seek out occasions for debates and confrontations with an opponent of such power, erudition, and cleverness. Herzen had then not yet published his well-known article, the very lively, despite its abstract philosophy, "Dilettantism in Science" (*Notes of the Fatherland*, 1842), in which he allowed science the right to have no regard whatsoever for precious traditions and beliefs which promoted peoples' and nations' ease of existence on earth, and to obliterate them without a qualm the moment they in any way contradicted its own, scientific, bases. In this privilege of science he also located the feature which distinguished it from dilettantism, which was incapable alike of devoting itself with childlike fervor to the poetry of national myths and of steadfastly following the path of analysis and rigorous investigation of things. It was this feature of dilettantism which was responsible for its natural ability to keep people from reaching final conclusions, under the pretext of gracious assistance to each of the sides. In place of, and in compensation for, any ensuing deprivations in life, the author promised, in the name of science, a number of distinguished intellectual pleasures and such sound convictions as would more than compensate for everything that might be undermined or destroyed by it. The article revealed a passionate and unqualified faith in the omnipotence of science (by which term was always meant, in any case, the philosophy of natural science) and was an article, despite its somewhat heavy-handed language, with a profoundly radical content. On first meeting with A. S. Khomyakov, Herzen came up against, in opposition to his own philosophical radicalism, another, similarly unqualified radicalism, but of a completely different kind.

Herzen himself reported, in one of his publications abroad, a part of the run-ins he had with Khomyakov having to do primarily with the tenor, spirit, and basic principles of German philosophy. From these reports it becomes clear that Khomyakov's main argument against the Hegelian system was provided by the proposition that no philosophy worthy of the name could be deduced from an analysis of the properties and phenomena of *Reason* alone, with all other, no less important, moral forces of mankind excluded. As concerns the other part of his arguments with Khomyakov, the theosophical part, Herzen hardly even mentions it in his memoirs, perhaps because it seemed to him considerably less important than the former part, but one may now be allowed to differ with him in that opinion.

The basic reason, though not yet clearly formulated as such, responsible for the second part of their disputes was A. S. Khomyakov's attempted rehabilitation of Byzantinism, so much an object of opprobrium among scholars in the West. The manner in which Byzantinism had been understood and applied by its proper and natural defenders in Russia—the preceptors at our theological seminaries and academies—had had the effect of further increasing aversion for it. With the appearance of Chaadayev's famous letter in 1836,[72] however, where Byzantinism was declared to be the source of the intellectual and spiritual stagnation of all of Russia and was all but consigned to the damnation of history, Byzantinism became an issue which no one who wanted his beliefs and convictions to have the aspect of something critically reasoned out and scrutinized could circumvent. A. S.

Khomyakov not only did not circumvent the issue, he persistently worked it into everything in life, including spheres of human activity where its presence was least to be expected, everywhere providing him a convenient device for measuring truth, good, and beauty. The key to an understanding of many of the Khomyakov school's extravagantly original opinions and verdicts, which went counter to all known facts and ideas, lies precisely in its invention and manipulation of this new criterion for evaluating historical phenomena. Its theses and ideas to the effect that the religious aspect of Western art and, especially, of pre-Raphaelite painting was a product of a feeble mysticism and not of direct Christian outlook, that the person of Tsar Fedor Ivanovich represented the attractive ideal of an old Russian ruler and that the reign of Elizaveta Petrovna, in our modern history, provided a superb model of rule in the national vein—all these theses and others even more daring and peculiar threw the Khomyakov school's opponents into such confusion for the very reason that these people were not fully aware of its secret and did not possess the key to decipher these puzzles.

That Khomyakov was acting with integrity and believed in his principles goes without saying, but one may surmise, at the same time, that for his mind, a predominantly dialectical mind, the idea of raising the banner of Byzantinism, of reversing the verdict of history and turning general opinion backward, that idea might have had an alluring aspect of its own. However that may have been, by declaring Byzantinism a great and still not fully appreciated phenomenon in mankind, A. S. Khomyakov thereby negated and wiped out the enormous mass of Western historical, critical, and theological works hostile to Eastern civilization and degraded the West's self-esteem as well as many of the things on which it prided itself, the eras of the Reformation and the Renaissance, for instance, to the level of secondary and even pathological phenomena of human thought. For him, the Reformation was a sorry attempt on the part of Western peoples to rectify their religion, its direct sources having become clogged with Catholicism, and the era of the Renaissance, which preceded it, was a desperate appeal, on the part of those same people, to the pagan world for help in creating for themselves something at least resembling science, art, and civilization.

The positive side of his defense of the all-saving grace of Byzantinism Khomyakov grounded in a conception and understanding of the Eastern church doctrine as one allowing complete freedom of thought under the unlimited authority of political or ecclesiastical dogma. A. S. Khomyakov was not the least bit embarrassed by the history of the Byzantine Empire, which could have contradicted his position. In the first place, as far as he was concerned, there was no thoroughgoing, impartial history of the Byzantine Greeks in existence anywhere in the world, and everything that claimed to be such a history in Europe seemed to him very nearly wholesale calumny or wretched misinterpretation. In the second place, even if such a history were to be in existence, it would not have been able to serve either as a confirmation or a refutation of his ideas. The principles underlying Eastern Christianity were so profound and exalted that the political and social development of the country itself could not keep up with them. One could imagine the corruption of the Court at Constantinople and of social mores and governmental practices in any way whatsoever, but still the spirit and the outlook preserved by the church of the nation and perpetuated by it for all ages remained the one single foundation on which a great, cultivated and moral Christian state could be predicated. It was the church doctrine in the Byzantine Empire that constituted its real history, its thought and its right to the gratitude of all peoples.

Later pamphlets, which A. S. Khomyakov published abroad in the 1850's under the pseudonym Ignotus, contain an exposition of the main points of the doctrine and of the view emanating from it as to the mutual relations between the people and their hierarchies and authorities in Christian community. Eastern Christianity, even in company with and in spite of the Asian despotism which sometimes stood at its head, retained the notion of the congregation of the faithful as a prototype of a state where each man depends on the other and where each man is at once both subject to and exerciser of authority. It allowed in practice, but did not recognize in principle, divisions of people into those who instruct and those who are instructed, into those responsible to command and those responsible to carry out commands, because all people had the same mission—to serve the *church* —and the least of them could stand side by side with an exalted member in the course of this unceasing service and as suited its needs. The dogmas elaborated by Eastern Christianity, for all their character of unimpeachableness and immutability, did not in the least hamper freedom of movement for philosophical thought thanks to the profound and all-encompassing quality they had obtained in the "councils": they surrounded human reason from all sides just as the atmosphere of air surrounds our earth. Furthermore, a philosophy which did not eschew theological truths or moral and social questions, a philosophy of the sort found in its rudiments in the Byzantine preceptors, met the requirements of the heart no less than the demands of the most subtle metaphysical analysis, and on account of this dual character had, sooner or later, to send out living shoots into all aspects of science, had to revitalize and renew the intellectual life of Europe.

Summoned to the great task of renewing the, morally speaking, deteriorated life of Europe was that nationality which, by the workings of history and Providence, had become heir to and representative of Byzantinism in the world, no matter, be it added, how poor, humble, and lowly a lot this chosen nationality might have had for the time being.

No more abstract and radical a kind of thinking could have been put in opposition to Herzen's philosophical radicalism, and Herzen acknowledged that because of A. S. Khomyakov, he was forced to read the voluminous histories of Neander and Gfrörer [73] and especially to study the history of the Ecumenical Councils, a history little known to him, in order to be able to establish some kind of balance in the argument with his opponent and to have the possibility of checking on the abundant references to laws and paragraphs of the council ordinances which Khomyakov poured out from memory, opposing them to Herzen's precise German theses.

If Khomyakov's basic position, the starting point of his system, had so radical a character, then it stands to reason that the conclusions, the practical applications, the political, historical, and literary judgments which it conditioned were bound to be even more strikingly colored by contempt for Western culture, by a harsh view of its development and by an emphatic rejection of the majority of its products. And that was precisely the case. A. S. Khomyakov himself diligently followed the progress and discoveries of science, the arts, and even the crafts in Europe, being one of the most cultivated men Russia has ever had, but the school he created, as always happens, plunged ahead in its set direction without the wariness and caution its founder continued to maintain. Everything our "Westerners" then enthused over, from the novels of G. Sand, which had great success with them owing to the social questions they raised, to the new attempts at formulating the political and social life of states (Comte, Proudhon, Michelet)—all these were dismissed by the Khomyakov school as things unworthy of attention. Europe was declared untenable ground for a vigorous art, for the satisfaction of the highest needs of human nature, for the gratification of the religious cravings of peoples and for the establishment among them of justice, law and order and love. To Europe were relegated the natural sciences, finance and technology, great industrial inventions, creation of enormous merchant fleets and navies, in short, fabulous achievements in all departments of knowledge promoting the material aspect of life. It was condemned for the development of comfort, luxury and riches which it went about amassing in measureless quantity. Europe's well-being, unprecedented in history, continued to grow even greater in detriment to its ever more deteriorating moral significance. It even closed its eyes to the doom rising up before it in the form of the proletariat, which was multiplying under its custody and threatened to bring on a return of the age of barbarism. From European literatures the Khomyakov school used and made mention of only passages taken from their satirists, moralists, and critics; the historians and writers of Europe were valued according to the number of rebukes and reproaches they had occasion to utter regarding their own time and the past of their native lands. The school's foreign literary anthology consisted almost exclusively of exemplary passages of that kind, which it eagerly and frequently quoted. According to the testimony of all who heard him, Khomyakov conducted his criticism of the social and intellectual situation in Europe with particular skill, brilliance and wit, although also within the bounds of decency and decorum, which were inherent properties of his keen intellect. However Herzen, on his part, might have tried to ward off and cool Khomyakov's critical enthusiasm, he himself was not exempt from the effect of that criticism. Khomyakov's words, in our opinion, left marks on Herzen's mind and heart, against his own will, perhaps, and were reflected in his later avowals of the insubstantiality and bankruptcy of Western life in general.

Encountered in the course of these heated debates, however, was a name around which the argument raged and foamed with particular fury, like a torrent encountering an immovable rock. This was the name of our colossus who, when receiving from the senate the title "Father of the Fatherland," delivered a speech which could be taken as a kind of comment out of the depths of the preceding century on the issues of the day agitating his descendants: "It behooves us always to bear in mind the fate of Tsargrad [Constantinople] and the Byzantine Empire so that we do not lose our realm over concern with trivial matters." It was for that reason the most zealous disciples of the Khomyakov school consigned the name of that personage to the ranks of the group of liberty-seekers, those alienated members of society and despisers of the Russian way of life, of whom Russia at all times had had a great abundance not only among minor officials and carousers at the public pothouses but also in respectable, and particularly strict, families. These domestic aliens went ahead and brought about their reforms when one of the greatest geniuses of all time became their representative and seized the reigns of government of the Muscovite tsardom. No more radical a comment could have been made to the Westerners with all their reverence for reform; and it was for that reason that the Westerners took revenge on their adversaries by holding up to execration, in their turn, everything the latter considered most hallow to the national spirit and national memory.

In the press, in the then modest field of publicistics, all this, needless to say, appeared toned down and was expressed less graphically and less frankly. People came out on stage somewhat dressed up—with a few, well-known exceptions. Nevertheless, traces of the turbulence behind the scenes were bound to be reflected in journalism and were, in fact, reflected there. The *Muscovite*, which had become the echo of the Slavophile school, went to the extreme of monomania in the defense of its basic stands—about the richness of the Russian national spirit, about its religious essence, about the elements of humility, meekness, endurance, and wisdom which made it unique—going so far as to assert, for instance, that the Russian land was fertilized for history with the tears of its inhabitants, not, as was true of the lands of Western nations, with their blood. *Notes of the Fatherland,* the rallying center for Westerners from 1840 on, in promulgating universal human development, the laws of which, it argued, were the same for all countries, very often carried its denial of national distinctions to such a pitch of incomprehension that it seemed deliberately put on. Both journals conducted furious polemics and, of course, neither lacked its complement of crackbrains, its *"enfants perdus,"* whom the editors sent out as skirmishers; and it was these people who produced the eccentricities and absurdities of which one can harvest a fair collection from both the one and the other side. Many people even to this day have assumed that these eccentricities and absurdities are what comprise the characteristic features of the journalism of the time, but it is beyond any possibility to share this view. Behind both journals stood other people who saw considerably further than the horizon to which the public organs they supported were forced to limit themselves. So, for instance, Belinsky understood all questions far more profoundly than *Notes of the Fatherland* for which he wrote, and behind Belinsky stood Granovsky, Herzen, and others who often far from shared the views of their journals. The case of the *Muscovite* was even plainer and more acute. People like the Kireevsky brothers, Khomyakov, and the Aksakovs can by no means be held responsible for all the provocative sallies of the journal's editors. In breadth of understanding of the Slavophile question and in the competence and intrinsic value of their convictions, they stood much higher than the *Muscovite,* which was constantly regarded as their organ and which was supported by them on the surface.

Thus, both literary parties at the time described (1843) stood like two camps opposite one another, each with its own sabres. It seemed as if they would never meet except under provocation to exchange blows and cast defiance in each other's teeth. But time—years of cumulative deliberation—arranged things otherwise. Already at the midpoint of the period, 1845-46, a change had come about in the minds of the leading people of both camps, and the feeling began to arise that each of the two embodied some essential requirement of development, some one of the principal forces that gave it shape. The parties were bound to fight the way they did fight, out in public, precisely in order to bring out clearly the full importance of the content contained in the ideas they upheld. Only after their efforts, labors, and struggle was it possible to discern how much vital truth lay in the idea of the national, the ethnic.

CHAPTER

[XIX]

AT THE CLOSE OF 1843, Belinsky, now a married man, occupied a small apartment on the courtyard side of the Lopatin house the outer side of which faced Anichkov Bridge and Nevsky Prospect.

On those premises Belinsky had taken three small rooms for his own use. The most spacious room was called the dining room, the second largest passed for a parlor and was graced with a Morocco leather couch and the mandatory armchairs placed around it, and the third room, something on the order of a short, dead-end corridor with one window, was meant to be his library and study, as the bookshelf by the wall and the desk at the window led one to believe. However, the master of the house himself did not at all abide by this distribution of functions: he always used the dining room for working and reading; the couch in the parlor served him for the most part as a sick bed during his frequent indispositions; and he looked into the study only for the purpose of fetching a book he needed from the shelf. Two rooms in the rear of the apartment were occupied by his family which was soon increased by the addition of a daughter, Olga.

His daughter and, later on, a son, who lived but a short while and took to the grave with him his father's last energies, and also the flowers on the windowsill comprised the objects of Belinsky's care, efforts, and most tender solicitations. They alone were his life, a life which was beginning to ebb away from him and bit by bit grow dimmer. Soon he was required to wear a respirator when going outdoors, and he remarked to me in jest: "Look what a rich man I've become! Griboyedov's Maksim Petrovich ate on gold, but I breathe through gold: that's a step up, I should think!" I often found him on his parlor couch in complete prostration, especially after intensive labors over some urgent article which left him with an aching head and in a fever. It must be added, however, that he recovered very rapidly from these paroxysms, sustained as he was by that intensity of will and

spirit which never abandoned him from 1842 on and which, often raising him up from his sick bed and endowing him with the deceptive
look of a man full of life and energy, kept undermining, at the same
time, the last reserves of his afflicted organism.

This high-strung state of his spirit eventually became his normal
condition. His moral sensibility knew practically not a moment of
peace or relaxation until his illness broke him utterly. The quietest,
most friendly chats were interspersed with his outbursts of anger or
indignation, which could be provoked by some mere anecdote from
daily life or even a tale about some outlandish custom in another,
quite distant country. Someone once described in his presence the
means by which the old Egyptian pasha, Mehemet Ali, acquired
eunuchs of good stock. What he would do was to make a raid on
some neighboring Negro tribe and order that all the male children be
seized; then a meticulous selection was made from among the prisoners and the chosen specimens were subjected to the operation in
question, after which they were immediately buried in hot desert sand
up to the waist. Half the children died, and the half that withstood
the ordeal was distributed by the old villain among various Turkish
notables of whom he had need for some reason. The blood rushed to
Belinsky's face; he went up to the storyteller and declared in a com-
plaining tone of voice: "Why did you tell that story? Now I shall have
to face a sleepless night." Belinsky's wife was altogether in dread of
those nights when he sat up late in conversation with his friends.

Owing to the effect of his incredibly well-developed powers of
imagination and representation, Belinsky experienced feelings of
hatred for people long since departed into the domain of history and
for events already past which for some reason aroused his ire. He had
hosts of foes and antipathies both in the contemporary world and in
the realm of shades, about which he could not speak with equanimity.
His passionate nature simply did not know an objective attitude, that is,
to put it plainly, indifference toward historical personages and important facts of history. Belinsky became the contemporary, as it
were, of the various epochs he encountered in his reading: he would
choose the side proper to defend and would fight against the opposite,
long since silenced side, just as if it had that moment upset his moral
sense or violated his beliefs. Something similar, but in the opposite
sense, happened with objects of his sympathy which he found in various centuries and among various peoples: he would conceive passions
for the heroes of his contemplation, would jump up at the mere mention of their names, and would often defend them against contemporary criticism to the furthest possible extent. He was reluctant to
part with his friends. But most of all, however, he expended his ener-

gies on enmity and indignation. The circle of his foes, aside from the ones who were foes in actuality and in person, swelled with all that great number derived from his reading: he fought just as passionately with the shades of time past as he did with people and events of the present.

One can easily imagine what occurred when Belinsky left off prosecuting those who stood mute under his accusation and happened to encounter a living, contemporary personage standing right there in front of him, in plain sight, in possession of some limited notion of a serious subject or some obtuse and obscurantist theory. This was the time when people failed to distinguish between a man himself and his words and opinions, thinking that they inevitably comprised one and the same thing. Belinsky, least of anyone, admitted such a distinction, and his thundering criticisms in such instances shattered all ties with his opponent and left no hope for their resumption in the future. The consequence of behaving toward the world at large in such a manner was, of course, the necessity of living in solitude or in the company only of one's intimates, a situation to which Belinsky willingly condemned himself, refusing to change his way of expressing his thoughts and judgments in the slightest whenever unavoidable circumstances or chance brought him into a different milieu.

Of course, his reading was carried on in this same state of intensity, even when it dwelt on things of a scientific or abstract nature. We have already mentioned that his reading during this period of his life reached out progressively more and more into economic and political questions. The manner of reading Belinsky adopted for himself would have been enough to tax even a stronger organism than his. To a book or an article, to any doctrine or opinion, from the most conscientious treatises encompassing the profoundest interests of society and mankind on down to the most trivial pieces of Russian writing, he paid a more than serious attention—he paid a passionate attention, attempting to elicit the psychological reasons for their appearance, constructing their genealogies and scrutinizing one by one each of the features of their moral physiognomy. This provided him numerous reasons for outbursts of enthusiasm or anger. How many times we would find him, after he had finished reading some book, article, or chapter, pacing in and out his three rooms in an attitude expressing extraordinary agitation. He would instantly launch into a heated and wholly unconstrained improvisation, relating his impressions from his reading. I thought his improvisation even better than his articles, but, then, articles were not written in that tone and could not have been so written. If one were to judge by the number and mass of sensations, excitements, and thoughts which that extraordinary man experienced every day, one might call his all too brief life, a life so swiftly consumed before our eyes, a rather long and full one. To this we must add that Belinsky so insinuated himself, we venture to put it, into the authors he studied that he was continually discovering their covert, unuttered thought, continually correcting them when they forsook or deliberately obscured it, and continually divulging their ultimate expression, which they themselves were afraid or unwilling to make. Revelations of that sort were the strongest side of his criticism. Thus, in many foreign, predominantly economic and social writers, he surmised the direction they would or must take. So, for example, he said of George Sand, whom, incidentally, he respected very much, that she was far more bound by the ideas and principles she rejected than she herself thought; about Thiers he observed that the revolution in his *History of the French Revolution* takes on the aspect of some kind of *divine dispensation* which makes a great deal in the book incomprehensible despite a very lucid and smooth exposition; Pierre Leroux he called an insurgent Catholic priest, etc. And as concerns people active in Russian affairs, it hardly needs to be said that he almost infallibly defined their entire future activity on the basis of the first signs they supplied of it.

There was good reason why, with his mind engaged in this constant work, his friends should have found that Belinsky, on each new meeting, was no longer where they had seen him the time before: the ceaseless wheel of his thought often carried him far out of their sight. His polemics were destined to express precisely that aspect of his spiritual nature, a nature craving combat and movement, just as his critico-publicistic articles revealed his faculty for self-command and control over his own thinking.

After this, one should have little difficulty understanding why, in the war between the Slavophiles and the Westerners, Belinsky turned out to be an inexorable foe, whereas other comrades in arms of his, such as Herzen, Granovsky, and their like, secretly considered themselves only temporary foes of our nationalist party, only awaiting a clarification of its program from its worthier representatives before extending their hand to them. True, Belinsky also came to the idea later that it was essential to discriminate what was relevant in the Slavophiles' doctrine from the less relevant silt, and he admitted, moreover, certain qualifications which were meant to protect his own Western viewpoint from the charge of blind devotion to all European institutions, but he was the last to leave the breach which he fanatically defended against incursions of elements of obscure and crude thinking emanating directly from the mass of the people, and raised the banner of universal human education against all the pretensions and declarations of so-called national cultures.

The point of departure for all his vehement polemics against such cultures and against their defenders was the conviction that they could arise under any order of things and be assimilated within any pattern of life to which they had grown accustomed or which they favored for some reason. On the other hand, the basic character of universal education seemed to him to consist precisely in that people who acquired it were able to subject all forms of existence to criticism and argument, and could choose to be satisfied only with those which accorded with logic and withstood the most rigorous analysis. On this basis Belinsky divided the world into clear-eyed and blind peoples, abhorring the latter on principle no matter what virtues, lofty qualities of soul, talents, and other distinguished merits they might otherwise possess.

It need hardly be added that there was, in this instance, no question whatsoever of doing justice to people, nations, and things; in the heat of battle, Belinsky simply did not give a thought to doing justice, thereby completely matching his adversaries, who acted in exactly the same way. Both he and they acted only to preserve their own conceptions, conceptions which seemed to them salutary in their consequences, and no one gave a thought as to how many needless victims fell during their clashes, how many crass and wholly unjustified blows were administered to ideas and beliefs, and how many reputations and personalities suffered for no good reason. All of that was left for later history to delve into and to render each person what was due and proper. For the people of the time, however, the situation was one of bitter, stubborn battle and desperate, longlived hatred for one another, a hatred so deep-rooted that it even survived many of the combatants and continued in their names over their graves.

In 1842, before my return home, Belinsky, soon after his pamphlet "The Pedant," about which I have already remarked, delivered still another severe blow to a certain very respectable personage of the Moscow circle—the now deceased K. S. Aksakov. It is well-known that K. S. Aksakov, on the appearance of the first part of *Dead Souls* in that same year of 1842, wrote an article in which he proffered the idea of Gogol's resemblance to Homer and Shakespeare with respect to act of creation and power of work created, finding that only those writers and our author displayed the gift for bringing out in vulgar characters and even in vice itself a certain inner strength and unique power which they could draw on simply out of belonging to a mighty and thriving nationality. K. S. Aksakov, placing Gogol on a level with

Homer in terms of act of creation, neglected any mention of the great numbers of European writers of genius who were also distinguished by extraordinary creative abilities and who, by being so treated, were all implicitly placed lower than Gogol; and what is more, Aksakov outrightly declared that in the case of the novel, understood as a continuation of the ancient Greek epic, not a single *contemporary European name* could, under any circumstances, be placed on a level with Gogol's. Nothing could have enraged Belinsky more than these aphorisms. That very same Belinsky who had been first to proclaim Gogol an artist of genius now declared, both in print and by word of mouth, that Gogol's genius as the creator of types and characters, while it could not be denied, nevertheless had a relative significance. Owing to the content and inner meaning of the problems the Russian author was trying to solve, his genius was limited by the intellectual and moral situation of his country, and the work he produced could not be made to compare with the issues and themes of European art or with the aims it had set and still continued to set itself in the persons of its best representatives. Furthermore, no such strength and power as had been proposed was to be found in the characters Gogol brought on the scene, and it was unlikely that the author had even thought about such a meaning for them, and if he had, then he had fallen into childish error. Belinsky added, moreover, that Gogol was not only not higher than all European novelists but, though surpassing many of them by his gift for unmediated creativity, observation, and poetic feeling, he yielded to certain, and not even especially outstanding, manifestations of European literature in scope and significance of ideas. All these remarks administered a rather heavy blow to the newly advanced interpretation of Gogol, but Belinsky added to this also a few sarcastic conclusions from his opponent's postulations and concluded the argument with ridicule. The final blow—the coup de grâce—of the polemic on Belinsky's side was his declaration that, if one were to judge by certain lyrical passages in the first part of *Dead Souls*, in which astonishing revelations of the inner and outer beauty of Russian life were promised, Gogol could, perhaps, lose his significance as a great *Russian* artist also. From that moment on, Belinsky's name was anathema in the Slavophile camp and even became for them something of the embodiment of the fortuitous and extraneous civilization alien to the Russian people, which was identified with Petersburg, whereas for themselves they laid claim to Moscow as being a city particularly alive with and conducive to a keen understanding of the Russian national spirit with all its hopes and conceptions.

CHAPTER

[XX]

I FOUND BELINSKY still under the influence of the polemics, exacerbated by them to the highest pitch and preparing himself for new engagements. Not a day passed without a conversation getting underway about the Moscow version of the moral and political problems in Europe and Russia, about the Moscow interpretation of Gogol and the aspects of Russian life exposed by him, about the Moscow conception of the institutions of old Russian life and about the morality which derived from the Slavophiles' doctrine or was implicit in it. We repeat, he had not the slightest intention of doing justice to his opponents, and his opponents paid back their Petersburg adversary and his party in exactly the same coin. The argument came down to a matter of enmity and wrangling between the two cities. Patriotism on both sides consisted in disparaging the one capital in favor of the other. There was no possibility for a man tending not to share the passions in which both parties were embroiled to hold anything like an independent opinion. One faced the necessity of choosing between the parties and sacrificing whatever objections might have occurred to one's mind in the course of their mutual name-calling, the necessity, so to speak, of suppressing one's personal self in the interests of one's personal allegiance.

No one felt the effect of this cross fire between the two centers of our national development more completely or more painfully than I. S. Turgenev, who found himself right in the middle of things when he returned from abroad and soon thereafter entered on the literary scene with his poem *Parasha* (1843). Suspecting a true-blue Westerner in him from his very first steps, the party which looked askance at examples of foreign education and culture almost seemed to set out deliberately to place as many obstacles as possible in his life's path. A whole collection of inane anecdotes about his words, expressions, and and observations was carefully gathered together by his enemies and put into circulation with all the necessary embellishments and accretions. Turgenev's works up to his *Notes of a Hunter* were never spoken of except as monstrosities of Western culture transplanted without the slightest evidence of talent on Russian soil. Belinsky thought otherwise, having immediately discovered in *Parasha* the signs of the author's uncommon power of observation and ability to pick an original point of view on things. "What do I care about all those anecdotes about him," Belinsky said. "The person who wrote *Parasha* is a person who will know how to correct himself in whatever, and whenever, he needs to." His words once again proved to be right. The rapid and dazzling development of Turgenev's artistic talent in combination with the development of the qualities of his moral nature, his spirit of open-mindedness, his tolerance for people in general, and especially his just appreciation of their works and their beliefs—these things brought about a reconciliation between him and all his former persecutors and placed him in the center of the intellectual movement.

However, there was a certain under-cover connection, at the time, between the parties, a certain conciliating idea more than adequate for opening their eyes to the identicalness of the goal toward which they were striving from different sides. . . . But the time has not yet come to elucidate this conciliating principle, the kernel of which lay on the field of battle and was constantly trampled upon by the feet of the combatants. The kernel, however, did germinate despite all adversities, as we shall see. The connection consisted in their equal sympathy for the enslaved class of Russian people and in their equal ambition to abolish the order of life which allowed for such enslavement or even based itself precisely on it. No one, for the time being, was willing to see the similarity in the basic motive governing both parties, and when this motive came out in the open by itself, as it did from time to time, our parties hastened to suppress it as quickly as possible. For the sake of further bolstering their differences, they refused to put trust in each other's feelings, characters, and intentions. People in Moscow said with reference to the humanitarian protest in Petersburg: "Out of its liberalism and anguish Petersburg has made a comfortable Voltaire chair on which to take its ease." The response from Petersburg was: "It must be even cosier to sleep on age-old Muscovite feather beds—especially under the din of its 'forty times forty' bells." To all this an exchange of invectives in verse was added. Lampoons and epigrams on Belinsky were composed in Moscow and composed, what is more, by people whose behavior in ordinary life was of an unquestionably spotless moral character. And the answer that came from Petersburg was a scurrilous song containing, among other things, the following verse:

> Taken your way, we'd have Russia
> What it was till Peter's day:
> With its belly full of kasha
> Belching all the night away.

What kind of agreement could there be here?

Exacerbated by the polemic, Belinsky became suspicious to an extreme degree. So, for instance, impelled by that same constant concern of his for elements of European development, he looked askance even at our provincial literature, at those literary compilations which came out at that time in Kharkov, Archangel, and elsewhere, detecting in this the intention to create small centers of civilization in opposition to the big national centers of Petersburg and Moscow and to develop the idea, on the local level and behind the scenes, of an independent national culture which would be capable of finding all the necessary bases for itself on its own.

The gulf separating the parties became especially wide when public discussion arose in Russia about the rights of all Slavs of other nations—of Austria, Hungary, and Turkey—to our patriotic and national sympathy. The discussion, raised first by M. P. Pogodin,[74] reached the press from private and official circles, where it had been kept confidential since the beginning of the 1830's, and reached it in so bombastic a tone that, in its early stages, it provoked Belinsky's mockery of its form and content. The position he took on the Slav question had the same source as the position he chose regarding things Slavic in general. The reason for his negative attitude toward the question was once again his assumption that it screened an attempt to glorify unsophisticated national cultures and an effort, with some hope now of success, to oppose them to the consciously elaborated principles of European thought. Indeed, the attempt this time could rely on that spontaneous sympathy for oppressed ethnic groups and peoples, which was bound to exist, and did exist, among the Russian public. No one was more predisposed to sympathy of that kind than Belinsky, but at the thought that there might be a scheme here —a scheme to elevate modest folk creativity with its superstitions, delusions, and unconscious flashes of truth to a level equal to, or even higher than, the carefully thought out bases and principles of European sophistication—at that thought alone Belinsky dimissed all other considerations and not infrequently did violence to his own feelings. It turned out, in the present instance, that Belinsky maintained an attitude of unconcern for the valorous efforts and sacrifices of the foreign workers for the cause of Slavdom who rescued the language and the ethos of their peoples from utter destruction in the midst of other nations hostile to them.

Be that as it may, Belinsky himself was shown no greater justice by his adversaries when they undertook to disclose the bases of and motivations for his opposition. They declared him a man dedicated to the narrowest of interests in life and bereft even of the faculty for understanding patriotic or national instincts. They even went further. Because of his impassioned defense of the national policies of Peter I and because of his avowed sympathies with Petersburg, they declared him a petty and scarcely *altogether unself-seeking* centralist and bureaucrat. He indeed was a centralist, but not in the sense which his enemies maintained—not in favor of some already existent order of things, but in favor of that distant order of things which he conceived in the form of a union of all the nations of Europe on the grounds of one common civilization under the aegis of one set of laws for rational existence.

With what enthusiasm he spoke of the first glimmers of this future centralization, of this future order of life which he seemed to discern both in the rapprochement of European nations by way of new roads, international conventions, and the like and in their efforts to create, without destroying the distinctive indigenous and ethnic features of each country, a single common code for the political and social life of mankind! And in this connection, he was not able to contain his indignation, nor would he have wanted to do so, the instant he suspected the appearance of signs indicating interference with that code glimmering in the distance and still far from fully elaborated. Everything that hampered its realization, whether on the part of national vanity, the presumptuousness of ethnographers exalting one or another national group at the expense of all other nationalities, or on the part of a skepticism which adduced arguments from the negative and dubious details of contemporary European life in favor of its desisting from doing anything—all these things caused him to feel indescribable consternation.

In his ecstatic exposition of his hopes for the development of Europe Belinsky deluded himself about many things, as time proved, but he deluded himself valorously, as is the case with people who deeply believe in some lofty idea! Belinsky was so jealously protective of the good accumulated by the old and the new European civilization that he looked with mistrust at exemplary and extraordinary works of cultures other than, and alien to, Europe and was very reserved in his comments about them. When Zhukovsky's translation of the epic poem *Nal and Damayanti* appeared, Belinsky limited himself to reminding the reader how much higher the Greek epic, the *Iliad,* was than the fabrications of Indian folk art. The same thing happened when the superb translation by Ya. K. Grot acquainted the

Russian public with the Finnish heroic epic, the *Kalevala*, the great monument of the visions and conceptions of a people said once to have occupied the whole of Europe. Making a contrast once again between the Finnish epic and the Greek outlook on life, Belinsky found in the former only ungainly fantasy, monstrous images and concoctions belonging to a barbarous people which must repel anyone who has once acquainted himself with the harmony, measure, and refined workmanship of the Greeks.

Yet, however important all these questions may have been and however striking the polemic to which they gave rise, they could not for a minute overshadow in Belinsky's eyes the purely Russian question which for him had then become wholly focussed on one name, Gogol, and on Gogol's novel *Dead Souls*. This novel afforded criticism the only arena in which it could contend with an analysis of things pertaining to social life and mores; and Belinsky held fast to Gogol and his novel as to some sudden and unexpected assistance. It seemed as if he considered it the mission of his life to make the content of *Dead Souls* immune to any supposition that it harbored in it anything other than a true picture, artistically, spiritually, and ethnographically speaking, of the contemporary situation of Russian society. He exerted all the powers of his critical mind in the effort to repudiate and destroy attempts to entertain any conclusions from the famous novel other than, and tending to mitigate, the harsh, ruthlessly critical conclusions that directly issued from it. After all his digressions into the region of European literatures, into the region of Slavdom and the like, he returned from the field of those more or less successful battles to his perennial, domestic cause once again, all the more invigorated by his preceding campaigns. The domestic cause in question consisted primarily in routing from the literary arena once and for all, if possible, both the irresponsible, venal, and self-centered revilers of Gogol's epic and also its ecstatic partisans who claimed to see in it something other than that for which it actually allowed. He tirelessly pointed out, both by word of mouth and in print, what the right attitudes toward it were, urging his auditors and readers at every opportunity to think over, but to do so seriously and sincerely, the question as to why types of such repulsiveness as were brought out in the novel made their appearance in Russia, why such incredible happenings as were related in it could come about in Russia, why such statements, opinions, views as it conveyed could exist in Russia without horrifying anyone.

Belinsky believed that a conscientious answer to those questions could become, for a man who made the effort, a program of action for the rest of his life, and especially could have the effect of laying a solid foundation for his mode of thinking and for a proper judgment about himself and others.

To this same time also belongs the appearance in Russian letters of the so-called "Natural school" which ripened under the influence of Gogol—Gogol interpreted in the way Belinsky interpreted him. One could well claim that the real father of the Natural school was—Belinsky. This school had nothing else in mind than to point up those details of contemporary and cultural life which could not yet be pointed out and analyzed in any other way, whether by political or by scientific investigation. Let us note, incidentally, that the term "Natural" was given the school by the coryphaeus of the pompous, trite, and pseudo-beneficent interpretation of Russian life, Bulgarin, but out of enmity for Belinsky it was welcomed and adopted even by persons deeply averse to Bulgarin's literary and critical activity. It is still today in common use among us despite its origin and its meaninglessness.

CHAPTER

[XXIII[75]]

WHILE ALL THIS was going on around Gogol's name, Gogol himself turned in a direction in which even many people who thought they shared all his views did not follow him. In February 1844, unexpectedly and after a long silence, I received the following letter from him:

> February 10, Nice. 1844
> Ivanov sent me your address and informed me of your readiness to do anything for me I might ask of you. I thank you for your good will, of which, I might add, I was never in any doubt. But now to the matter at hand. Here are the things I should like you to do for me: the first. . . . (The first request consisted in my entreating N. Ya. Prokopovich, a schoolmate of Gogol's at Nezhin and now his agent for the publication of *Dead Souls,* to send him money received and on hand and the accounts as soon as possible. As something of minor interest, we shall omit it and turn directly to the second request, as the one of greatest moment for us, which we shall now quote in its entirety just as the author wrote it.)
> 2) The other request. Find out how the talk about *Dead Souls,* as well as about other works of mine, now stands and what character it has taken. In part, I know, this will be difficult for you to do because the circle in which you move has a good opinion of me, for the most part, and so, there's no getting anything worthwhile from it. Would it be possible to get hold of something outside that circle, even if via acquaintances of your acquaintances, at fourth or fifth hand? Many quite intelligent remarks can be heard from people who have no liking at all for my works. Would it be possible to find out also, at some opportune moment, what is being said about me in the salons of Bulgarin, Grech,

Senkowski, and Polevoy—what power and magnitude has their loathing for me reached or has it already turned into complete indifference? I recall that you could find out a thing or two from Romanovich,[76] whom you very likely will come across on the street. No doubt he still attends their evening gatherings as he did before. But do all this in such a way as to make it seem that it is you, not I, who is interested. It wouldn't be amiss also to find out Romanovich's own opinion about me.

In exchange, I shall give you a piece of advice which may reek awfully of old age but is, nevertheless, a very sound piece of advice. Mix with people as much as you can and always widen the circle of your acquaintances; and see to it that those acquaintances be, without fail, experienced and practical people with some business in hand; and, once making their acquaintance, abide by this rule: more strictness toward oneself, more indulgence toward others; and tag onto this advice my habit of not disregarding any talk about myself, whether intelligent or stupid talk, and never getting angry over anything! If you do this, grace will descend upon you and you will know that wisdom which you could never learn from books or from intellectual intercourse.

Let me know about yourself in all respects, how your life is getting on, how you pass the time, whose company you keep, whom you see, what everybody, both friend and stranger, is doing.

In what state generally are gambling and whoring, and what's the subject of conversation these days, both in major and minor fellowships, naturally in decent terms so as not to offend anybody. And so, sincerely and heartily embracing you and wishing you every real benefit and gain, I await your early reply.

Farewell. Yours, G.

Address your letter to Frankfort on the Main, in care of Zhukovsky, who has established himself there from now on, and where I myself intend to be in a month.

The letter was one of a number of letters which surprised people very close to Gogol, such as Pletnev, for example, on account of their endless questions about public talk and opinion on his works. Gogol requested, in particular, accounts of the most irresponsible and outrageous opinions. Even people not so well acquainted with Gogol were deluged by him with letters of this kind, making one suspect that this curiosity of his, under the plausible pretext of studying public attitudes toward his works, disguised a peculiar kind of consuming vanity in him which might even have provided him a sort of pleasure.

As for me, I was delighted with Gogol's letter and wrote back an extensive reply. And I did so with a candor and open-heartedness that brought back to me those unforgettable evenings in Rome, Albano, Frascati, and elsewhere, when we spent marvelous Southern nights endlessly chatting and conversing about anything and everything, when, on account of these conversations—as happened numerous times in Tivoli—we did not even go to bed but sat up until morning on the window seat of a trattoria, dozing to the murmur of a fountain monotonously splashing in the center of its plaza and cutting across the superb lines of an ancient Greek temple which loomed at the other end. Everything then was understood simply and was expressed the same way. But I was cruelly mistaken—the times had changed. With no presentiment yet of the new change of direction Gogol had taken, I unexpectedly and inadvertently struck the sore spot in his thinking and badly upset him. I well remember that, in answering his appeal, I presented him with a picture of party positions regarding his novel, and reported on the polemics Belinsky was conducting with them, not thinking it necessary, of course, to be careful about my remarks concerning either party. I believed that I was obliged to express my thoughts fully and completely, as he had requested, and, therefore, spoke with a certain, perhaps, excessive heat and indignation both about his enemies from the Bulgarin-Senkowski *salons* and about his friends from the Moscow party. Not suspecting the close ties which had been forming between Gogol and the latter at the time, I committed one of those rash acts of sincerity which make a man regret his own honesty. Gogol, who had asked for sincerity, could not tolerate this instance of it and misconstrued my friendly letter.

At the end of my letter, if my memory does not deceive me, there was also a remark to the effect that it was almost impossible even to imagine in the transitional epoch in which we lived some matter of ours which would find a response in posterity, inasmuch as posterity, probably, would not even want to know about certain hopes and ambitions of our time. The remark belonged, of course, to the category of high-sounding, but immature and presumptuous aphorisms such as in private, intimate correspondence not infrequently flow from the pen of a person desirous of saying more, rather than less, than seemed necessary and not foreseeing, moreover, that his words would be read, not by friendly eyes, but by the leery eyes of a judge and censor. It was reasonable to expect an objection and argument against the remark, but not, to be sure, what I did receive.

With an easy conscience, I sent my immoderately candid letter off, and two months later received a reply to it. I was simply baffled by this reply. It contained a very harsh reprimand, something more than a superior's dressing-down, but rather a kind of pastoral malediction, just as if Gogol were solemnly excommunicating me from his church. Instead of the person I had known, the kind-hearted, perceptive analyst of human life who understood everything and put everything in its proper place, I found myself confronted by a completely different person—and not so much just a person, but a kind of preacher on a pulpit which he himself had erected for his needs and from which he thundered out against the sins of poor folk left and right, on authority given him by someone and without always knowing exactly in what way they had sinned. The tone of his letter completely confounded me because I still did not know that Gogol had long since adopted the role of prophet and preacher and that he had already shown himself in that role to Mme Smirnov,[77] Pogodin, Yazykov,[78] and even Zhukovsky and many others, thundering and, at times, lashing out at them with the alacrity almost of a figure from the Old Testament. I quote this letter in its entirety.

Frankfort, May 10 (1844)

Thank you for certain pieces of information about talk of my book. But your own opinions—take care, they are prejudiced. Immoderate epithets scattered here and there in your letter are enough to show that they are prejudiced. A man of good sense would never have allowed himself such opinions. Anger or dissatisfaction, no matter who their object, is always unjust; in one case only can our dissatisfaction be just: when it is turned not against another person but against ourselves, against our own iniquities and against our own failings in our duty. And another thing: You think that you see further and more deeply than others, and you are surprised that many people, presumably intelligent people, do not observe what you have observed. But God only knows who's the one mistaken here. The *leading people* are not those who see some particular something that others do not see and are surprised that others do not see it; only those people can be called *leading people* who see precisely the whole of what others see (all others, not just some others), and, basing themselves upon the sum of the whole, see the whole that others do not see and are not surprised that others do not see the same thing. Your letter reflects a man who simply has become despondent and who has not taken a look at himself. If all of us were to take a proper look at ourselves, instead of deliberating about the spirit of the time, we would have substantially more to gain. In addition to getting to know better what it is we have within ourselves, we would acquire a more lucid and well-rounded view on all things in general and would see roads and ways for ourselves where our sinful despondency veils everything in darkness and reveals to us, instead of roads and ways, only itself, i. e., sinful despondency alone. Only the Evil Spirit could have insinuated in you the idea that you live in some kind of transitional age when all efforts and labors are bound to perish without any echo of them in posterity and without any immediate benefit to anyone. If only our eyes could be made lucid enough, we would see that, wherever it is our fortune to be and under whatever circumstances, propitious or the contrary, there is so much matter in our own, our private lives that our mind itself, perhaps, would swoon, appalled at the sight of all that we have left unfulfilled and neglected, and despondency would then creep into our hearts with good reason. At least it would be more excusable in that case than in the other.

I confess, I thought you (I don't know why) far more sensible. I felt an uneasiness in my very soul when I read your letter. But I shall leave off this matter, and let us never mention it. I cannot abide all these opinions about our age and time because they are all false, because they are uttered by people who are vexed or embittered about something. . . . Write me about yourself only at such time as you experience a strong feeling of dissatisfaction directed against yourself, when you make complaints, not about interference on the part of people or of the age or of whomsoever it might be, but only about interference on the part of your own passions, indolence, and mental torpidity. And another thing: Not in one line of your letter is there a ray of faith, nor is the least spark of a lofty humility to be detected in it! And how, after that, can you still want our minds not to be one-sided or to be impartial! There! I've dumped a whole load of reproaches on you. Don't be surprised, you asked for it yourself. You desired a refreshing letter from me. But I am refreshed now only by reproaches, and with them, therefore, I have done you the same service.

Instead of all your talk about how others are guilty or have failed in the performance of their duty, try and carry out the duties I am going to impose on you. Send me the catalog of the former, Smirdin's, *Library for Reading*, with all its supplements. It's the fullest booklist we have; and add to it a list of all books printed by the Synod press: you can find out about it at the Synod bookstore. And do one thing more: copy out in a close hand all Senkowski's critical articles in *Library for Reading* on *Dead Souls* and on my works in general, doing it in such a way as to be able to enclose it in a letter. I have asked and asked about this, but no one has done it for me. Prokopovich has my Smirdin catalog, I believe. Send it in the post, also; it now does accept parcels. Address it to Berlin, in care of Count Mikh. Mikh. Vielgorsky, Customs Commission official, for delivery to me, if the post office will not undertake to deliver it to me directly in Frankfort. Here, for the time being, are your duties, genuinely Christian duties. Prosecution of this responsibility is required of you directly and without reward. N. Gogol.

Despite the letter's tone of didactic displeasure, which took me utterly by surprise, it touched me very deeply, nevertheless: in the first place, because of its extraordinary literary merits, and in the second place, and primarily, because of a kind of boundless faith of his in the new outlook he was propounding. Only this one thing remained a puzzle to me: by what process of thought had Gogol transferred directly to my account everything I had said in general terms about contemporary people, and how had he come up in my reports with a personal problem—despondency, disgruntlement, dissatisfaction with fate, and other traits of an unsuccessful ambitiousness? But I particularly failed to understand how the additional question had ever cropped up here of my religious convictions and the state of my soul and conscience, since I had had not the slightest intention of making a confession to Gogol and he had not intimated any such question. By relaying public talk about *Dead Souls*, to impart, thereby, evidence of the more or the less satisfactory state of one's religious sentiments —who would ever have thought of such a thing?

Afterward, the whole matter was explained. Gogol's letter, as well as a great many other such letters received by various persons in Russia, was one patch of cloud in that cloud layer which preceded the appearance of his fateful book, *Correspondence with Friends*. The letters heralded its imminent rising on the horizon. Gogol, horrified at the success of his novel among the Westerners and people of unmediated feeling, was wholly engrossed in the idea of disclosing his real historical, patriotic, moral, and religious views, something that, in his opinion, was now essential for an understanding of the second part of the epic which was being prepared. At the same time, Gogol's mind was bringing ever closer to fruition an aspiration and a plan to endow the promiscuous life of Russia at last with a code of lofty rules and adamantine axioms which would assist it in ordering its own inner world and to be an example to all other nations. But that intention of his was still kept secret from everybody for the time being and could not have served to clarify Gogol's behavior. In the dark about these things, I answered Gogol that I had received his letter, thanked him for his concern about me, assured him that I was not distressed over his reprimands, and had no reason not to accept his advice, but thought it necessary to point out a curious mistake. He had treated me as a person with a very high opinion of himself, a haughty person suffering from pride, whereas he might have noticed in the course of our long relationship that I much sooner could claim to be the least worthy of the world's children, and without any reward such as the poet, who once used the expression, spoke about.

After that, our correspondence ceased for a long time, until 1847, when, living with the ailing Belinsky at a spa in Silesia, in Salzbrunn, I again received a letter from Gogol, but this time a mild and, in part, sad letter. His *Correspondence with Friends* had already appeared and brought upon him such a mass of grievances, reproaches, and, finally, slander and unmerited insult that under this storm of popular protest he bent down like a reed—to the ground. The state of his spirits was also reflected in the letter, but it shall concern us later. From that time on, Gogol never failed to show a kind, affectionate, and considerate attitude toward his old correspondent and companion, and each time we met, up until his very death, that attitude was displayed with renewed energy. In 1851, a year before his decease, seeing me out the door of his apartment in Moscow on Nikolaevsky Boulevard (Count Tolstoy's house), he stopped on the threshold and said to me in a tremulous voice: "Don't think ill of me, and do take my side with your friends, please. I value their opinion."

The figure of Gogol afflicted, humbled, and prepared for any eventuality—the Gogol of his last days—remains, equally with the figure of the slowly dying but ever restless Belinsky, my life's most moving recollection.

My poor, confused friend who died, willingly, an agonizing death precisely because he lived in the epoch of conflict between unfixed sets of beliefs, equally important and indispensable, an epoch which he so passionately defended against opinions as to its transitional status! The following circumstance is of extraordinary interest. In March 1848, engaged in working out the second part of *Dead Souls* in Moscow, he wrote his old school friend, the already mentioned N. Ya. Prokopovich, that his work was being hampered, in the first place, by his infirmities and, in the second, by the reflection on an author of all the unwholesome influences of the unstable, *transitional* time in which he lived. And so the horror and indignation aroused in Gogol by the mere suggestion that the epoch might be called transitional vanished four years later, and did not only vanish but the idea itself was recognized as an indisputable truth on the basis of personal experience. Here is that extraordinary passage in his letter, of which I made at the time an accurate copy, without, of course, explaining to anyone the reason why I considered it especially important.

Moscow, March 29 (1848)
My infirmities have brought my occupations with *Dead Souls* to a halt temporarily, when they seemed to be going so well. Perhaps it is not my infirmities, perhaps—also the fact that when you look and see what stupid readers have come our way, what senseless judges, what a lack of taste . . . you simply cannot lift a finger. *It is a strange thing, though you know that your work is not for some transitional, contemporary moment, still the contemporary disorder deprives you of the peace of mind necessary for work.*

How far this admission is from his exclamation: "Only the Evil Spirit could have insinuated in you the idea that we live in some kind of transitional age when all efforts and labors are bound to perish without any echo in posterity . . ."! Alas! However rash that contention may have appeared, however arrogant and false, awkwardly stated and untimely, Gogol himself, the man who passionately criticized it, still felt a doubt as to the use of his efforts and labors for *posterity*—a doubt which resulted, as we know, in the burning of the second part of *Dead Souls.* If it had been in his power then, the result of this mood might have been something even more extensive—I mean, the burning of all his works in toto. It is true, his mental sickness, the pathological condition of his brain, was involved here—but isn't it a fact, after all, that transitional epochs are characterized by these sicknesses which are themselves nothing but the product of a silent struggle of forces in the depths of the mind and soul of every well-developed person?

With all that, I can now easily confess and repeat that the remark about the futility of labors undertaken during a time of transition which I erred in making then and which caused such misunderstanding, was completely thoughtless and false in substance. Neither Gogol's work nor the work of Belinsky himself nor of the people of the 1840's generally from both our camps has failed to leave its mark and exert its influence on their immediate posterity, and there is every indication that they will still find more than one response among generations even further removed from us. It is only this conviction that could have stimulated the compilation of the present "Reminiscences."

[XXIV]

I MUST NOW SAY SOMETHING about that remarkable year in the history of our literary parties, 1845, and proceed to a brief bibliographical account of certain articles in the *Muscovite* when it was—for too short a time—under the direct editorship of I. Kireevsky. These articles comprised an important event in the period we are describing, and without analysis of them further discussion of the period would lose its real meaning, for these articles marked the moment the dispute between the Slavophiles and Westerners took on a new, less relentless and short-sighted character than previously. Although it was not lacking in militant spirit then or for a long time afterward, still its tone did become different. The change of tone and the change in what was said, changes which the Slavophiles were first to broach, had important consequences with respect to the internal affairs and the position of personages in both parties.

We know that the question concerning the relationship of national culture to European education occupied, beside Belinsky, Granovsky, Herzen, and their friends, as well. Considering their close relations with those working for the Slavic cause, it was this question that kept them from coming together on some neutral ground with the people of the opposite camp, people whose moral value they knew very well. And indeed, as long as complete rejection of Europeanism dominated the Slavic party, no reconciliation or agreement was possible. It was exactly this obstacle the Kireevskys, Khomyakov, and their friends crossed over when, in 1845, they took upon themselves the editorship of the *Muscovite*. They made the first step toward a rapprochement with the Westerners. It could be said that, in taking possession of the journal, the new editors had nothing else in mind than properly—from their point of view—posing and resolving that question. Thereupon it became clear from the very first that European civilization was just as valuable, as a *type* of civilization, for the Slavic party as it was to any European, valuable, however, not as a ready-made model for imitation, but as a sound depositor in the capital of intellectual resources of Russian national culture itself and as a worthy adviser in its cultivation of its capital on its own.

The editors' first task, therefore, was to dismiss and refute those opinions held by confederates of theirs which expressed contempt for the European type of civilization or contrasted it with Slavic culture as something inimical or inapplicable to the latter. The leading article by I. V. Kireevsky in the first issue of the *Muscovite* for 1845 ("Survey of the Contemporary Condition of Literature") dealt heavy blows to the persecutors of the West and, above all, to the former critic of that same journal, S. Shevyrev, who in his article of 1841, "A View of European Education," had expressed the opinion that Russia, not having undergone either reformation or revolution and, for that reason, preserving a great moral unity, could not share a spiritual life with the diseased European world, but more likely was meant to cure and renew that world. I. V. Kireevsky believed no less than S. Shevyrev in all the dogmas, so to speak, of the Slavophile party, in the distressing dichotomy of European life and in the necessity and possibility of its being renewed by principles of Eastern philosophy, all of which he acknowledged in his treatise. But I. V. Kireevsky, at the same time, had a conception of the role of the West in the cause of civilization that was considerably wider than the one held by the ultra-Slavists from his own party to whom he did not hesitate to tell the bitter truth.

In his second article (*Muscovite*, No. 2, 1845), he declared both our trends, the purely Russian one and the purely Western one, equally false, and did so on grounds far more offensive for his own party than for the party hostile to it. The purely Russian trend was false because, he observed, it inevitably and fatally came to expect a miracle and to summon it to the aid of its faith, since only a miracle could resurrect the corpse—the Russian past over which people of that persuasion so bitterly lamented. This trend, in addition, did not see that, be European enlightenment what it may, it was already beyond our power to eradicate its influence, after our once having become involved in it; and even if it were possible to do so, it would be a great catastrophe. Were we to tear ourselves away from Europe, he added, we would cease being a nationality belonging to mankind as a whole and we would deprive ourselves of all the benefits of Greco-Roman culture (*Muscovite*, No. 2, pp. 63–78).

The Westerners, by which he meant primarily Belinsky, as the most extreme of them, were also rather severely upbraided. Their trend was accused of failing to understand that the truths of the West were only the remains of Christian principles, and the rebuke was supplemented by the assertion that they were "behaving like women" in being governed by their single passion for the object of their adoration, that passion being what brought them to the absurd idea that Europe had supposedly found the solution for everything and that it was merely a matter of picking up and making a fetish of everything it gave off, necessary or not (p. 73). Instead of these vacuous trends, the only thing that existed and was important for Kireevsky was a conception of two kinds of education, one of them being the kind that comes about through the inner ordering of spirit by the power of the truth informing it. This is the most rational, the highest form of education, and one which could not possibly dispense with a knowledge of Europe. The other, the lower form, took place through formal development of the intellect and the acquisition of higher knowledge with the help solely of imitation and borrowing; it made a man something resembling a logical and technological factor devoid of national or any other kind of convictions (p. 74). At the end of his investigations, Kireevsky presented a thesis summarizing his position, which reads: "Therefore, love for European education and, equally, love for our own—both coincide at their final point of development in the same love, the same aspiration toward living, total, universally human, and truly Christian enlightenment."

Both of I. V. Kireevsky's articles made an enormous impression and found sympathy and censure among people from both camps —from the Slavophile and from the Western camp—equally. Belinsky belonged among those who expressed censure. He detected in the article's makeup, in part, a certain German trait of skillful but specious generalization, and, in addition, a certain lack of consistency: "How in the world," he said, "has Kireevsky managed to find a race capable of filling out the development of Europe with fresh elements of its own making, while at the same time recommending to that race ideals of civilization of his own invention? After all, the ideal of civilization is this very chosen race itself! No, that won't do: if you are not deceiving yourself by saying that you have been deemed worthy to read in the book of destiny about the mission of the Russian people, then don't be ashamed to lie in the dust at its feet. I much prefer Sh. [Shevyrev] and P. [Pogodin] who don't shilly-shally and simply blare out: 'We are the saviors, we are the regenerators!'—at least you know what answer to give them to that."

I. Kireevsky's third article, the one which, according to his prospectus, was to have concerned itself with current happenings in literature, unfortunately did not appear in print.

Our homegrown persecutors of the West were no less decisively and severely treated by A. S. Khomyakov in two superb articles of his: (1) "Letter to Petersburg" (*Muscovite*, No, 2, 1845 on the topic of Russian railroads) and (2) "Foreigners' Opinion of Russia" (*Muscovite*, No. 4, 1845). The latter article was unsigned and had in view, of course, the well-known book by Custine,[79] which, despite a strict ban, was read everywhere in Russia and aroused, by its way of characterizing certain persons and events, sarcastic behind-the-scenes talk which, though innocent enough, alarmed people in the government administration of the time, nevertheless. The usual Slavophile apologetics were also found in his articles in great abundance. Just as Kireevsky, Khomyakov, in the first of the articles, declared enlightenment to be nothing else than the illumination of the entire reasoning faculty in man or in a nation, and he supplemented this thought with the observation that such an illumination could coincide with learning, but could also exist without it and not lose its beneficial effect thereby.[80] Again just as Kireevsky, he prefaced his criticism of friends with criticism of the Westerners and the Belinsky school, accusing it of unpardonable one-sidedness. In their literary judgments both I. V. Kireevsky and A. S. Khomyakov came very close to Belinsky and often even went further. Take, for instance, the following passage from Kireevsky's second article: "The works of our literature, as reflections of European literary works, cannot be of any interest for other nations except as a matter of statistics, as an index of our scholastic achievements in studying their models" (*Muscovite*, No. 2, p. 63). Belinsky never said anything more emphatic than that. And what abuse he had to put up with on account of similar, now wholly justified, dicta! The Slavic party, it is true, while secretly agreeing with the positions of the critic they abhorred, often tried in every way to keep apart from him, at times going to rather ingenious lengths to make it possible to contradict Belinsky while sharing his opinion. There are a great many examples of this.

With his convictions thus shielded against any suspicion of abetting his enemies, Khomyakov turned with that much more energy to the diehards of his own party who exorcised the West as if it were the pestilence. "Do not think," he exclaimed, "that on the pretext of preserving the wholeness of life and avoiding European duality, you have the right to reject any European intellectual or material advance whatsoever. . . . There is something ridiculous," he continued, "and even something immoral about this fanaticism of immobility" (*Ibid.*, pp. 82–83). "You must know," he elaborated further on, "that assimilation of foreign elements is brought about by force of the laws of the moral nature of a people and brings about new phenomena which manifest its uniqueness, versatility, and independence." He even denounced our ultrapatriots and persecutors of the West by calling them simply skeptics bereft of any faith in the power of the truth and wholesome principles of Russian life which they defended and which had already in our time, despite the character of imitativeness belonging to it, forged far ahead of its teachers in many things—for instance, in Russian life it would be unthinkable to have such a thing as *Bavarian* art engaged in reproducing, all at the same time, the monuments of Greece, Byzantium, and the Middle Ages.

It was a rather peculiar thing to praise Russian life for what it did not do, not having as yet any conception of the history of art in general, but the aptness of all Khomyakov's other formulations was acknowledged by the Slavophiles with regard to the Westerners, and by the Westerners with regard to Slavophiles.

Khomyakov's second article, "Foreigners' Opinion of Russia," was noteworthy for the fact that it exonerated the foreign authors and their Russian informers from responsibility for the absurdities which they spread about Russia. "What else could they have said?" Khomyakov noted. The fundamental principle of life of a people from which everything ensued was very often not only misunderstood by other peoples but not infrequently misunderstood by the first people itself. An example of this was furnished by England, which up to that day was misunderstood, in the author's opinion, both by foreigners and by *its own* writers.[81] With only a formal-scientific education and only logical procedures for extracting ideas, he added, there was no possibility of grasping the soul of a nation, of apprehending the principles by which it lived. That is why our simple people, without having gone on to higher classes in logic and formal education, had rendered, according to Khomyakov, an enormous service to Russia. "What came into effect here," the author said, "was the unconscious clairvoyance of human intelligence which can prognosticate much that still cannot be given a name or a definite description" (*Muscovite*, No. 4, p. 38). By preserving its national culture, the Russian people had prepared precious materials for a national consciousness which was to grow even stauncher and reach more powerful expression after assimilating elements of European civilization, and which, once that had happened, would make fallacies about Russian life on the part of our own, as well as foreign investigators, an impossibility.

Even a man so taken up with his work as P. V. Kireevsky, who had consecrated himself to the collection of monuments of folk creativity and who made only reluctant appearances in the arena of journalism, participated in the activity of forging secure bases for his party. In the third issue of the *Muscovite*, he criticized M. P. Pogodin's contention, according to which the Russian people were always noted for mildness and submissiveness, had not known class discord and easily yielded to demands made on it. P. V. Kireevsky considered this contention a slur on the Russian people, proposed a different interpretation of its history, and provoked a heated rebuttal from M. P. Pogodin who reaffirmed his earlier thesis on the submissiveness of the Russian people with citations from the ancient chronicles.

From all this, one may well suppose that the former editor of the journal had reason to regret having turned his periodical over to other hands, despite the rapid moral and material importance the *Muscovite* had acquired under its new editors. As early as the third issue, Pogodin hastened to protect himself against the attacks of his overly conscientious and candid friends whose demands continued to grow and grow, threatening to leave him and a good share of his party behind. In a short article of his, "In Favor of Old Russia" (*Muscovite*, p. 27), he objected with unconcealed pique to the reproach or, as he expressed himself, to the *slander* that the Slavophiles supposedly did not respect the West, supposedly wanted to raise up a dead corpse, supposedly worshipped impiously a static ancient order of things. The ruffled editor rather ironically made clear that the Slavophiles were waging a campaign in favor of the Russian spirit emanating from ancient times, in favor of independence of life and, after that, also in favor of unconstrained appreciation of all the benefits of West, East, North, and South (p. 31). That amounted to wholly avoiding an answer to the real issue of the question.

At the end of the year, M. P. Pogodin hastened to take the journal back into his own hands and easily managed to strip it of the importance it had begun to acquire. The *Muscovite* dragged on a rather wan existence, putting its issues out late and at rare moments coming to life with polemical sparks, sparks which soon died out and disappeared in a heap of literary rubbish. So it continued until 1850 when a new generation, an exclusively Moscow-educated generation, brought the public's attention back to the journal. The names of the fresh forces which then revitalized the editorship of the journal, under the standard of which they banded together, are now well-known. They were: A. Ostrovski, A. Pisemsky, A. Potekhin, Kokorev, and others, specializing in artistic production, and A. Grigoriev, Edelson, T. Filippov, and others, specializing in criticism and philosophy. Petersburg immediately set about polemicizing also with them, taking them to be epigones—the residue of the mighty old party. But this has to do with another period of literature and national development.

The Moscow Westerners with Granovsky and Herzen at their head did not leave the Slavophile party's gesture of magnanimously extending its hand without response. They simply welcomed the opportunity to begin again a certain exchange of ideas with their highly cultivated opponents, now that the major fosse which had kept the two camps from any sort of communication with each other was, if not completely, at least half filled in. The combatants turned once again to talk, for they now could understand one another. Retaining all their distinctive features and their independence, without acknowledging very many of the Slavophile positions and using those they did to embellish and supplement their main theme of the benefit and necessity of studying Europe, and especially without repudiating their right and duty to exert energetic opposition, when applicable, to conclusions the Slavophiles might make from both Russian history and the history of Europe in general, the Moscow party of Westerners, nevertheless, acknowledged the importance of the Slavophiles' latest *profession de foi* and understood the necessity and legitimacy of concessions on their part. And these concessions were made, as we shall see. But Belinsky remained outside this entire movement.

CHAPTER

[XXV]

SIMULTANEOUSLY WITH THE SPLIT in the camp of the "Slavs," a split of the same sort ensued among the Westerners. The *Muscovite* had caused many a storm deep within this party, and at the outbreak of one such storm, in the summer of 1845, I myself was present.

The summer of 1845 has left me with recollections so vivid that even now (1870), after the passage of more than twenty-five years, I seem to see before me each of the members of the Moscow circle of the time and seem to hear their every word. For me this is no distant, half-forgotten past but seems an event of yesterday. The voices, facial expressions, and postures of these people remain in my memory just as vividly as if we had parted company only a little while ago. I shall try to give as faithful an account as possible of my recollections.

Granovsky, Ketcher, and Herzen had informed their friends that they were going to move to the village of Sokolovo—some 15 to 20 miles from Moscow—for the summer (of 1845). The village belonged to the landowner Divov, who retained the large mansion there for himself for any trips he might take to his family estate, but leased to tenants the two wings of the mansion and a cottage behind it plus a magnificent linden and birch grove that ran from the house down a hill to the river. On the other side of the river and hill, in keeping with the common character of Russian landscapes, a solid line of peasant huts was strung out. The Herzen and Granovsky familes occupied the wings and Ketcher—the rear cottage. The landowner did not disturb his tenants. During his rare visits all he did was *order* the peasants, both men and women, to walk *freely* around his garden, filing past the windows of the mansion. However light, to all appearances, this corvée, it still aroused a strong resentment on the part of those liable to it, as the tenants themselves had more than one occasion to witness.

In all likelihood, Sokolovo never had before or has since presented so astounding a scene of noise and commotion as it did in the summer of 1845. Visiting the vacationers was done on a fabulous, massive scale. The lawn fronting the mansion was the site of almost colossal dinners, and both hostesses, Natalya Aleksandrovna, Herzen's wife, and Elizaveta Bogdanovna Granovsky, once they became accustomed to this flood of visitors, managed the huge crowd with incredible dexterity. They themselves were very different types of persons, though theirs was a very close friendship. Herzen's wife with her soft, barely audible voice, with her affectionate and feverish smile, with all her look of childlike tenderness, frailty, and suffering, possessed, in addition, a passionate nature, a fiery imagination, and a very strong will, of which she gave concrete proof at the beginning and at the end of her life. Elizaveta Bogdanovna Granovsky was the embodiment of tranquil, unobtrusively noble, and inwardly joyous acceptance of the fate which had determined her position both as wife and as woman. Both were capable, each in her own way and with different motives, of very considerable sacrifices and feats, whenever there was need. Always surrounded by their women friends from Moscow, they served for the time as that tempering, aesthetic force which kept the friendly carouses, where there was no skimping on champagne, within the tone of gay, but far from loose, sociality.

I appeared in the midst of the Sokolovo assembly at the end of June and was received by them with the greatest cordiality but with a certain tinge to it that I could not fail to notice. As a guest from Petersburg and from Belinsky's inner circle, I was bound to be made sensible of that note, lodged in the friendliest effusions, of discord, of dissonance which already existed between the two sections of the Western party. This note rang in the ironic jokes Herzen made, in Ketcher's nervous guffaws, and in the semiserious expression on Granovsky's face which alternately faded and grew darker. Everybody felt it essential to sound this ugly note out loud and finish with it as quickly as possible so as to be able to return again to simple, candid relationships with one another. And that is just what did happen without delay.

That very day, the whole company assembled for a walk in the fields surrounding Sokolovo, which were then swarming with activity on account of an early harvest. Peasants—both men and women— were harvesting the fields in dress that was almost rudimentary, and this gave occasion for someone to remark that, of all women, the Russian woman was the only one who felt no embarrassment in front of anyone and in front of whom no one had any cause to feel embarrassed. The remark was enough to bring on the storm to clear the air that everyone was expecting. Granovsky halted and with unusual seriousness made objection to the joke: "One should add," he said, "that this fact is the shame not of the Russian peasant woman but of those who brought her to it and who are accustomed to treat her cynically. Our Russian literature is especially guilty of the latter. I can by no means agree that our literature has done well by indirectly abetting this kind of cynicism through dissemination of an attitude of contempt for folk character." With that the argument began.

I did not mention that also among the permanent guests at Sokolovo was Evgeny Korsh,[82] the editor of *Moscow News* and an influential member of the circle. In his convictions he belonged wholly to the party of extreme Westerners, sharing with them a quest for bases for life and thought in philosophy and history, keeping in touch with the theories of socialism and being far from apprehensive about whatever results might finally come out at the end of their investigation; but, at the same time, he did not take on faith any alluring prospects a doctrine offered, whatever the doctrine's source, if it even slightly veered toward Utopia or showed a penchant for arbitrary conclusions. He waged constant war against ideals of existence, of which there arose then a great abundance. Generally speaking, he was a critic of the convictions and beliefs of his circle, while sharing many of its hopes and all its basic postulates. He stood with one foot raised, so to speak, from his own camp over the opposite one, dampening the overly rosy expectations or excessively sanguine outbursts of enthusiasm of his friends. His vast erudition and truly remarkable endowment of keen and acerbic wit, the effect of which was even enhanced by the contrast of a speech defect, made of Evgeny Korsh an outstanding member of the circle.[83] He understood immediately that the quarrel started was not a decisive battle of any sort that would end by changing the positions of the embattled sides, but only a simple exchange between them, and, therefore, he ranged freely between the sides without joining either the one or the other. The issue was otherwise understood by Ketcher,[84] who felt it incumbent upon him to make himself the advocate of the absent Petersburg faction, however little he himself then shared all its views. He took up Granovsky's gauntlet and began an argument with him about *principles,* and did so in an extremely heated manner, as will be evident, I hope, from my abridged version of this noteworthy altercation. I can vouch for the accuracy and order of the ideas and for a close approximation of the words in which they were expressed.[85]

"Excuse me," Ketcher exclaimed, "but how can you take every trivial remark and turn it into a generalization that way! What person could keep his head on his shoulders if people started drawing various meanings out of every casual word of his? Why, we'd have a regular

Preobrazhensky bureau of investigation going! But if you're going to start making generalizations, Granovsky, then you'd do better to ask yourself the question: Didn't the people themselves participate in forming our bad habits and aren't our bad habits precisely the people's habits?"

"Hold on, my dear Ketcher," Granovsky objected. "You say: One oughtn't make generalizations from casual remarks. In the first place, my good friend, casual remarks are closely related to our intimate thought, and, in the second place, a collection of such remarks can sometimes comprise a whole doctrine, as, for example, in Belinsky's case. And I must tell you straight out," Granovsky added, putting particular emphasis on these words of his, "that in outlook on our Russian nationality and with respect to many other literary and moral questions, I sympathize far more with the Slavophiles than with Belinsky, *Notes of the Fatherland,* and the Westerners."

A momentary silence followed this categorical statement. Much later on, the idea Granovsky had articulatd was repeated numerous times by Herzen on his own part in his publications abroad, but it was Granovsky who first stated the idea, and did so at Sokolovo. Herzen, of course, took part in the argument which had started, not having the slightest suspicion that he would himself come into conflict with Granovsky over a question exactly matching the one then being discussed.[86] He now supported Granovsky, but not as decisively as might have been expected, judging by the outward signs of similarity in their attitude of mind. Belinsky's forthright, undeviating, candid endeavors had always had an appeal for him, despite the many reservations he had about them, and, in addition, some suspicion of the imminence of his bitter reckoning with Granovsky himself had, most likely, already occurred to him and placed a certain restraint on what he would say. His intervention into the discussion was of an amicable kind.

"But you must understand, my good fellow," he said, turning to Ketcher, "that beside the general national question, a question over which we can deliberate this way and that way, we are talking about a moral question. We must behave decently toward the lower orders of society who work for but are not responsible to us. Every sally made against them, deliberate or not, is like insulting a child. Who is going to speak for them, if not we ourselves? They have no official advocates; in that case, you understand, everyone must become their advocate. It is especially not amiss to understand that now (1845), when we are making efforts to get rid of all sorts of constabularies. It's not for the sake of giving ourselves free rein to cut capers that we need to send seen and unseen constables packing."

Ketcher did not relish letting his opponent have the last word. He inveighed against the attempt to mix morality, after nationality, into this trivial issue which had grown into such a debate; he asserted that the exposure of any indisputable fact, even of the most deplorable character, could never be immoral; and, finally, after some jocular remarks on the new upcoming Russophiles (no one stinted adding spicy sauce of that kind to arguments those days), he came around to Belinsky, who actually was the real subject of the whole conversation. Ketcher observed that we hardly even had the right to make any judgment about Belinsky's views on nationality since he had never expressed his real views completely and, indeed, because of the censorship, could not relay all of his thinking on this subject and on many others, as well. At that point, Granovsky once again stopped Ketcher and ended the argument with a remark that stunned everybody by its unexpectedness. I quote the remark word for word.

"Do you know, my dear Ketcher, what I have to say to you on your remark about the censorship? As concerns Belinsky's intelligence, talent, and integrity, we can have no quarrel. But here's what I'll say about the censorship. If Belinsky has become a force among us, he owes it, in the first place, to himself, of course, but in the second place —to the censorship. It not only has not harmed him, it has rendered him a great service. With his nervous, irascible character, his caustic expression and obsessions, he never would have been able to cope with his material without the censorship. It, the censorship, forced him to think out plans for his critical articles and their means of expression, and has made him what he is. It's my firm conviction that Belinsky has no right to complain about the censorship, though there's no reason to thank it, either: it, of course, also did not know what it was doing."

The argument was consummated once that declaration of Granovsky's was made. Everything Granovsky had wanted to say was said. When someone remarked afterward that all Belinsky's trenchant, antinational sallies stemmed also from a feeling of democratic fervor aroused by the condition to which the masses of the people had been reduced, Granovsky eagerly concurred with the opinion, seeing in it the key to many of the critic's excesses, which he considered, nevertheless, abnormal and regrettable. The argument ended. It had done its work in having cleared everyone's conscience and allowing them to return, without further obstacle, back to simple, friendly, and sincere relations.

As I conceived of it, this argument had still another significance. It was the first major manifestation of an idea, long held secretly in mind, concerning the necessity of a more reasonable attitude toward the simple people than was current in literature and in certain strata of the class of thinking people. Literature and our cultivated minds had long ago relinquished the notion of the people as a human entity ordained to live without rights of citizenship and to serve the interests of others only, but they had not relinquished the notion of the people as a brutish mass without any ideas and with never a thought in its head. The argument signalized a sharp change which had come about in the conceptions of one section of the Westerners regarding ways of judging and evaluating the home-grown culture and moral physiognomy of the crowd.

Two or three years earlier, it would not have occurred to any member of the Western party to examine its boldest assertions about the customs, beliefs, and moral characteristics of the people or to be concerned about the soundness and justness of its views on their life, hopes, and expectations. All of that was a matter of personal taste, and it was left to the individual to think about these things as he liked, without being called to account in the least for his opinions and his point of view. Unnoticed, a tone of haughty, half-patrician and half-pedantic contempt for the way of life and turn of mind of that realm of toil and darkness took hold among the educated circles. It was especially glaring in the case of ardent enthusiasts and supporters of the doctrine of personal energy and personal initiative, the presence of which they saw no evidence of in the Russian world. Often their reactions to this world smacked of the arriviste's or merchant-baron's putting on airs before his less successful confreres. *Conceit over one's education* sometimes tainted even the most substantial minds of the time and was by and large *the* unwholesome side to our Westernism. However, it—this Westernism—did finally curb this kind of perverted application of its principles to life. The argument recounted above was the result of a long-held desire on the part of one section of our Westerners to lodge a formal protest against the shallow treatment of questions regarding the life of the people, of which certain segments of their own party were guilty.

Perhaps no one took this newly arisen question about the special mentality of unlearned people so much to heart as did one of the most trusted and ardent friends of the circle, K. D. Kavelin,[87] a man who was in the custom of infusing all his convictions, those pertaining to practical life as well as those pertaining to science, with a spirit of enthusiasm. The habit of disdaining the people had been so general that even persons who later became the most fervent advocates of their rights and interests were affected by it. Considerably later on, in Petersburg, where he had moved and where there was the greatest need of clearing the way for a favorable attitude toward all types of folk creativity, Kavelin's propaganda went on unabated straight to the end of the 1850's. Here is the place also to mention that another person who contributed not a little toward a change in the manner of regarding the people and toward an awareness of their mental life was the very person once so ridiculed by the Slavophiles—Turgenev. His first stories for *Notes of a Hunter*, appearing in the *Contemporary* of 1847, put an end to any possibility of holding the mass of the people in derision. But the ground for *Notes of a Hunter* had already been prepared, and Turgenev gave clear and artistic expression to the essence of an attitude of mind which was already, so to speak, in the air.

CHAPTER

[XXVI]

I RETURN to Sokolovo.

In midsummer this village outside Moscow took on the semblance of a perpetual congress of writers, professors, actors, and friends who were incessantly arriving and disappearing, all apparently with the object in mind of exchanging ideas and news with one another. The hosts and hostesses lived in terribly crowded conditions and had no time, it appeared, to concentrate on any special occupation of their own. Guests changed in kaleidoscopic succession. Beside Panaev, who himself has left a description of life at Sokolovo, there flickered before my eyes N. A. Nekrasov, an old acquaintance of mine whose career and poetry were then arousing everyone's sympathetic attention, and next, Ivan Vasilevich Pavlov, whom I met there for the first time and who made a big impression by the singular uncouthness of his manners, under which was hidden considerable thought, observation, and humor, and others; Evgeny Fedorovich Korsh, old Shchepkin, the young Zasyadko, who met an early death, the novice painter Gorbunov, who made a lithographic collection of portraits of the whole circle,[88] were constant visitors at Sokolovo. The summer hosts themselves did not live as idly in this whirl of guests and of people dropping in from all sides as might have appeared at first sight. So, for example, Herzen was engaged in publishing and continuing his letters on the study of nature; Granovsky was preparing himself for his second series of public lectures; Ketcher was hard at work translating Shakespeare. Sometimes Ketcher would disappear from Sokolovo for whole days at a time. Dressed in a dirty, grey smock and having taken with him only a piece of bread, he would roam through the woods surrounding Moscow. In the woods he once met a haggard army deserter with an injured foot, who regarded him with less than friendly eyes. Ketcher extracted a splinter from his foot, bandaged the wound, and gave him his piece of bread.

When Sokolovo's population of natives and newcomers gathered for a meeting at one or another of its forums (in addition to Sokolovo's populous dinners, a circular clearing surrounded by magnificent lindens deep in the park served as such a forum), the conversations, discussions, and telling of stories that went on there, reflecting all the great diversity of character, mind, and attitude, bore a certain common tone, which was the dominant tone of all social discourse of the epoch. Almost no political conversations, in the strict sense of the word, ever occurred at these improvised academes. Public life of the period equipped people only with humorous anecdotes and provided nothing more for the time being. The basic principles governing society received, as such, no attention whatever. To deliberate over them was considered an idle pastime, and they would be spoken of when it happened that, in their application, they reached the extreme of either comic or tragic absurdity. Up to that time, they were considered by everyone matters long since dead and buried. They were recalled to mind particularly on those occasions when the necessity arose of escaping from the clutches of one or another of them risen from the dead and walking the earth, having taken suddenly to persecuting the living. Instead, European affairs, doctrines, and discoveries stood in the foreground; these topics comprised the dominant note in conversations. At the same time, there was another thread running through the entire patchwork of casual conversation at Sokolovo, and it was that which gave one a sense of the common origin and kinship of all the opinions and ideas expressed then, despite their frequent contrariety. Above all, it should be noted that only one thing was not allowed at Sokolovo—to be a limited person. Not that one was peremptorily required to be an effective speaker and display flashes of brilliant capabilities in general; quite the contrary, people wholly engrossed by their own specialties exclusively were held in very high esteem there. What was required were a certain intellectual level and a certain dignity of character. All the discourse of the circle was devoted to refining people's intellect and character, no matter what the talk was about, and that is what gave it the monotone already mentioned.

One other characteristic feature: the circle shunned contact with the unwholesome elements lying off to the side of it, and would become disturbed should any, even accidental or remote, reference be made to them. The circle had not withdrawn from the world, but stood apart from it—which was the reason it attracted attention; but precisely on account of that situation, a special sensitivity developed in its midst toward all that was artificial and sham. Any evidence of a questionable sentiment, crafty expression, empty motto, specious assurance was instantly surmised by the circle and, whenever these things showed themselves, they provoked a storm of ridicule, irony, and devastating criticism. Sokolovo in this respect was no exception to the general rule. Generally speaking, this circle, the main representatives of which had gathered for a while at Sokolovo, resembled a militant order of knights which was without a written charter but which knew all its members scattered over the broad face of this earth of ours and which, nevertheless, by some kind of agreement no one in actual fact had brought about, stood athwart the whole current of contemporary life, keeping it from taking free rein, hated by some and passionately admired by others.

CHAPTER

[XXVII]

THE HISTORY of the "Western" party's presently ensuing internal disagreements is no less worthy of attention than the history of its emergence and effect in society. A split in the Moscow section of the Westerners ensued after the Moscow friends protested against Belinsky's
exclusive Europeanism. Its two most important representatives, Herzen and Granovsky, parted company over issues arising, in the final
analysis, on the grounds of that very Western civilization with whose
features they were so concerned. The ideas of socialism and the
change of manner in treating metaphysical concepts, which those
ideas entailed, now supplied the impetus for a new subdivision of the
party. The very first sparks of that disagreement among the friends
had occurred, again, at Sokolovo, but the brunt of the argument, with
all its aftermath, belongs to the following year, 1846. I shall now take
the opportunity to pause and consider this detail which, in various
shapes and forms, was repeated in many other circles and sections of
our "Westernism."

Everybody is familiar with the fact that a specifically *Russian* socialism, or what could be called popular or folk economic concepts,
had very clear-cut and narrow limits and consisted of the doctrine involving the principles of the village commune [*obshchina*] and the
guild [*artel*], i. e., the doctrine on the possession and utilization in
common of the means of production. In the modest and limited form
which our entire history gave it, *Russian* socialism was, in fact, first
advanced by the Slavophiles with the amendment, however, that it
served not only as a model of economic organization for anything pertaining to agriculture and the trades but also as an example of com-
bining the idea of Christianity with the needs of external, material
existence. It was this amendment to which our Westerners would not
agree and which they repudiated in no uncertain terms. While acknowledging that the Russian *obshchina* was preserving the interests

139

of the people at the given moment and was providing them the means to struggle against the adverse circumstances surrounding them, they did not acknowledge that the *obshchina*-type of property ownership contained a universal economic principle that might be valid for any economy. The temporary significance of the *obshchina* and the *artel* was, for the Westerners, confirmed by the example of exactly the same kind of institution being found among all primitive peoples, and they believed that, with further advances in freedom and well-being, the Russian people themselves would abandon this form of labor and communal life. These convictions also belonged to contemporary political-economic science, which, in company with the Westerners, acknowledged the *obshchina*-type of production of goods and equal distribution of land and work tools as nothing more than a measure against famine taken by the indigent and childlike mode of life of the people, and saw no reason to nurture hopes of its acquiring any political or economic significance in the future. Such was the form in which the Westerners conceived "Russian socialism."

It was quite otherwise that they perceived "European socialism." To begin with, it opened up brilliant prospects on all sides and unfolded before their eyes a dazzling, fantastically illuminated vista to which there was no end in sight. As has already been mentioned, European socialistic theories were very diligently studied then, but all that was derived from these theories were only more or less fortuitously combined and coordinated collections of startling, stupefying and imperious aphorisms. The European socialism of the period did not yet stand on practical and scientific grounds but, for the time being, only worked at producing something on the order of "visions" of the future structure of social life, a life which it designed to suit its own fancy. The substantive part of its content was vehement criticism of all economic codes and active religious beliefs and convictions, by which means it intended to clear a place for itself in people's minds: this criticism was what gave it its sharply etched, militant character. And in what forceful terms this character was expressed! Not to mention the famed exclamation of Proudhon's—"*la propriété c'est le vol*," —and the no less acclaimed apothegm of the tailor Weitling—"Only one form of free labor is open to us—robbery"—there were many, many others, likewise blinding and deafening theses of the young socialism of the time over which its neophytes had to set their minds working: "Commerce and the merchant class which it has created are nothing but parasites in the economic life of nations"; "the results of the *collective* labor of workers are reaped free of charge by the employer who always pays for piece-work only"; "the correct association distributes work according to each person's capabilities and reward according to each person's need"; "a worker's abilities do not entitle him to a larger share of the reward since these abilities are themselves a gift of chance"; "art and talent are deformities of the moral world, counterparts to the physical deformities, and do not deserve to be valued and paid for"; "the worker has just the same right to the good he produces as the man who orders it"; "the civilization of Europe is the direct offspring of its leisure classes"—and so on and so forth. I have quoted here only a random sampling of the theses and postulations of the new socialism, but there were hosts of them; and they all taxed the imagination far more than did whole systems in the same line of thinking, such as the systems of Saint-Simon and Fourier, inasmuch as the hierarchical character of Saint-Simon's teaching and the artificial harmony of temperaments and psychological gradations of Fourier's aroused puzzlement and humor on account of many of their aspects. But when it came to the aphorisms and theses of "militant" socialism, quite the contrary—no one made demands for plain and convincing proof. The strength of these thunder-bearing postulations consisted, not in their logical inevitability, but in the fact that they heralded some new order of things and seemed to throw beams of light into the dark vista of the future, making discovery there of unknown and felicitous domains of work and pleasure about which each person judged according to the impressions he received in the brief instant of one or another such flash of light.

These *insights* into the future, however, had an extremely varied effect on the members of the circle itself. Granovsky, for instance, was not the least bit seduced by them. While acknowledging that European socialism was something that could not be ignored by the historians or by thinking people in general, Granovsky regarded it as the malady of the age, all the more dangerous for its not expecting and not seeking aid from any quarter. "Socialism is extremely dangerous," he said, "in that it teaches one to look for solutions to the problems of social life, not in the arena of politics, which it despises, but apart from that arena, whereby it undermines both it and itself." Herzen and Belinsky took a different attitude. Socialism's militant manifestoes, heralding its campaign of extermination against European civilization, did not horrify them. Of course, neither the one nor the other had any such intention as adopting all its prescriptions or converting all its claims into dogmas of their own personal "faith" (in their position it would have been absurd to do so). Many of socialism's subversive decrees seemed, even to them, puerile outbursts, but they viewed with far greater equanimity, dispassion, and aplomb than did Granovsky the fate of contemporary culture and learning should they have to suffer a certain detriment. That that culture and learning faced no small ordeal no one doubted: in all of Europe then it was thought that, with the advent of socialism, Europe would be beset with a terrible hurricane supposed to shake all the beliefs, convictions, habits, ideas, and historical bases which it had taken so much time and effort to acquire. The difference in ways of regarding these premonitions of an upheaval was what shaped the *dissension* within the Moscow circle about which we are now talking. Herzen was of one mind with Belinsky, and they both honestly and directly beheld the symptoms of disintegration which threatened Europe, in their opinion, from socialism, without calling for, but also without terror of, the havoc it was supposed to bring. They believed that from the ashes of the old civilization of Europe would arise a phoenix—a new order of things to be the crowning achievement and the last word of its thousand-year-long development.

All the premonitions of an upheaval had the contrary effect on Granovsky: they filled him with extreme alarm, and the upheaval itself, as he envisioned it, did not elicit his slightest sympathy, did not arouse any rosy hopes or expectations. The disagreement between the friends was, as we see, of a completely innocuous character with nothing more substantial to it than suppositions and conjectures, but, still, it was accompanied by ironies and arguments which brought out the views of the two sides on other subjects of a moral character. Once having started up, the dispute was kept going by a number of inflammatory elements added to it from the side, from scientific and other features of the life of the time.

Among such inflammatory materials one must include, incidentally, Feuerbach's famous book, which was then in everybody's hands. It could be said that Feuerbach's book [89] had nowhere produced so powerful an impression as it did in our "Western" circle, and nowhere did it so rapidly obliterate the remnants of all preceding outlooks. Herzen, needless to say, was a fervent expositor of its propositions and conclusions; among other things, he connected the upheaval it revealed in the realm of metaphysical ideas with the political upheaval heralded by the socialists, in which respect Herzen once again coincided with Belinsky.[90] But Granovsky, bitter at heart and upset by doubts, kept avoiding the ultimate statement that his friends were insisting he make regarding all the phenomena in question, and did not make it, but endeavored, instead, to keep underfoot the concrete, historical basis of existence which was being washed away from all sides. He began to be at odds with his own circle, with the circle in which, as he himself said, his heart and the whole moral part of his being were totally lodged.

An attitude of coolness and a difference of opinion had already covertly existed between the friends before coming out in the open. Granovsky had once said in my presence, back at Sokolovo, jokingly asking the company's leave to go to Moscow and visit other friends of his who had remained there (meaning, primarily, the Elagin salon), "I have to go so as not to degenerate completely in your company. Why, look here, you've already deprived me of immortality of soul!" These words, despite their jocular character, stunned me then as a revelation. A year later, in 1846 that is, Granovsky's decision was made final. Herzen relates in his "Memoirs" that Granovsky once announced to him in no uncertain terms, after a heated controversy between them, that he, Granovsky, could not go along any further with his former comrades in the direction they were making more and more their own and from which he could see no reasonable way out; that he felt compelled, though it grieved him deeply, to disengage himself from the circle dear to him on account of many religious, moral, and historical issues, and to make a firm and sincere announcement to this effect. Herzen was dumbfounded: he was losing a friend—and what a friend!—of his youth, and he could see, furthermore, with how wretched an expression and in what a tone of voice Granovsky had presented his ultimatum! Astounded and abashed, Herzen turned immediately to E. F. Korsh for help in clearing up the matter and, if possible, for his intercession, but he met with an evasive answer from Korsh which indicated that not all the members of the circle were inclined to regard Granovsky's announcement as a momentary and capricious outburst. E. Korsh did not approve of the point-blank manner in which Granovsky had posed the issue, but one could have surmised from his explanations that Korsh himself appreciated, nevertheless, the soundness of the reasons which compelled Granovsky to make his announcement. The breach took on the meaning of an indubitable fact and needed, just as a bone fracture in the body, to be immediately bound up and then to be left to the healing action of time—to knit the limb together. That is just what was done. However, a complete, perfect healing between the broken members of the circle did not ensue. Be that as it may, I was witness to the fact that until the end of their lives Granovsky, Herzen, and Belinsky could not speak of one another without affection and without the most heartfelt emotion.

CHAPTER

[XXVIII]

AND WHAT INDEED had Belinsky been doing all this time? At the end of
the summer of that year (1845), Belinsky was living at a summer cottage on the Pargolovo Road, across from the pine forest surrounding
Pargolovo Lake. He and I had retired there together when, after my
arrival back in Petersburg, I had paid him a visit to inform him about
and talk over all that I had seen during the summer. I gave him a detailed account of the impressions I had gained from my stay at Sokolovo. He listened attentively to my sympathetic description of what
was done and said there, and then remarked: "Yes, Moscow man is a
splendid man, but aside from that, it appears he will never become
anything more."

Belinsky was now almost the only person left with the banner
and emblem of implacable enmity. He thought it his duty to raise that
banner conspicuously higher ever since the ranks of its defenders had
begun to disperse. He could not regard, without a feeling of bitterness, the rapprochement of the warring parties in Moscow, a rapprochement made possible, as he believed, only because one party had not
fully stated its idea and had not fully revealed its ultimate goals, and
the other party—the Westerners—had welcomed sympathetic expressions and had given itself over, with eyes closed, to its favorite
pleasure—embracing its enemies and making haste to sit them down
at the same table. The cause of strife between the friends grew constantly greater: in his struggle against the Slavophiles, Belinsky found
himself harassing both all their old confederates and their new ones.
Therefore, at almost every exchange of ideas between the old friends,
misunderstandings piled up in the Western camp. Only one feature of
their usual relations remained intact. The friends did not stint on mutual criticism and severe reproach when they stood face to face with
one another, but instantly resumed their former roles as friends and
true comrades once the talk stopped and they parted. It was a matter

of necessity then for all of them to preserve the sympathies they had acquired in the course of long contact, which did not in the least prevent each one of them from advocating and promulgating his own individual convictions.

Belinsky instantly set about with his usual fervor and sincerity to define and clarify the points of disagreement that had cropped up between the Moscow and Petersburg Westerners. First of all, he took a skeptical and derisive stand toward the grim earnestness with which scholars in Moscow treated questions of Russian life, transposing them into terms of science, philosophy, philosophically oriented history, and the like. In his opinion, these questions had no need of so elaborate a formulation and could be solved by very simple, unsubtle and uncomplicated means and principles in the reach of every, even most elementary, understanding. Likewise, in the matter of literature's relation to the educated classes of society, Belinsky believed that the latter were sooner in need of setting their frame of mind in proper order than of knowing about the latest results of European science. Belinsky immediately made the first graphic application of his systematic rejection of subtle explications and abstruse exercises in the sphere of ideas to Herzen's letters on the study of nature, which had begun to appear then in *Notes of the Fatherland.* He acknowledged that the ideas, as well as the aims, of these extremely intelligent articles were of the highest importance, but did not acknowledge the possibility of extracting from the revelations of natural science the moral and educational guidance needed, particularly by the Russian public, the majority of whom had not yet acquired the faculty for understanding the most rudimentary moral principles. "And in what an abstract language, almost unintelligible jargon, these articles are written," Belinsky commented, "just as if Herzen had composed them for his own entertainment. If I was able to understand anything in them, it was only because I have a dozen years of rambling through German philosophy behind me; but not everybody is obliged to possess such an advantage!"

There is no doubt that through these declarations of Belinsky's and others like them ran the undercurrent of his desire to deal with social literature concerned with the vital issues of the day and with popular expositions of scientific and moral truths (he expressed a yearning for literature of that type also in one of those yearly surveys of literature he used to write then), but, nevertheless, the bases for his verdict seemed very harsh. They would deprive the intellectuals of the epoch of the last refuge from life's emptiness, the refuge they had found in science and in abstract formulation of problems. They would cut off the only arena in which thought was allowed to manifest itself.

To aid in the destruction of that arena or to demean its importance publicly simply meant, Belinsky's opponents felt, to play the same game as, and into the hands of, the obscurantists. In Moscow, people regarded this opposition of Belinsky's to erudition and pure thought as a formidable mistake committed by the critic out of obsession and, furthermore, as an error in judgment. It was impossible, they said there, to call for popular propaganda of science while cutting off or undermining the real source of science itself, while putting pressure on or dismissing those engaged in science and supplanting present-day conditions of intellectual life with nothing more than reproaches, passionate appeals, and wishes for something better, the futility of which must have been clearer to this most volatile of critics than to anyone else. In this way, the Moscow Westerners departed further and further from the center of Westernism formed by Belinsky in Petersburg.

I remember an interesting scene which occurred at that same time; by chance I was a witness to it. P. N. Kudryavtsev,[91] on his way to Berlin, where he was being sent to complete his training for a professorial career, made it a point, needless to say, to visit Belinsky in Petersburg, since Belinsky had been a friend in his youthful days, one who had once discovered in the author of *The Flute* the ideal of innate aesthetic taste and understanding. But this meeting now turned out to be highly constrained, cold, and tense—it would have been hard to guess, judging by that meeting, the kinship that once had bound these two people together. Kudryavtsev was the perfect representative of the Moscow view of the Petersburg critic's present activity, and the whole trend of the conversation in which the two old friends engaged clearly indicated the presence, in hidden form, of dissension of a rather advanced stage of development. I see, as if this moment, the tall figure of P. N. Kudryavtsev in a blue frock coat with shiny metal buttons; he sat slumped back in an armchair in Belinsky's dining room-parlor and stopped his companion's outbursts with abrupt and curt utterances which, said in his usual hollow voice and with a stony expression on his face, came out sounding like sentences read by a judge. Belinsky again chose Herzen's articles to use as a means of relaying his reproaches to the people in Moscow for their abstract attitudes toward life and science. Kudryavtsev answered tersely: "There's no getting around abstractions when it comes to a great many scientific problems—logical necessity is to be held to blame for that, not people." Belinsky tried in vain to develop the idea about it being essential to prefer those scientific propositions most applicable to contemporary life and about it being essential to treat those propositions in the way most easily understandable for the reader. Kudryavtsev replied: "'Where do you get this hierarchy of sciences? Abstract sciences are just as essential as political sciences, and they are mutually helpful. Why not occupy yourself with those you're most familiar with and in the form handiest for you?" The talk went on in that tone for a while. All Belinsky's ardor could not, however, withstand that decisive rebuttal of all his contentions—rebuttal seemingly very calm but in actuality full of anger and enmity. The conversation collapsed of itself and the old friends parted coldly, exchanging the most banal inquiries at leave-taking, just as if they were strangers. Through Kurdryavtsev's mouth had spoken a certain part of Moscow University.

And that very same Kudryavtsev, a year later when I visited him in Berlin, in my presence, very severely and emphatically stopped short a certain gentleman by the name of Sazonov, a student and disciple of Schelling's—but only of a very low-grade variety—when the latter had the foolhardy notion to denounce Belinsky vehemently. It must be pointed out that, as the pretext for his denunciations, Sazonov took an unfavorable comment on Schelling Belinsky had once uttered (in his article on Count Sollogub's *Tarantas*, I believe), and that Kudryavtsev was himself at the time under the overwhelming influence of Schelling's "Philosophy of Revelation" and spoke of it in glowing terms, which did not prevent him, as already said, from pulling his confederate up short. That was the way Belinsky's opponents almost always behaved, as he did also himself, all of them belonging to a special class of opponents, now completely died out.

No greater resentment or rancor was kept by Herzen, aware of the critic's reaction to his articles and afterward remarking on his reactions numerous times. "That strange fellow," he said, "deigns to find that it is difficult to display more intelligence and competence in a subject in the more obscure kinds of expression, but he forgets that it isn't posssible to show intelligence and competence in any other way in Russian." However, Herzen was soon more than amply compensated for the critic's harsh verdict. Following his letters about the study of nature, the first chapters of Herzen's well-known novel [92] appeared in *Notes of the Fatherland,* and the author had the pleasure immediately thereupon of seeing Belinsky's whole attitude toward his work as a writer suddenly change. The initial chapters of the novel sent Belinsky literally into raptures, increasing as the novel itself developed. Our critic did not, of course, overlook the romantic coloration with which the novel's protagonists were overlaid, but the author's own relation to his characters, the acid truth with which he depicted their dreams and enthusiasms—which did not exclude his showing profound sympathy for them—and, finally, the picture of an instructive true-life drama stemming from their false positions in society—all these things struck the critic as something almost totally unexpected. He had expected a great deal from Herzen's lucid mind, but such mastery of "composition" he had not expected: "That's where his strength lies," he said, "that's where he is in his element and where an arena has opened for the mighty literary exercises to which he is inclined." Herzen was touched by the unexpected success of his novel, which demolished the critic's arid attitude. "Vissarion Grigorievich," he remarked later on, jokingly but very pleased with the judgment, "likes our little tales better than he does our treatises, and he's right, of course. In our treatises, we are forever changing our dress to escape surveillance and we politely greet the policemen on every corner. But in the tale we move along proudly and wish to have nothing to do with anyone because we have a permit in our pocket that entitles it to pass and to be put up for the night and fed." Herzen reaffirmed his view about the "tale" and also justified Belinsky's prophecy when, in 1847 (in the *Contemporary*), he published his so-called "Memoirs," and etc. (about mental diseases in general, and the like).[93] This, too, was a tale, but a tale encompassing profound psychological and social problems.

There was, however, still another reason for these sympathetic effusions of Belinsky's, aside from the one engendered by the literary merit of Herzen's work: Belinsky inclined more and more toward avowing the great importance of what he called "belles lettres," that variegated, clever, and absorbing body of semi- and nonfiction such as existed in all European countries, constituting just as vital an element of their social development as works of imaginative literature, and often serving as a guidebook to the understanding of the latter. This introduction, on Belinsky's part, of a new factor into the domain of art and his equipping it with citizenship papers did not amount to betraying the critic's earlier positions in 1840–45, but only to something supplementing them. "Great, exemplary works of art and science," he said, "have been and will remain the sole elucidators of all the problems of life, knowledge, and morality. But until the appearance of such works, works which sometimes keep us waiting a long time, the activity of belles lettres is essential. During the long intervals, their role is to occupy, nourish, and encourage minds which would be doomed to idleness or to rehashing old models and traditions without them." To desire the rise of belles lettres and not to give them the significance of ultimate judge of all contemporary problems meant, for Belinsky, simply to desire an exchange of ideas, and a sorting out of essential materials in expectation of a solution of those problems by science and creative art when their time comes. The first stirrings of such belles lettres Belinsky discerned precisely in that novel of Herzen's mentioned above, a fact which he once made public in an analysis of it where, without attaching any artistic importance to it, he placed it very high as the work of an intelligent, observant, and cultivated man. Along the same lines, the first works of another writer, D. V. Grigorovich—who came out with his story *The Village* in 1846, following it with another one, *Anton Goremyka,* the same year, both stories arousing much talk—were received by our critic with extreme sympathy. He saw in them the beginning of an era of talented exposés and shrewd examinations of features from our rural life, the importance of which was for him now beyond dispute.

However modest might have been the role Belinsky had assigned belles lettres generally in literature, still, his intercession on their behalf and his claiming for them rights to attention seemed heresy to many people. What was new and peculiar was the critic's recognition that society's preceptors were now not only the geniuses or the major talents, as was the case before, but also the whole nameless mass of men of letters and men of public affairs engaged in dealing with the issues of their life and age to the best of their ability and understanding. The first to catch sight of this new direction of Belinsky's was, of course, the Slavic party, which had always been particularly sensitive to changes in his thought. It declared his whole program in belles lettres a glorification of public "chit chat," and a disparagement of serious-minded, hardworking people in favor of "big mouths." I myself had occasion to hear from certain, by no means obscure, members of the party the remark that placing belles lettres on a par with poetic endeavors was something like offending the "Holy Spirit."

To the moderate Moscow Westerners, Belinsky's new propaganda seemed neither very strange nor so perilous for the cause of education: they were aware of the participation of belles lettres in the creation of the general intellectual tenor of contemporary Europe. Moreover, within the circle there existed the conviction that the attacks of Belinsky's enemies were brought about simply by a misapprehension, in many cases—a deliberate one, inasmuch as it was impossible even to imagine Belinsky as a persecutor of artistry, of pure creativity and serious endeavors. And they were right, as proved by Belinsky's ecstasy when, in that same 1845, he saw the manuscript of Dostoevski's *Poor Folk,* which, from the beginning, he considered an extraordinary work of art.

[XXIX]

ON ONE OF MY VISITS to Belinsky, before dinnertime, when he used to rest from his morning writing, I saw him from the courtyard of his house standing at his parlor window and holding a large copybook in his hands, his face showing all the signs of excitement. He noticed me, too, and shouted: "Come up quickly, I have something new to tell you about." "You see this manuscript?" he continued, after we shook hands. "I haven't been able to tear myself away from it for almost two days now. It's a novel by a beginner, a new talent; what this gentleman looks like and what his mental capacity is I do not know as yet, but his novel reveals such secrets of life and characters in Russia as no one before him even dreamed of. Just think of it—it's the first attempt at a social novel we've had, and done, moreover, in the way artists usually do their work, I mean, without themselves suspecting what will come out of it. The matter in it is simple: it concerns some good-hearted folk who assume that to love the whole world is an extraordinary pleasure and duty for every one. They cannot comprehend a thing when the wheel of life with all its rules and regulations runs over them and fractures their limbs and bones without a word. That's all there is—but what drama, what types! And yes, I forgot to tell you, the artist's name is *Dostoevski*. And I'm going to give you some samples of his motifs right now." And with extraordinary emotion Belinsky started reading the passages that struck him most, informing them with an even higher color by his intonation and his nervous recitation. That is how he received the first work of our novelist.[94]

And that was not the end of it. Belinsky wanted to do for the young writer what he already had done for many others, such as Koltsov and Nekrasov, i.e., liberate his talent from rhetorical-moralizing tendencies and endow it with strong nerves and muscles, so to speak, such as would be able to take hold of things directly, immediately, without straining in the attempt, but in this the critic now encountered decisive opposition. At Belinsky's, the new author read his second story, *The Double,* a sensational depiction of a person whose existence moves between two worlds—the real world and the world of fantasy—without allowing him the possibility of fixing completely on either one of them. Belinsky liked this story, too, owing to the power and scope of its handling of an original and strange theme, but it seemed to me (I also was present at this reading) that the critic had something in the back of his mind which he did not think essential to articulate immediately. He constantly drew Dostoevski's attention to the necessity of *getting the knack,* which is what they called in the literary profession acquiring a facility in rendering one's thoughts, ridding oneself of the complexities of exposition. Belinsky apparently could not accustom himself to the author's then still diffuse manner of narration with its incessant returns to what had already been said, its repetitions and rephrasings ad infinitum; and Belinsky put this manner down to the young writer's inexperience, his failure as yet to surmount the stumbling blocks of language and form. But Belinsky was mistaken: he had encountered, not a beginner, but an already fully formed writer in possession, consequently, of his own ingrained professional habits, despite the fact that, on the face of it, he had only his first work to his name. Dostoevski heard the critic's recommendations out in a mood of affable indifference. The sudden success won by his novelette had instantly brought to fruition those seeds and germs of high self-regard and high self-esteem already present in his soul. That success did more than rid him of the doubts and hesitations that normally accompany writers' first steps: he took it also as a prophetic dream auguring laurel wreaths and chaplets. Thus, when deciding whether to submit his novel to a collection then being prepared, the author demanded, with utter aplomb and as a special consideration to which he was in his rights to expect, that his novel be printed in some special way to set it off from the other contributions to the book, for instance, with a border around it.

Subsequently, as we know, from Dostoevski emerged a marvelous prospector of rare and astounding phenomena of human thought and consciousness who was equally famous both for the veracity, worth, and interest of his psychological discoveries and for a number of fraudulent images and conclusions which he derived via the same exceedingly subtle and surgically incisive, so to speak, psychological analysis as had helped him create all his most vivid character types. He soon parted company with Belinsky—life had separated them and sent them in different directions, although for a fairly long time their views and outlook on things had been the same.

I have not yet mentioned that for two winters (in 1844 and

1845) Petersburg housed within its walls its unfailing antagonist, N. Ketcher. N. Ketcher spent those two winters in Petersburg on official business; he missed his native city terribly and returned there once and for all in the summer of 1845, where, as we have seen, I found him in the country at Sokolovo. In Petersburg he was working on a translation from German of some book of therapeutics or pharmacology which was supposed to serve as a textbook for the medical schools run by the government's Medical Office. But in addition to that book, he always had on his desk volumes of Shakespeare's plays in the original and in German, and he would turn at will from his translation of the textbook to his rendition of the poetic creations of the British dramatist. During the intervals between these occupations, he attended the theater and gatherings of Petersburg actors whose company he cultivated in a rather peculiar way, denouncing almost everything which they admired and on which they placed their highest hopes. He sometimes held gatherings of his actor friends at his apartment on Vladimirskaya. There I once met V. A. Karatygin,[95] who was then at the apogee of his fame. The noted tragic actor of the period struck me as somewhat outlandish, with his huge frame, his deep and hollow bass voice, his regal appearance, and his obtusely circumspect and sententious way of expressing himself. His frenzied gestures, affected posings and exaggerated expressions made him rather often outlandish on the stage, as well, but there he redeemed those deficiencies by his intuitive grasp of the main feature of the character he was portraying, his infusing the whole role with that feature and projecting it in as vivid and egregious a way as he could, in which respect he sometimes achieved extraordinary effects.

Ketcher's presence in Petersburg was marked by constant, unending talk about the difference between and opposite merits of our two capitals. Belinsky, embittered by the *deals* between the parties in Moscow, thundered out against the city that had had a corrupting influence on the most sound-minded people, while Ketcher now played the role of Moscow's advocate, which was entirely in accord with the practice he had adopted in the circle of always standing up for those who were not present. We have seen how, in the summer of his return to his native haunts in Moscow, he had, on the contrary, proved to be an ardent defender of the Petersburg views. However, there was nothing new in the arguments between the friends excepting one feature: the dispute was carried on, not by representatives of two hostile parties, but by representatives of one and the same friendly party, which confirmed the dissolution of the party. The two capitals, Moscow and Petersburg, were again utilized, as they had been before in the struggle against the bona fide Slavophiles, to designate the spirit and content of the new sections of the divided party of Westernism. Moscow and Petersburg were ordained, as before, to bear the brunt of contemporary people's biased emotion, passions, and outbursts of anger and to serve them as weapons in their struggle. Petersburg "Westernism" spoke through the mouth of Belinsky. "Between the Petersburgher and the Muscovite," Belinsky said, now with only Westerners in mind (I retain here the meaning of what he said though not the actual form of it), "no sharing of views can last long: the former is a *dry* person by nature and the latter *unctuous* in everything he says and thinks. They have different roles; they can only interfere with and do dirt to one another when they get together." I have given this aphorism almost word for word, having heard it so often from Belinsky. For that reason, in Belinsky's opinion, if it were permissible to dream about our having a major literary and social party sometime in the future, it could only be expected to come out of Petersburg because only in Petersburg did people know the true worth of things, of words and actions, and because, furthermore, only in Petersburg were the people not to be taken in by anything and did they accept all gifts and favors without gratitude and sentimentality as something due them, and, finally, also because they were able, without heartache, to detach themselves from obsolete ideas and from admirable people, if they led nowhere or interfered with the attainment of an already established goal. How far Belinsky had departed from his still fairly recent pining for Moscow and his tender remembrances about it! Ketcher, in behalf of the Moscow Westerners, expressed a completely different opinion. According to his interpretation, all a man of Petersburg's efforts consisted in being *reputed* a clever man, with such things as points of view, convictions, tendencies being considered by him various kinds of tomfoolery interfering with one's making a career; and then, once reputed a clever man, the Petersburgher slept and dreamed of ways of selling himself, bag and baggage, as dearly as possible.

In a short article, "Petersburg and Moscow," written by Belinsky in 1846 for Nekrasov's miscellany and providing a good reflection of his argument with his friend, the critic admitted that Moscow did more reading and thinking, and did it better, but in conversations he supplemented this remark with the comment that people in Petersburg had more dignity and conducted themselves with greater propriety, giving the impression of preparing themselves for some serious business; on this basis, a tried and true, disorderly Muscovite could not help feeling queer on the banks of the Neva. Ketcher had an answer to that contention, too. The idea he expressed was approximately that the excesses, disorders, and various kinds of gross behavior of the

Muscovite were even more honorable than the respectability and discreetness of the Petersburgher. In Moscow, all atrocities were atrocities pure and simple and were not said to be something else, whereas here you could not tell the whole year long whether the person right before your eyes was a hero of virtue or an inveterate scoundrel. It is remarkable that the debate between the friends, carried on in such terms, could have lasted as long as it did—for whole months on end—but that was because the argument incorporated a great many personal matters and a great many issues engendered by the day to day life and happenings in both capitals. Moreover, this was then a widespread, popular argument which kept occurring, one way or another, in every house wherever people not unsusceptible to literature and problems of culture came together.

However strange, shallow, and inane all arguments of that sort might have seemed to people of the time, it cannot be maintained that they were completely devoid of relevant bases and causes for their emergence in the epoch in which they flourished: the Western party, for instance, through Moscow and Petersburg, discerned shades of opinion in people according to their sympathy for the one or the other city, shades of opinion which it would have been very difficult to discover any other way; they immediately saw by a person's favoring one or the other center of the Western trend that person's true allegiance and his real views on the general issue of enlightenment; and, finally, they surmised the color and shade in which all his convictions would show up. Belinsky was inclined to recognize allies and antagonists even by the degree of sympathy shown to one or the other of the capitals. All that lasted, however, but a short time, as we shall soon see, because the character of the objects of comparison began, with the shift of participants and representatives of the trend to other grounds and with the total disappearance from the party's midst of some of them, to undergo frequent change: the unit of measure for evaluating and defining the factors contrasted to one another constantly proved inaccurate and inapplicable.

Of far longer duration than the argument were talk and discussion on the well-known *fiction,* the conventional notion according to which Moscow was the acknowledged seat of Slavophilism and Petersburg of Westerner tendencies. The controversies provoked by this *fiction* were renewed several times afterward, but they, too, now seem an occupation invented for and by people overburdened with unused energies. It is extremely difficult for the eye of a person of the present day to detect in all these arguments an historically valid fact, since what he sees now are only tag ends of things and he does not discern their connections with the spiritual life of the epoch and is distracted by the fact that all these remnants of our recent past confront him in a new, completely done over and almost unrecognizable shape such as the later stage of our ideas and of our press gave them when it, in turn, undertook to rehabilitate them.

But talk and heated discussion never did constitute for Belinsky a real matter of concern, being only preliminary to it. Very often his articles were preceded by a long exchange of ideas with those around him or by exposition of the ideas occupying his mind in friendly conversations, by which means he would equally clarify for himself his themes and the future order of their development. That is also what happened now.

Belinsky took advantage of the appearance of Count Sollogub's novel *Tarantas* to have a serious and detailed talk, this time in print, with his Moscow friends. We know that the Westerners were extraordinarily frank in their relationships with one another in the intimacy of their own circle, but Belinsky was very nearly the first to extend that frankness to the printed word. True, the Slavic party had given the example in the *Muscovite,* as we have seen. It undertook to wash its dirty linen and to square accounts with its own members, but it immediately relinquished the attempt, probably finding that the small size of its family required extreme caution and consideration in the mutual dealings among its members. Only on the condition of reciprocal support could the party maintain its integrity and keep all its personnel, needed for the struggle, intact. The requirement of keeping ranks closed, as far as possible, in the face of its enemies brought it later to the constant practice not only of putting the best side of its participants on permanent public display, carefully passing over in silence, while doing so, all the particular disagreements it had with them, but also of discovering brilliant aspects in the work of those people of the circle who had nothing of the sort. There was never any place in Belinsky's mind for such considerations and calculations and they never could have stopped him. In this instance, too, he gave himself over completely to his intention without the slightest hesitation. Belinsky's article on Count Sollogub's *Tarantas* can be called a paragon of masterful polemic which communicated far more than what was formally said in it. It produced a powerful impression on people capable of detecting behind the words they heard another, hidden voice—and who then did not have that ability? With consummate skill Belinsky criticized the dual character of the work analyzed, its portraying very faithfully, sometimes even with genuine humor, the meager arena of mental and practical life through which representatives of both our old, original Russia and our up-to-date and dandified Russia moved, but at the same time adding to its portrayals fantasies about the future brilliant development of the same sorry milieu that it depicted. The way it came out, the roughness and infertility of the soil were what gave one the right to depend on obtaining from it an abundant harvest and dazzling results. Belinsky gave full credit for the realistic depiction of things and images which he found in the novel, and regarded with contempt its fantastic prophecies and elucidations which, he said, proved nothing but the poverty of the author's own judgment and outlook on things, if one discounted the possibility of his having intended to be *ironic*. Belinsky termed all these infantile *insights into the future* of Russia Quixotry, but added that this Quixotry was something innocuous and still of a very low-grade, secondary quality, there being another, more dangerous and better thought out variety. Thereupon the critic went back to a description of this higher grade and type of Quixotry, the beginning of which he descried abroad in the sphere of the science of history and philosophy, presumably in the sphere of highly developed people,[96] and warned against its appearance among us. This Quixotry of higher calibre, according to Belinsky, believed in the possibility of reconciling diametrically opposed principles and mutually exclusive points of view, and was concerned with discovering some corner in the domain of thought where the forced marriage it was arranging, the unnatural union of disparate trends, could be consummated without trouble. However grand this pseudo-scientific Quixotry might have appeared, having at its disposal enormous powers of erudition, dialectics, and philosophical resourcefulness, it was, nevertheless, Belinsky maintained, akin to the banal Quixotry of Sollogub's novel. They had in common the ambition to find salvation from the hard truths of life in the realm of falsehood and fantasy. All the intentions and aims of this polemical article were clear and transparent enough for everyone initiated in literary affairs, but Belinsky wanted to have his say out completely. He held to the author's credit the detail of his having given the silly dreamer-hero of his novel a generic name by calling him "Ivan Vasilievich." "We shall now know," Belinsky said, "how all fantasizers of this type among us are to be called." The fact is, of course, that I. V. Kireevsky, the author of those remarkable articles in the *Muscovite,* had exactly that name and patronymic.

How this article affected Belinsky's Moscow friends is apparent from their words and opinions in the country at Sokolovo, about which we spoke earlier.

CHAPTER

[XXX]

MEANWHILE, the time of a very important change in Belinsky's life was approaching.

Sooner than might have been expected, Belinsky proved to have been mistaken when, owing to the debilitation of our parties, he had prophesied the imminent enthronement of indifference toward vital questions of Russian life or when he had expressed apprehension that the parties would completely merge on the ground of some fantastic notion out of the realm of history, law, and national life which would not have the slightest connection with the contemporary state of affairs. Nothing of the sort occurred or could have occurred. Whatever steps the moderate sections of our two parties might have taken toward a rapprochement, they still could by no means merge, as the following period showed—and showed very quickly. Between the parties lay a gulf formed by the disparate conceptions of the role of the Russian people in history and disparate judgments on all other factors and elements of that history. The "Slavs," as we know, assigned the most insignificant part in the development of the state to elements coming from outside, from other national groups, with the exception of the Byzantines, and in many instances regarded these elements as a misfortune preventing the people from expressing their spiritual essence fully. The "Europeans," on the contrary, ascribed to the intervention of other nationalities a great part in the formation of the Moscow State, in the determination of the whole course of its history, and even were of the opinion that these ethnographic elements introduced by alien nationalities were responsible for what was now called the Russian national physiognomy. The disagreement amounted ultimately to the question of the cultural capabilities of the Russian people, and this question proved to be so formidable that it laid down an impassable demarcation line between the parties.

The "Slavic" party did not want to be, and could not have been, satisfied by its enemies' concessions—for example, the conception of the people as one of numerous factors making up our history—and even less could it have been satisfied by recognition of the people's possessing certain sympathetic, morally ingratiating aspects of character to which its opponents were willing to agree. It demanded for the Russian people something greater. What it demanded was affirmation of the people's possessing an enormous political, creative, and moral reputation and great powers of organization as evinced in the creation of the Moscow State and in the discovery of social, familial, and religious ideals against which our later and modern orders of life could offer nothing of equal weight. On this basis, and without troubling itself about historical facts contradicting its dogma or ingeniously interpreting them in its favor, the party undertook to fashion piece by piece a colossal image of the Russian people with the aim of creating of it a type worthy of homage. From the very first sign of this work at erecting an apotheosis, personified in the people, of the moral bases and ideals of olden times, and without waiting for the completion of that work, the Moscow Westerners as a whole made it their task unremittingly to denounce the Russian people of the Slavophiles' concept as a *pseudo*people, as the fabrication of a barefaced sophistry which invented the historical features and material it needed. They particularly rebuked their learned opponents for their tendency to undertake the defense, by necessity, even of very shameful facts in the life and history of the Russian people, if it proved impossible to pass over them in silence or impossible to repudiate them in toto as falsification by the enemies of the Russian land.

This polemic lasted a long time and raged especially later on, in the 1850's, during the period which saw the appearance of extraordinary Slavophile publications (1852–55: *The Moscow Miscellany, The Simbirsk Miscellany, The Colloquium*). The animating spirit of this polemic, after Belinsky had passed on, was that very same Granovsky who had once been suspected by his Petersburg friends of complicity with the enemy, although he himself seldom made appearance in the arena. It is true that he was always a magnanimous foe. We know that pertinent things were said in the heat of the argument on both sides and many talented people were brought to light who later succeeded in acquiring honorable names. From the very start, not one of them passed Granovsky by unnoticed. This man possessed in the highest degree a lively sense of conscience which obliged him to point out distinction and merit wherever he might encounter them, unhampered by any extrinsic, partisan or tactical considerations. It was no rare occurrence for any of us to hear him treat his personal enemies and the enemies of his trend in terms even their most favorably inclined biographers might have accepted for their pages. Among other instances, he held in very high esteem the young Valuev,[97] the author of a well-known article on protocol for one of the Slavophile miscellanies, who met so early a death for the fatherland, and could not speak of him without affection.

Relieved of the fear of seeing the argument which had cost him so much concluded by some simple compromise between the parties, Belinsky now took a calmer and more objective stand on the question of what share folk elements should have and have had in the cultural development of the country. When now (1846) it turned out that the cause of exposing the presumptuous propaganda and excesses of the nationalist party could count on its old confederates, a calm response to the question was made considerably easier. One could no longer help but see that the doctrine on nationality, as a factor leading to a change of the prevailing conditions of national existence, had a very serious side to it; only on the basis of that doctrine was the possibility afforded of speaking of the mistakes made by Russian society in detriment to the honor and dignity of the state. The example was plain to see. The "Slavic" party, despite all objections to and criticisms of it, acquired more influence with each passing day and brought under its sway minds of the kind not especially submissive by nature, and did so by its preachings about the unrecognized, improperly appreciated, and shamelessly disparaged Russian nationality.

And indeed, however questionable the idealization of the people made by the "Slavs" might have seemed and however shaky the bases for their doing so might have been declared, the work of the "Slavs" was still virtually the only cause of the epoch in which our society took substantial part and which overcame the coldness and suspiciousness of official circles. This work captivated everyone alike, making it possible to celebrate the discovery within the depths of the Russian world and in the midst of general moral poverty of a rich deposit of moral capital obtained at almost no cost. Everyone felt himself better off. The "Westerners" had nothing of the kind they could propose; they had no unified and elaborated political theorem; they were concerned with investigation of current problems, with criticism and analysis of contemporary phenomena, and did not venture to compose anything like an ideal of civic existence with the materials that Russian and European life provided them. The conscientiousness of the "Westerners" left them empty-handed, and it is easy to understand that the positive image of national political wisdom which the Slavophiles had found began, therefore, to play a very prominent role in our society.

The arbitrary treatment of history, which was constantly pointed out to the Slavophiles, did not in the least arrest the growth of this ideal or its development; on the contrary, freedom in interpretation of facts helped to make it thrive by allowing features and details to be introduced into its makeup which had the greatest appeal for the national pride and the greatest effect on the masses. Mistakes, inaccuracies, abuses of evidence in this instance worked for the health of the ideal, so to speak, and toward bolstering the party that fostered it. Meanwhile, with the aid of its disputed ideal, the party achieved some undeniably very important goals—whether consciously or unconsciously makes little difference. What happened in this instance was what had already happened often enough in the world: positions involving risk and license brought far more benefit to society and to people than did the cautious, reasoned out, and, therefore, timid steps of impartial inquiry. The party succeeded in expanding the horizon of the Russian intelligentsia with a new element, a new active member and agent for thought—I mean, the element of the nation, and once it had promulgated its creed, neither science, in general, nor the science of government, in particular, could now avoid keeping it in mind and taking it into account when making various political and social decisions. This was the great service rendered by the party, whatever might have been its price. Later on, when he was already living abroad, Herzen understood very well the meaning of the structure erected by the Slavophiles and said with good reason: "Our European Westerner party will not secure the position and significance of a social force until it masters the themes and issues put into circulation by the Slavophiles."

But if that was impossible for the while, at least the time was already approaching for understanding the importance of such themes. No later than 1847, Belinsky was already speaking of the absurdity of opposing nationality to the universal development of mankind, as if these two things were supposed, without fail, to exclude one another whereas in fact they constantly coincided. The universal development of mankind could not express itself otherwise than through one or another nationality, the terms were even unthinkable one without the other. He developed his idea in detail in the article, "Survey of Literature in 1846." One passage in it is particularly noteworthy. Belinsky approached it through a preliminary and very detailed exposition of the view that just as an individual, who has not stamped the imprint of his own spirit and own substance on the ideas and notions he has come by, would never be an influential person, so also a nation which has failed to communicate some special, unique mark and expression to the moral bases of human existence would always remain an inert mass usable for the performance on it of any sort of experiment.

Belinsky concluded the lengthy development of this contention with words almost literally repeating those Granovsky had spoken at Sokolovo with regard to the sympathy which the basic position of the "Slavs" often elicited, although the critic had not actually heard Granovsky's words himself. Here is the passage: "What *individuality* is with respect to the idea of a person, *nationality* is with respect to mankind. Without nationalities mankind would be a lifeless logical abstraction, a word without content, a sound without meaning. *With regard to this problem, I would sooner go over to the side of the Slavophiles than remain on the side of the humanistic cosmopolites* because, if the former are in error, they err as human beings, as living creatures, whereas the latter even tell the truth like such and such an edition of such and such a Logic. But, fortunately, I have hopes of remaining in my own position without going over to anyone's side. . . ." The young editors of the new *Contemporary* of 1847, for which the article was written and where it was published, had other thoughts on this subject, however. Since the struggle with the Slavophile party and, in addition, an interest in more or less artistically done exposé literature comprised, for the while, the entire program of the new journal, it is understandable that its critic's move in the direction of the usual enemies of Petersburg journalism obscured one part —and a vital part—of the journal's program. Later I heard that the editors were very disgruntled by the article with its strange and unheard of tendency for the Petersburg Westerner press, and one with which they were obliged to inaugurate their new organ on the public forum.

Thus Belinsky's long polemic with his bitterest foes came to an end.

The founding of the *Contemporary* in 1847 terminated Belinsky's collaboration on *Notes of the Fatherland*, which he had served so diligently over the course of six years that he had secured the journal an honorable name and position and had lost his own health. Beginning in mid-1845, the thought of leaving *Notes of the Fatherland* was constantly on Belinsky's mind, N. A. Nekrasov lending him particular support in this from a practical point of view. The fact was that Belinsky's material situation kept deteriorating from year to year and no solution presented itself from any quarter. His energies weakened. His family needed increased means for its existence, and in the event of a catastrophe, which he already foresaw would come, it would be left without a crust of bread. Possibly no other writer of ours found himself in a situation more like that of the European workmen or proletarians of the time. Like them, he had no one personally to accuse for the formation of the oppressive conditions of his life—everybody conscientiously carried out their obligations in his regard, he was not under anyone's thumb, no excessive demands were made on him and no one made attempts to evade mutually agreed upon conditions. Thus, everything around him was in due and proper order—was respectable, as the English say. All the same, his labor acquired its value only after leaving his hands and brought all the profit to be expected from it to the publication and not to the person who produced it. There was no possibility of improving matters without changing the usual economic arrangements, the permanency of which had already been secured. With each passing day Belinsky became more and more convinced that the more effort he put into his work and the more brilliant its results in literary and social respects, the worse his situation would become in view of the inevitable depletion of creative material and deterioration of his own working capacity as a consequence of his redoubled effort. The future thus appeared to him in very grim colors, and from mid-1845, we heard his bitter complaints about his fate, complaints in which he did not spare even his own person. "And what in the world is this fate to do," he would say in conclusion, "with a fool who could not put anything it provided him to good use." [98]

And indeed, with the end of the year 1845, Belinsky did abandon journalism for a while and parted company with *Notes of the Fatherland*. This event produced something of a commotion in the little literary world of the time. With Belinsky's retirement, the decline of the journal was prophesied, but the journal held steady, as does any enterprise once it has secured firm foundations and has, moreover, a ready-made arena for literary activity to offer upcoming talents. Such a talent was the young Maykov who took over what Belinsky had bequeathed—the literary critical section of the journal; and this section found in Maykov [99] a new and fresh energy instead of the atrophy and debilitation which threatened it.

V. N. Maykov put aside all Belinsky's aesthetic, moral, and polemical baggage and took as his norm for the evaluation of works of art the quantity and importance of the issues of life and society which they raised and the means which the authors used to focus on and deal with them. His premature death prevented him from developing his conception of things fully. [100]

With the rupture of old ties, not all had yet ended for Belinsky; he had to find the means for existence. Belinsky had foreseen this and had turned to his friends, before the rupture occurred, for advice and help, proposing a plan for their consideration of publishing, now directly in his own name, a voluminous collection of their combined works, if they agreed to go along with his plans and intentions. The answer was not long in coming. From all sides our well-known and lesser known writers hastened to put at his disposal all that they had on hand, and by the beginning of 1846 Belinsky had accumulated a considerable quantity of manuscript material, in part very valuable, as its subsequent publication showed. The importance of the material collected could not have escaped the notice of Belinsky himself or the attention of his closest associates in the whole matter, N. A. Nekrasov and I. I. Panaev. The latter had long been searching for the chance to do independent publishing and had tried it several times, issuing miscellanies and collections, but now they were given the opportunity of establishing a large enterprise—a new periodical. Belinsky's material could serve the journal, in its initial stages, as ready-made support. It was thus that the idea arose of acquiring the old *Contemporary* of Pushkin's, which was carrying on a modest and almost unacknowledged existence under the directorship of P. A. Pletnev; and the idea was put into effect by Nekrasov and Panaev. At the same time, they purchased all of Belinsky's "material" (Panaev was the main backer in all of these dealings), which enabled Belinsky to pay off his debts and for the first time to feel himself a free man. Moreover, the new editors of the *Contemporary* of 1847 provided him also with a future prospect that must have been especially appreciated by Belinsky. They had in mind to include his name on the list of unofficial coeditors of the journal (the official editor put forward as security in the face of the censorship was Professor A. V. Nikitenko [101]) and to furnish him, in addition to payment for his articles, with a share of whatever profits the publication would bring in, as well. It would indeed have been difficult for the venture to get along without Belinsky's popular name, but with this was also combined the hope, shared by Belinsky, that all the best men in the field from Moscow would follow him to the new publication and would sever ties with *Notes of the Fatherland*. This hope, however, was fated not to be fulfilled. Moscow literary men and, also, certain literary men of Petersburg, while wishing the *Contemporary* complete success, thought that two liberal organs in Russia were better than one, that the division of the trend into two representatives would even better provide for the lot and freedom of hard-working journalists and that, finally, owing to the commercial character of any journalistic venture, it was unlikely that the new one would be able to go any other way in its dealings with people than the way the old one had gone. All this occurred at a time when I (since February of 1846) was abroad.

CHAPTER

[XXXI]

ONE MORNING, IN LATE FALL 1847, in the minute parlor of my Paris
apartment, Rue Caumartin 41, appeared a gentleman with hair neatly
combed straight back, as was the Russian custom, and dressed in a
long surtout which strangely hampered his motions. It was Herzen,
his appearance still bearing the stamp of a Moscow resident but who
soon was to become transformed, thanks to Parisian tailors and other
artificers, into a perfect gentleman of the Western race with close-
cropped hair, an elegant beard that very rapidly assumed all the essential outlines and a suit coat smartly and smoothly draping his
shoulders. I was terribly glad to see him and listened to his humorous
tale about the trouble and effort he had had to go to in order to leave
the country and then about his long voyage, by post chaise what is
more, across all of Germany. He had arrived in Paris with his whole
family, had put up at Place Vendôme, and had come to me, as a long-
time resident of Paris (I had already spent a whole year in the French
capital), to ask about conditions, way of life, and habits of his new
place of residence, to all of which, as was also the Russian custom, he
very soon applied himself. And it was not he alone, but also his family, who submitted to that kind of transformation and change of exterior and, with it, of way of life itself; and they did so with a facility
and nonchalance that would have been considered astonishing, had
they not been common and well-known properties of our Russian nature. Herzen's wife, after her first week in Paris, was already a completely different type of person than the type she had been in Moscow. However, the inner alteration that changed her personal character had begun back there—as I shall relate—and was only brought to
completion in Paris. From a quiet, pensive, romantic lady of the circle
of friends, aspiring to ideal cultivation of her mind and soul and making no demands on or concessions to the outside world, she suddenly
became a splendid traveler with every right to occupy an honorable

position in the great, cosmopolitan city in which she had arrived, although she made no claim whatever to such a position. The new forms and conditions of her existence soon dislodged from her mind the last vestiges of her memory of Moscow. The rapidity of all such external and internal metamorphoses experienced by Russians depended on, in addition to their predisposition, a great many other causes besides.

For instance, the Paris of the distinguished bourgeois king, Louis Philippe, owing to various aspects of its political life, had a captivating effect on Russians who made their way there always in a more or less secret, stealthy way, since it was officially forbidden those days to have the word France inscribed in one's passport. The impression Paris produced on the travelers from the North was something like what ensues upon a sudden windfall: they flung themselves on the city with the passion and enthusiasm of a wayfarer who comes out of a desert wasteland and finds the long-expected fountainhead. The first thing that struck one on encountering the capital of France was, of course, its social movements. Everywhere throughout Europe there already existed parties which were subjecting the conditions and institutions of European life to analysis, and everywhere there had already formed societies for the consideration of measures to halt, change, and redirect the course of contemporary life, but only in Paris did this critical activity enter into, so to speak, the ordinary, daily run of things. In Paris, moreover, it was decked out most effectively in all the lights of the French national spirit, that spirit skilled at arranging people, doctrines, and ideas into picturesque groups and making public displays and pageants of them before they became the directors and transformers of society. One could not resist feeling drawn to this activity which was made up of shrewd and clever articles from the world of journalism, propaganda in the theater, series of lectures and discussions by professors and nonprofessors. For example, I spent three Sundays in a row listening to A. Comte himself expatiating, in the hall of a certain arcade, on the basic features of his theory before a crowd of people who could have had no inkling of what that theory would become later on. This activity was supplemented by a huge number of books on social topics, which began the well-known war against the official political economy, and also by affiliations of honest, well-read, and well-developed workers who had already taken account of the new socialist positions and had revised them in their own fashion, such as Corbon, a future deputy, who was a watchmaker by trade and whom I also had the chance to see in the shop that served him also as the office of his journal, L'Atelier. All these were the flames that preceded the famous Revolution of 1848, something which, it should be added, no one then had any premonition of and which, incidentally, extinguished all those flames by its sudden oncoming.

I arrived in Paris at the end of spring 1846, and found a whole Russian colony already established there, its chief and outstanding members being Bakunin and Sazonov,[102] and busy with incessant pursuit and discussion of practical, historical, philosophical, and other issues such as the social life of Paris under the liberal King Louis Philippe continually aroused. However, for the while there was no other term by which to call this type of concern with European issues such as existed then among Russians than—an amusement.

The matter at stake was primarily one of satisfying a curiosity unceasingly aroused by the events of each passing day, of doing the duty of standing on the alert for every significant and insignificant happening in the city and of procuring material for analysis, for the exercise of critical faculties and, lastly but most importantly, for the manufacture of the endless, variegated, gold-embroidered fabric of conversations, arguments, conclusions, propositions, and counter-propositions. In this no one had any notion yet of a responsibility to one's own conscience or of some mandatory precept for the management of one's personal life and behavior. Nor was the necessity of some sort of self-discipline in the future foreseen.

No such thing as a Russian political emigration was even thought of yet; it came about only when the thunder of the 1848 Revolution resounded and forced many people to turn to their past, to tally it up and to take some clear and definite stand both on the menace that had suddenly burst out over Europe and on the governments that were alarmed by it. True, from time to time reminders about demands for a different order of life than the one they were enjoying made their way into the midst of our people amusing themselves with Paris. Such was the case with the well-known Golovin,[103] who had received an official recall to Russia because of a trifling little book which he had had published in French in Paris without *permission*. The book, an essay in political economy, was something even less than a text-book—it was a simple set of extracts from student notebooks, and not altogether coherent extracts at that, but in any case quite innocuous. I would venture to say that I have never in my life met a writer less worthy of attention than this Golovin, who at one time played the stock market and a role in the *opposition*, wormed his way into the Jockey Club, into the world of libertines, and into democratic *consiliabula*—a brazen and childishly craven man. Despite the recall, he remained in Paris and became, before anybody else, a Russian political émigré and, at that, on a very special principle, out of fear: he was haunted by terrors of all possible kinds, which were simply unthinkable in connection with him.[104] After *reminders* of the sort Golovin had received, the circle of our dilettante politicians and socialists deliberated over the fact from various points of view and then once again lapsed into the enthralling flow of their occupations and their impassioned, though amateur, involvement in the private affairs of the French nation.

One should not suppose that this game of chance with the whole content of Paris was carried on solely by people well-versed in literary and political matters: persons with quite different aims in life, not cultural ones, often became involved in it. For instance, on my way to Europe I received a letter of introduction to the famous Marx from a certain steppe landowner of ours, also well-known in his own circle as a fine singer of gypsy songs, a skillful gambler, and experienced hunter. As it turned out, he was on the friendliest of terms with Lassalle's teacher and the future head of the International; he had assured Marx that, as a person dedicated heart and soul to his glowing creed and to the cause of establishing economic order in Europe, he was returning to Russia with the intention of selling his entire estate and casting himself and all his capital into the chute of the oncoming revolution. No obsession could have gone any further than that, but I am convinced that the spirited landowner was being sincere at the moment he made all those promises. After returning home, first to his estate and later to Moscow, he did not give so much as a thought to those fervid words of his that once had rung out with such effect in the presence of the astonished Marx, and died, not too long ago, a very old, but nonetheless jaunty, bachelor in Moscow. It is not hard to understand, however, that after such goings on, both Marx and many others became, and for a long time remained, convinced that any Russian who came to them should be looked upon first of all as someone sent to spy on them or as some conscienceless deceiver. Actually, a far simpler explanation can be given this matter, though without making it any the less reprehensible.

In any case, I took advantage of the letter from my jaunty landowner, who, at the time he handed it over to me, was still in an enthusiastic frame of mind, and met with a very friendly reception from Marx in Brussels. Marx was under the influence of his recollection of the sample of expansive Russian nature that he had so accidentally come across and spoke of it with appreciation, detecting in this new phenomenon for him, as it seemed to me, signs of genuine power in the Russian national element in general. Marx himself was a man of the type made up of energy, will power, and invincible conviction—a type of man extremely remarkable also in outward appearance. With a thick mop of black hair on his head, his hairy hands, dressed in a coat buttoned diagonally across his chest, he maintained the appearance of a man with the right and authority to command respect, whatever guise he took and whatever he did. All his motions were awkward but vigorous and self-confident, all his manners ran athwart conventional usages in social intercourse but were proud and somehow guarded, and his shrill voice with its metallic ring marvelously suited the radical pronouncements over things and people which he uttered. Marx was now in the habit of speaking no other way than in such categorical pronouncements over which still reigned, it should be added, a certain shrill note superimposed on everything he said. This note expressed his firm conviction that it was his mission to control minds, to legislate over them and to lead them in his train. Before me stood the figure of the democratic dictator incarnate, just as it might be pictured in one's imagination during times devoted to fantasy. The contrast with the types of people I had left behind in Russia was of the most emphatic kind.

On my first meeting with Marx, he invited me to attend a conference scheduled for the following evening with the tailor Weitling who had a rather large following of workers back in Germany. The conference was being called in order to determine, insofar as possible, the overall mode of operation among the leaders of the workers' movement. I unhesitatingly accepted the invitation and came to the meeting.

The tailor-agitator Weitling turned out to be a fair-haired, handsome young man, wearing an elegant style of surtout and a coquettishly close-cropped beard, looking more like a traveling *salesman* than the stern and wrathful zealot I had presumed I would meet. Quickly exchanging greetings, with an added touch of exquisite politeness on Weitling's part, we sat down at a small green table at one narrow end of which Marx placed himself, pencil in hand and his leonine head bent over a sheet of paper. His inseparable companion and colleague in propaganda, the tall and erect Engels, with his British air of dignity and gravity, opened the meeting with a speech. In it he spoke of the necessity for people dedicated to the cause of transforming labor to expound their common views and establish one overall doctrine which would serve as the standard for all their followers who had neither the time nor the opportunity to concern themselves with theoretical issues. Engels had not yet concluded his speech when Marx looked up and addressed a question directly to Weitling: "Tell us, Weitling, you people who have made such a rumpus in Germany with your communist preachings and have won over so many workers, causing them to lose their jobs and their crust of bread, with what fundamental principles do you justify your revolutionary and social

activity and on what basis do you intend affirming it in the future?" I
remember the actual form of this trenchant question very well because it began a very heated debate among the conference participants which lasted, however, as will be shown, but a very short
time.

Weitling apparently wanted to confine the conference to the
platitudes of liberal colloquy. With an expression on his face suggest-
ing earnestness and anxiety, he began to explain that his aim was not
to create new economic theories but to make use of those that were
best able, as experience in France had shown, to open the workers'
eyes to the horror of their situation and all the injustices that had,
with regard to them, become the bywords of governments and societies, to teach them not to put trust any longer in promises on the part
of the latter and to rely only on themselves, organizing into democratic and communist communes. He spoke at length but, to my surprise and in contrast with Engels' speech, diffusely, not altogether lit-
erately, repeating his words and often correcting them, and experiencing difficulty in coming to conclusions which either were made be-
latedly or came ahead of the arguments for them. He had a far different audience now than the one that usually crowded around his work
bench or read his newspapers and printed pamphlets on contemporary economic practices, and, in consequence, he had lost the facility
of both his thought and his tongue. Weitling likely would have talked
even longer, if Marx, his brows angrily knit, had not interrupted him
and begun to voice his objection. The gist of his sarcastic speech was
that to arouse the population without giving it firm and thoroughly
reasoned out bases for its actions meant simply to deceive it. The
stimulation of fantastic hopes that had just been mentioned—Marx
observed further on—led only to the ultimate ruin, and not the salvation, of the oppressed. Especially in Germany, to appeal to the workers without a rigorous scientific idea and without a positive doctrine
had the same value as an empty and dishonest game at playing
preacher, with someone supposed to be an inspired prophet on the
one side and only asses listening to him with mouths agape allowed
on the other. "Look here," he added, suddenly jerking out his hand
and pointing at me, "we have a Russian with us. In his country, Weitling, your role might be suitable: there, indeed, associations of nonsensical prophets and nonsensical followers are the only things that
can be put together and made to work successfully." In a civilized
country like Germany, Marx continued, developing his idea, people
could do nothing without a positive doctrine and, in fact, had done
nothing up to now except to make noise, cause harmful outbreaks,
and ruin the very cause they had espoused. The color rose in Weit-

ling's pale cheeks and he recovered his genuine, fluent speech. In a voice quivering with emotion he began to argue that a man who had gathered hundreds of people together in the name of the idea of justice, solidarity, and brotherly mutual aid under one banner could not be called a vain and worthless person, that he, Weitling, consoled himself in the face of the day's attacks with the recollection of the hundreds of letters and expressions of gratitude he had received from every corner of his fatherland, and that his modest, preparatory work was, perhaps, more important for the general cause than criticism and closet analyses of doctrines in seclusion from the suffering world and the miseries of the people. On hearing these last words, Marx, at the height of fury, slammed his fist down on the table so hard that the lamp on the table reverberated and tottered, and jumping up from his place, said at the same time: "Ignorance has never yet helped anybody." We all followed his example and also got up from the table. The meeting had ended. While Marx paced the room back and forth in extreme anger and irritation, I hastily bid him and his companions good-bye and went home, astounded by everything I had seen and heard.

My relations with Marx did not end even after my departure from Brussels. I met him again, in company with Engels, in 1848 in Paris where they had both come immediately after the February Revolution, intending to make a study of the French socialist movement, which now found itself at large. They soon relinquished this intention because French socialism was completely dominated by purely local political issues and already had a program from which it had no desire to be distracted, a program aimed at attaining, with weapons in hand, a controlling position in the state for the workers. But even before that period there were instances when I was in contact with Marx by correspondence, and these were of particular interest for me. I was treated to one such instance in 1846 when Marx wrote me a long letter in French in connection with Proudhon's well-known book *Système des contradictions économiques,* and expounded his view on Proudhon's theory. The letter was remarkable in the extreme; with respect to two of its features, it was in advance of the time when it was written—its criticism of Proudhon's postulates, which anticipated in their entirety all the objections subsequently raised against them, and also the novelty of its view on the significance of the *economic* history of nations. Marx was one of the first to say that forms of government and also the whole social life of nations with their morality, philosophy, art, and science are only the direct results of the economic relations among people, and that with a change in those relations they, too, are changed or even completely abolished. The whole matter consisted in discovering and defining the laws that caused the changes in people's economic relations which had such momentous consequences. In Proudhon's antinomies, however, in his opposing certain economic phenomena to certain others arbitrarily associated with one another and, on *historical evidence,* not in the slightest derived from one another, Marx discerned only the author's tendency to assuage the conscience of the bourgeoisie by casting the facts of contemporary economic practices unpleasant for it into laws supposedly belonging to the very nature of things. It was on this basis that he denounced Proudhon as a *theologian* of socialism and as a petty bourgeois from head to toe. I quote the last part of this letter in literal translation since it can serve as a good commentary to the scene related above and gives the key for understanding it.

In only one thing do I concur with Monsieur Proudhon (*N. B.,* Marx everywhere wrote *"monsieur Pr"*)—in his aversion for softhearted socialism (*sensiblerie sociale*). Before him, I had already brought a pack of enemies on myself by my ridiculing sentimental, Utopian, *sheepish* socialism (*socialisme moutonier*). But M. Proudhon makes a curious error when he replaces one kind of sentimentalism with another, I mean—the sentimentalism of the petty bourgeois and his declamations on the sanctity of the domestic hearth, conjugal love, and other, similar things—that sentimentality which, moreover, was even more profoundly expressed by Fourier than in all the self-satisfied banalities of our dear M. Proudhon. What is more, he himself is quite aware of his inability to treat these subjects because, on account of them, he gets himself into an unspeakable rage—*irae hominis probi:* he foams, swears, denounces, screams shame and plague, beats his breast, and calls men and God to witness that he is not party to the abominations of the socialists. He is concerned not with criticism of their sentimentalism, but, like a true holyman or pope, with excommunicating the wretched sinners while singing the praises of the petty bourgeoisie and its cheap patriarchal prowesses and its exercises in love. And this is not a case of mere accident. M. Proudhon from head to toe is a philosopher and economist of the petty bourgeoisie. What is a petty bourgeois? In a well-developed society he inevitably becomes, owing to his position, an economist on the one side and a socialist on the other: at one and the same he is blinded by the splendors of the bourgeois elite and sympathizes with the people's sufferings. He is a man of the middle class and of the common people together. Deep in his conscience he praises himself for his impartiality, for the fact that he has found the secret of an equilibrium, which supposedly is not like the *juste milieu*, the golden mean. A bourgeois of that sort believes in contradictions because he himself is nothing but a social contradiction in action. He represents in practice what is said by theory, and M. Proudhon is deserving of the honor of being the scientific representative of the French petty bourgeoisie. It is his positive service because the petty bourgeoisie will certainly figure as an important integral part in future social upheavals. I very much wanted to send you together with this letter a copy of my book "On Political Economy," but I have not yet been able to find anyone who would undertake to publish my work and my criticism of the German philosophers and socialists about which I spoke to you in Brussels. You would not believe what difficulties such a publication encounters in Germany from the police, in the first place, and, in the second, from the booksellers themselves, who are the venal representatives of the tendencies I have put under attack. And as for our own party, it, to begin with, is extremely poor and, besides, a good part of it is still extremely vexed with me for my opposition to its declamations and Utopias.

The book "On Political Economy" Marx mentioned in his letter was, I assume, his last work, *Capital*, which has only recently been issued. I admit that I, as was true of many others, did not believe Marx's eye-opening letter, taken as I was, in company with the majority of the public, with the élan and dialectical qualities of Proudhon's opus. With my return to Russia in October 1848, my relations with Marx ceased and never were again resumed. The time of hopes, conjectures, and all manner of *aspirations* had by then already passed, and the practical activity later chosen by Marx went so far afield of Russian life in general that from the position of the latter it was impossible to follow the former other than at a distance, indirectly and inadequately, by way of newspapers and journals.

The episode with Marx I have recounted here will perhaps not seem irrelevant to my picture of Paris, if I add that precisely the same kind of scenes and on the same issues were taking place in all the big cities in Europe and, of course, in Paris more so than anywhere else: the people changed and the settings changed in accordance with the difference in the development and education of the characters; the essence of the debates and conflicts within the democratic circles remained the same. Everywhere people were in search of *integrated* doctrines of socialism, of scientific explanations and justifications for the *feeling* of dissatisfaction out of which socialism arose, of plans for a commune where work and pleasure would go hand in hand. The need to do away with the mass of absurd, immature, and fruitless experiments undertaken for the realization of this ideal by uninitiated, poorly prepared and fantastically inclined minds was felt everywhere. That is what explains the combined efforts of the best of the socialists to find a type of workers' commune which would make it possible to prove without a doubt that a man's every moral and material need could find in it suitable and comfortable accommodation. The movement of minds both in the realm of theories and in the efforts at testing the ground for practical solution of economic difficulties was universal until the point where it came up against the "national workshops" in which it was crushed in order that it might be reengendered on different principles.

From his very first steps in Paris, Herzen, once moved into his permanent residence on Avenue Marigny, from where he wrote to the *Contemporary* of 1847—Herzen, with his particular cast of mind and penchant for taking energetic action when presented with any problem—found himself, as it were, in his native element. He immediately threw himself into that sparkling sea of daring assumptions, merciless polemics, and high feelings of every sort, and came out of it a new and extremely nervous man. His mind, feelings, and imagination had acquired a morbid irritability which revealed itself, above all, in his indignation at the political regime in power that busied itself with watering down doctrines by using one against the other. Anger and vexation were aroused in him by the transparency of reform projects which falsely promised to put an end to all debate and were already celebrating a victory before the battle had begun. Both the one and the other seemed to him equally signs of the insubstantiality of society, and in one of those moments of his soul-searching analysis of the impressions he had received on first acquaintance with European socialism he wrote one of those articles which can be termed the most pessimistic view of Western culture as has ever been expressed in Russian; but the fact is that it was written by him *from the other shore* —he now saw with his own eyes what till then had been known to him from afar.[105]

Despite that confession of his, Herzen devoted himself almost without reservation to the very movement he had considered futile. His prolonged concern with his object of study drew him into its interests, its problems and intentions, as often happens to people with passionate natures who encounter on their way blind but unshakable beliefs. There was not another person who would have reacted against the insubstantiality of the European order of life more mercilessly and who would have at the same time so decisively adjusted himself to it, judging his work and the habits of his mental and material life in its light. Herzen's letters from Avenue Marigny already bore a definite, though cautiously imprinted, stamp of humanitarian ideas with hints of issues of a new kind, and therefore they should be considered the first attempts at applying the sociological way of apprehending and discussing things in Russian writing. From his analysis of Felix Pyat's drama to the detailed descriptions of Paris life, everything in them reflected an attitude derived from sources unlike the ones that nourished our philosophical, masked-liberal, and philanthropical tendencies. Herzen's Moscow and Petersburg friends took pleasure in this original, always brilliant, but at the same time, new turn of his talent and had no premonition of something beginning here that would carry the author of the letters off to the side far away from them, and even the author himself had as yet given no thought to where he would end up by logical development of principles and their consequences.

It should be added that, while Herzen's Moscow friends admired the satirical adroitness of his letters, enjoyed the cleverness of their commentaries and exposés, and often dwelt at length on their flashes of profound thought in definitions of the current phenomena of French society, those friends nevertheless, did not fully believe in the objective truth of the letters and considered them partly the product of the usual frondeurism typical of travelers who feel embarrassed at giving in to a foreign country from the very start and at not making reservations while entering into close relations with it. An echo of this opinion was expressed most strongly by V. P. Botkin, for which reason I now quote the following excerpt from his letter to me of October 12, 1847, from Moscow:

> By the way, I read H.'s three letters from Avenue Marigny in number ten of the *Contemporary*, and read them with keenest pleasure. The first letter is not as good as the other two—there is even a certain forced wit evident in it: of course, not everywhere, but here and there a witticism doesn't seem to jibe with his pen, with the tone. As for his view of the theaters and the city, for all his superiority and for all his brilliance and profundity, I still think that this is a *first graphic* impression. *Je ne cherche pas chicane à sa manière de voir*—and while respecting his right to look at things from his own angle, I stand by my earlier opinion, nevertheless, and will not start imitating the Slavic intolerance shown by Herzen when he took me to task because I had the temerity not to agree with his opinion. In the other two instances, I read his letters with pleasure: they are so engaging, so playful —an arabesque in which joke and profound idea, deeply felt outburst and sprightly witticism interwine; and what difference

does it make that I have completely different opinions about a great many things: anybody has the right to look at things his own way, and Herzen looks at them in such a lively way, so engagingly that I completely lose my desire to argue: pleasure overpowers all other feeling. But their main deficiency, in my opinion, lies in the indeterminateness of their point of view: I would venture to say that Herzen failed to ascertain clearly the meaning both of the old aristocracy, which he so admires, and of the bourgeoisie, which he so despises. What does he have left? The workingman. And what about the farmer? Does he really think that by lowering the electoral standards the situation of the bourgeoisie will be changed? I think not. I am no partisan of the bourgeoisie and I am no less revolted than any other man by the grossness of its mores and its blatant prosaicalness, but in this instance what is important for me is fact. I am a skeptic; when I see that on each of the two contending sides of the argument there are equal amounts of good sense and nonsense, I am unable to join either one of them, although the working class, as the oppressed class, undoubtedly has all my sympathy, and yet, at the same time, I cannot help but add: God grant we have a bourgeoisie! *Cet air de matador* with which Herzen settles everything that has to do with Paris is very cute, engaging—I cannot resist admiring it in him precisely because I know that matador's soft and gentle heart, but the fact is that Herzen's conclusions elucidate exactly nothing: they only gloss over things. All these problems are complex to such a degree that it is impossible to raise one of them without raising several others together with it. . . .

Thus, even leaving aside V. P. Botkin's personal accounts with Herzen, who was in the habit of enunciating the bitter truth to him about his reprehensible indulgence in all the superficial attractions of Parisian life, the passage cited still expressed an opinion shared by other friends of Herzen's who understood quite well the causes and reasons for his democratic pronouncements over the bourgeoisie in its own homeland but who considered such pronouncements unsuitable for Russian society which was still lacking the formative elements that had once brought that very bourgeoisie into history. Moreover, his friends could not know where Herzen's wholesale condemnation of Europe would yet lead him and they feared that his authoritative word would find twisted reflection in the minds and notions of Russian readers. They feared the same thing from the confession of Belinsky when he went abroad and brought to light views on Western culture closely approximating Herzen's, about which we shall have something more to say. Perhaps among the reasons prompting Herzen to write, later on, the article mentioned above was his desire to make clear to his friends what his true relations to the European world were and what place he intended to occupy in it. We know that the article countered the situation of impasse of European society with the appearance of the people whose presence alone in Europe troubled minds and only whose grim aspects were known, but who brought with them folk culture and qualities of mind and heart that appeared to have a great future. To this note, which Herzen sounded for the first time in the article mentioned, he frequently returned, endeavoring to take it in a great many different registers, but it did not elicit sympathy from all his friends, some of whom found it strained and false despite whatever variations and mollifications with which the author frequently tried to accompany it.

Meanwhile, Herzen's life went on with noise and cheer as before, despite his sudden pauses in the midst of the distractions and entertainments of Paris and the anxious gropings for a solid footing that followed them; but these intervals were not long—the circle of his acquaintances became larger and larger, the discussions proliferated and the din rose.[106] Neither he nor any of his Russian friends thought at all about the possibility of a moment coming when the opportunity of living like an amphibian between two worlds—the Western and Russian worlds—would disappear and one would have to choose between the two spheres, each as powerfully and jealously as the other, although on different bases, claiming rights to possession of the whole man. That moment was not far distant (only one year separated it from people), but when it came, there ensued bitter reckonings, painful sacrifices, compulsory and unnatural repudiations which utterly ruined Herzen's life and the lives of many other persons together with him.

[XXXII]

Having started speaking about the beginnings of a future Russian emigration, I cannot pass over in silence a new element of a movement with which Paris had become enriched by that time, I mean— the Polish element. This element had, of course, existed earlier but had now become completely transformed.

It had cast off the mystical tint with which Towianski and Mickiewicz [107] had imbued it five years before, it no longer preached the doctrine of messianism with its solution of national and all other problems through the agency of persons who were the elect of Eternity expressly sent to earth for that purpose, and it no longer spoke of the brotherhood of all Slavic peoples as the ultimate goal of their historical development. Instead, meetings were then held in Paris of the so-called Polish Central Revolutionary Committee, which had declared itself the sole plenipotentiary of the Polish people and whose purpose was to direct the cause of restoring the fallen kingdom within its old boundaries, demanding blind obedience to its categorical decrees from every person who so much as spoke a Polish dialect, and which attained its goal completely. The committee had no thought whatever about a reconciliation among the Slavs on any bases common to them, but simply enjoined them to wage war against the governments under which they lived. With the help of its agents, its proclamations, its administrators and generals, who were sent out to various and highly dangerous areas within the Slavic territories, it held the threads of a vast republican conspiracy in its hands and had just brought about the Galician movement of 1846, [108] which had ended with the massacre of landowners and the fall of Cracow, after which the committee had paused for a while, considering new plans for uprisings and movements. Since forcefulness of action was the only justification the committee had for its existence and the only authority it could assert in the face of its detractors, such as the aristocratic party

of Czartoryski,[109] all members of this association distinguished themselves or tried to distinguish themselves, therefore, by that same forcefulness. Among other things, this forcefulness made room for the
power-hungry within the committee itself and had many other benefits besides. Above all, it relieved people of over-demanding inquiries
on the part of foreigners: what could be demanded of heroes? This
proven revolutionary forcefulness alone answered for everything, conveniently supplanting all other qualities that people might lack; it hid
all their inadequacies in education and intellectual development and it
took the place even of virtues and moral character when they were
not in evidence; in short, the host of Polish émigrés lived in Paris as a
special, privileged category of people. It was to them that one of the
Russian prospectors for political causes attached himself. This was
Bakunin, whom we have already met.

Already back in 1842, Bakunin had shown signs of what he was
going to become at a later time. That year, under the pseudonym
Elyzard, he had had an article published in A. Ruge's well-known
journal, an article [110] which aroused the attention of savant German
burghers by its *skillfully constructed* accusations against the German
genius for its unproductive ability to transfer all the demands of the
time and of social development to the grounds of scholasticism and
then, after having viewed them in the garb and sumptuous ornaments
of philosophical theory, to feel reassured and to take up new exercises
of the same kind. Being himself one of German philosophy's ardent
adepts, Bakunin broke off all relations with it and, in order to put
sufficient physical and moral distance between it and himself, moved
from Berlin to Paris. There he began looking for political work, trying
the editorial offices of journals, working men's workshops, the democratic cafés, and finally succeeded in finding something like his real
specialty and calling in Polish propaganda. After some hesitation, occasioned by the very onesidedness of that propaganda to which he
often referred in talking with friends, he ended up by accepting it
completely and devoting himself to it without reservation, openly and
decisively, burning all his bridges behind him and not leaving the
slightest avenue of escape for himself in case of a retreat. Not a single
Russian before him had so boldly cut himself off from his household
gods, his former cast of mind, his old remembrances and conceptions
in favor of the clandestine religion of the Polish cause. The fascination
of this religion consisted for him primarily in its revolutionary character for the sake of which its many narrow ambitions and many questionable instincts were forgiven. This was something like a special sort
of revolutionary romanticism where apparitions and phantoms took
precedence over logic, the guidance of history and the considerations

of reason and experience. Under the aegis of such a romanticism, it was possible to deplore the existence in mankind of its various antagonistic nationalities and, at the same time, to serve the most exclusive of nationalistic causes that the world has ever known; it was possible to renounce patriotic prejudices in general and to inculcate in oneself the views and feelings of a Polish ultrapatriot; it was possible, finally, to consider oneself free of all religious and class affiliations and to live in intimate accord with militant Catholicism and the Polish nobility. Not even socialism could have provided so wide a road for radical dilettantism, since socialism at least required of a person in each of its subsections (and there were not a few of these then) repudiation of other, competing sectors.

At this same time there arose the line of thought about the necessity of grafting Polish oppositional energy onto Russian nationality, which lacked it by nature. Bakunin took upon himself the development of that line of thought and in no small measure was influential in making Europe conscious of it for a while via newspapers, pamphlets, speeches, and treatises. He believed that he was performing, in doing so, a double service—arousing sympathy for one Slavic people victimized by the injustice of history and fostering the bases for independent judgment in another Slavic people, that is, among his fellow countrymen. Since the number of like-minded people in the Russian world determined the greater or lesser importance of his own position in the emigration, Bakunin was not very rigorous or particular in his recruitment of adherents, enrolling in their ranks, in company with minds inclined toward study of political problems, also people who were simply curious or of the kind in search of more or less interesting and piquant acquaintanceships in Paris. He himself, however, provided the example of outright profession of one's beliefs which seeks opportunities to make its positions public knowledge and does not, in pursuit of that aim, retreat in the face of street demonstrations and political scandal. Such was the phase of his life that he was then passing through and which preceded its final period during which Bakunin fashioned out of himself a consummate type of cosmopolite, so consummate that he seemed an abstraction and became virtually incomprehensible from the point of view of the real conditions of human existence—a type according no recognition to the effect of historical, geographical, or living conditions on the determination of the fates and endeavors of nations, a type abolishing races, ethnic groups, established states, and societies for the sake of constructing on their rubble a single, common model of life and labor.

Bakunin soon reached the apogee of subversive philosophical and economic romanticism, but that was still ahead; now, in his capacity

only as a Polish agitator, he was awaiting his chance to announce triumphantly and officially, so to speak, his choice of party. The chance
presented itself almost on the eve of the 1848 Revolution when the
Polish colony was celebrating the anniversary of the Warsaw Uprising
of 1830. At the jubilee, before a numerous gathering and in a public
hall, Bakunin delivered his famous speech in which he cautioned the
Poles against attempts, such as were already being made by some of
their fellow countrymen, to reach a reconciliation with their enemies,
and urged them instead to war to the death for their national idea, in
doing which he did not stint, of course, in making grim characterizations of the opponents of that idea. Guizot's administration, so fearful
in general of the passion of the populace and any provocation for it
(especially of Polish origin), did not fail to make a response to this
speech and, two days after its delivery, deported the orator from
Paris, in connection with which Guizot, in answer to an inquiry on
this matter in the Chamber of Deputies, said that one could not, after
all, tolerate boisterous individuals (*une personalité violente*) like
Bakunin disturbing the public order and international decorum. Bakunin then left Paris for Brussels, having written in advance a letter to
the minister of internal affairs, Count Duchâtel, in which, reproach-
ing him for exceeding his authority, he observed that the future belonged, not to him and his party, but to those whom he was now op-
pressing and persecuting.

Despite the power of attraction Bakunin possessed and owing to
his sensitivity to all problems of conscience that arise in men's minds,
owing, in addition, to his constant readiness to concern himself with
the solution of the moral and intellectual difficulties which beset men
in search of a way out of the contradictions between their thought
and their upbringing and natural inclinations, Bakunin, nevertheless,
could not establish frank relations between the Russian colony and the
Polish emigration, no matter how often he brought them together and
however skillfully he manipulated their discussions. There was a kind
of *fraud* like a subtle effluvium running through the relations between
the two sides, almost imperceptible to an outsider but intimately
sensed by all participants in the matter. Herzen detected it the moment he found himself among them. On both sides there were a number of mental reservations, what in the Jesuits' teaching are called *restrictions mentales,* and the tricks and devices associated with them
were nowhere more abundant than in precisely those moments of high
feeling when the two sides came together on some general grounds
and amicably shook each other's hands, jubilant over the unity and
harmony of their liberal ideas. Each side had something else in mind
besides, which it did not express openly, and what was left unex-

pressed was the most important thing. One must remember that the Polish emigration of the time, following its leading people and with the overt or covert approval of Europe, lived on the thought of the necessity for Polish supremacy, Polish hegemony in the future federal union of Slavic peoples, and stood for Poland's rights to demand of its fellow Slavs near and far, in the name of its superior civilization and its age-old affiliation with European culture, voluntary submission and the necessary sacrifices to bring about the protectorate. Understanding the awkwardness of expounding its leading idea in front of its Russian friends, the Polish emigration did not display that idea whenever discussions were launched on the role and mission of the various nationalities of the Slavic world; and that kind of discussion was launched constantly.

Many other curious considerations and, at times, also revelations of ethnic spirit and character were enunciated at those conferences, but the scope and aims of our essay preclude relating them here. Among other things, Lelewel, living in Brussels in extreme and honorable poverty, once astonished me by the truth and candor of certain views of his which other of his fellow countrymen kept only to themselves. As a matter of fact, he astonished them, too, in the same way on more than one occasion, for instance, in his well-known Polish history where he spoke out the bitter truth to his people in such quantity. I met Lelewel,[111] on my way through Brussels, at his favorite café, over which he lived, enjoying the benefit of the pipe from its stove, which passed alongside his room and heated it in the wintertime. Regularly each evening he went down to the café to drink his cup of coffee, paying the bill with a couple of sous carefully twisted up in a strip of paper. After my brief conversation with the veteran of the Polish cause, I thought never again to hear his voice, but the following day he came to see me and, not finding me in, left a note in French. To my great surprise, I found in it a minute treatise on the subject of the Russian language's supposed lack of words to express the concepts of personal honor and virtue—*honneur, vertu.* The word *chest* [honor], which did exist in Russian, expressed, supposedly, only the concept of a generic or functional distinction and had been understood by us in that way from time immemorial; and *dobrodetel* [virtue] was a compound word invented by us out of need to denote a *psychological* quality, which, however, it does not convey in the least. Thus, the old man had issued forth to negotiate with his visor raised and without concealing his opinion about the counteragent with whom he intended to strike a bargain.

The Polish emigration could not, however, conceal the truth from the eyes of their Russian sympathizers of the moment and aroused in them the same sort of secretly held, nationalistic train of thought. The Russians displayed before their political enemies an exemplary magnanimity, made all manner of concessions to Polish patriotic feelings, gave credence to their accusations and rebukes, and, at the same time, kept intact their own ulterior thought which intimated that the right to some sort of supremacy in the Slavic world, if one might even yet think of it, could only belong to a strong political body like their fatherland, which, in fact, was the real representative of that world. It was necessary to take many precautions to keep these secret, undivulged thoughts from coming out in the open and obliterating the international mirage that had succeeded in forming in Paris thanks to Bakunin. Owing to an instinctive fear of losing the possibility of coming together, which, even if no decisions were reached, at least allowed people to get familiar with one another (and that was a matter of no small importance then), there was a mutual implicit agreement to leave aside all burning national issues full of friction and controversy, relegating their solution to some future time, and to limit matters for the time being to exercises in humanitarian and noble feelings which were so effortlessly, conveniently, and effectively put on display. On this basis, good feeling among the members of the circle was assured, and in Paris one more fête was added. Thus originated the Polish question in the Russian world, and I am here presenting only the fact without analyzing it either from a political or moral point of view and without making mention of its repercussions.

I should note in this connection that Bakunin himself confessed that the Polish question was valuable for him particularly because it gave him the chance to locate his aims in life somewhere and to join in some kind of activity. In October 1847, after having been deported from Paris, he wrote his friends remaining in Paris a letter from Brussels from which I extract the following lines:

I shall very likely soon have to make speeches again; keep this quiet for the time being, except for Turgenev—the matter isn't quite settled yet. It could happen that I shall be banished from here, too—let them do their banishing, I'll speak all the more boldly, better, and more easily for it. All my life so far has been marked out in almost involuntary twists and turns independent of my own intentions; where will it take me? God knows! I feel only that I cannot turn back and that I shall never betray my own convictions. And therein lie all my strength and all my merit, and also all the reality and all the truth of my life, therein lie my faith and my duty; and I have no concern for all the rest: what shall be, shall be. There you have my credo. There's much mysticism in all this, you'll say—but who, then, is not a mystic? Could there be the least drop of life without mysticism? Life exists only where there is a broad, unbounded, and, therefore, also somewhat hazy, mystical horizon; really, we all of us know practically nothing, we live in an alive sphere surrounded by the miracles, by the powers of life, and each step of ours could bring them forth without our knowledge and often even independently of our will. . . . The reception the Poles gave me has placed me under an enormous obligation but also *has shown me and given me the chance to act.* I know that you take a somewhat skeptical attitude toward all this; and you, from your own standpoint, are right, and I, also, at times shift to your point of view. But what can one do—there's no changing one's nature. You are a skeptic, I—a believer; each of us has his own work cut out for him. But enough of this. G. sends you regards. Marx *treibt hier dieselbe eitle Wirtschaft, wie vorher,* ruining the workers by making casuists out of them. The same theoretical madness and dissatisfaction etc.

This letter, aside from testifying to the fact that it was not the substance of Polish propaganda that attracted Bakunin (his remarks about it were very casual), but the arena of political and demagogic activity it opened for him—this letter, I say, is curious also in another respect. It shows the author in his true light as a romantic, mystical anarchist, which is what he always was and which explains his hatred for the authoritative, positive-minded, and law-giving Marx—a hatred that lasted for twenty-five years and culminated in a scandal and complete break between them. Before too long, however, another, new path of activity was opened up for Bakunin. Hardly six months had passed when the 1848 Revolution opened the doors of Paris to Bakunin again, and he went there and took up residence in a barracks belonging to the workers who formed the guard and entourage of the revolutionary Prefect of Police, the famous Casidier. Until then, Bakunin had given ear to socialism and had made the acquaintance of its leaders only as a new element on which future, contemplated political upheavals could rely. Now he was convinced that the workers and socialism were forces in their own right, able by themselves alone to carry aloft on their shoulders a man with a gift for words, critical talent, and natural resourcefulness in the field of theories, abstract constructs, and grandiose illusions. He devoted himself to fantastic socialism with the same obsessiveness and the same readiness to make sacrifices as he had the fantastic Polonism that preceded it.

While the inspired Russo-Polish fêtes were celebrating the establishment of eternal peace in the north of Europe, the same kind of celebrations were going on, for a variety of reasons and in a variety of forms, in all corners of Paris. Educated foreigners had congregated there for just such fêtes with their magnificent spectacles and apotheoses of the future, drawing information from them on the condition and direction of thought in the homeland of attempted reforms of all sorts. The Russian colony did not lag behind anyone in this matter, and Herzen was often the animating spirit and hero of such fêtes. He very rapidly turned himself, as had Bakunin, from a gallery spectator into a participant and *soloist* in the democratic and social choruses of Paris. Under the electrifying effect of all the city's stimulating elements, Herzen's vibrant nature instantly branched out with exceptional power and luxuriousness, giving its all to these new branches and doing violence to its normal existence. Herzen's cultivated versatility began to serve him to the full extent of its capacity—he understood the sources of ideas better than the people who promulgated them and discovered extensions of them and very often corrections and limitations to them that escaped the specialists on the matters in question. He began to *amaze* people, and, not too long after his arrival, a circle began to form around him consisting of people who were more than admirers but, so to speak, his *adorers*, bearing all the signs of a passionate devotion. Among the latter was a well-known émigré, the poet Herwegh,[112] who later brought such misery and suffering into his personal and family life. More than once during the height of these intellectual festivities in Paris, I was reminded of the intellectual festivities at Sokolovo, festivities accompanied by the same nervous excitement of intellectual and physical powers but with what a difference in content and attitude!

With respect to the astonishment aroused in foreigners by the breadth of understanding shown by certain Russians, by their manner of posing questions and, in general, by their indications of extraordinary abilities, one could cite many curious details. Herzen and Bakunin reaped the tribute of this astonishment, admixed with something close to fear, at almost every step of the way. After meeting persons known and unknown to them, they continually left them wondering about the enigmatic natures of such power and such daring in conception and expression that remained isolated examples of culturedness among their countrymen. Michelet, who was even confounded by the élan, wit, and broad scope of a book of Herzen's he had read, made a well-known remark indicating that the author of *History of France* had gone to rather painstaking efforts to find an explanation for this new phenomenon for him and thought to have found it in the author's Swabian-Russian, rather than purely Slavic, extraction. As concerns Bakunin, even then people came to him for advice and for elucidation on questions of abstract philosophical thinking, including people such as Proudhon, for example. A certain intelligent and cultivated Frenchman who could see the gaps in the intellectual development of his own country called his friends together on Bakunin's account and said in this connection: "I shall show you a monstrosity (*une monstruosité*) in compact dialectics and in luminous conception of the essence of ideas (*par sa dialectique serrée et par sa perception lumineuse des idées dans leur essence*)."

If Herzen, as we noted above, began to bear on his person the marks of Parisian life, then so much the less could his quiet and intense wife have avoided infection by the intoxicating atmosphere of the big city. She became transformed into a genuine Parisienne, imbued her person with democratic tints and took the interests of French life warmly to heart, filled with rapture and admiration for various more or less indigent and miserable people whom French life had thrown out on the street and especially for those half-workers, half-bourgeois who, aside from ruminating over the form of the future, inevitable upheaval, had not another concern in the world. The Herzen house became a sort of Dionysius' "ear" where all the noise of Paris, the least movement and perturbation playing over the surface of its street and intellectual life were clearly echoed.

Only M. F. Korsh,[113] who had accompanied the Herzens on their trip, was not caught up in this whirlpool and served as a living reminder of the Moscow they had only recently left and had already forgotten. Ailing, rarely going outdoors, devoting herself to the care of the children and mindful only from afar of the tumult reverberating from the cosmopolitan city, she became a sort of anachronism in the family, a family, it should be added, that very much loved and respected her. No matter how interesting in its content and variety the milieu in which this intelligent and well-rounded woman found herself, her thoughts lived in constant association with the circle of far-off friends left behind in Moscow and occupied with a task neither spectacular nor sensational—the task of saving people's minds from the crudity that hedged them round from all sides. By her presence alone in the Herzen household she spoke to her hosts and to certain of their Russian guests about another culture and about already neglected friends of the recent past who were occupied at home with the unglamorous, preparatory spade work of enlightenment. Could any thought be spared for them now in view of such brilliance, such fascinating roads open on all sides for every intellectual and moral impulse and even every mental caprice! In the figure of M. F. Korsh, before the Herzens stood *elegy* personified with its ardent sympathies for the past, and who of those now reeling in the vortex of delight with the European world and new-found freedom—who had time to pause before elegies and give ear to them?!

[XXXIII]

SOON IT BECAME CLEAR to me that there were other reasons for the coolness between the friends—between those who had gone abroad and those who remained at home—of a more substantive nature than the diversions of Paris. After a number of candid and confiding talks, which we usually held at night in Paris, I could no longer doubt, to my great surprise, that, in Herzen's eyes and in the eyes of his family, Moscow had gone completely blank, been divested of its colors, and had lost the magic charm that opens hearts. All the old life in Moscow now seemed to Herzen and his wife an arid steppe; no touching remembrances could grow on it any longer, and those that remained from recent time had apparently withered, unsustained by that diligent care which is just as essential for remembrances as for children and flowers.

It is not quite a simple matter to explain this drastic change because it ensued from a rather complex psychological process and was fostered by a mass of very subtle nervous irritations, but it is beyond doubt that the change had begun back in Moscow and had only culminated abroad. This circumstance threw much light for me on all of Herzen's behavior in Paris, on all his feverish haste to place himself in the center of his new life: the other, old life, which could have acted as a counterbalance to it, was for him already hidden in fog, and no longer existed. No one had ever aroused in me so great a premonition as did Herzen, from his first steps on the ground of Europeanism, that he would take root there forever, that that ground would claim him utterly and not be displaced by any other, although there were as yet no concrete reasons for this prophecy anywhere in evidence. But I did not know then that Herzen was simply trying to acquire a second, spiritual homeland for himself, since the first one had already lost its power of attraction and existed only as a cause of pity, friendly compassion, and magnanimous offers of whatever services he was capable of rendering, should they be required.

We know that, shortly before leaving for abroad, Herzen had lost his father and had received a rather substantial inheritance making him a comparatively rich man. The framework within which his Moscow existence had been confined until then expanded, but it seemed to him even more restrictive and oppressive than before; with the increase in his material means, desires arose and spread their wings; and the desires of this supremely sanguine personality were on a par with his education and intelligence. Moreover, Herzen had entered that time of life when a man usually experiences an excruciating need for the most intense kind of activity (he was then thirty-four years old); but he could not, of course, find latitude for activity in the form and on the scale he needed. He was left with the prospect of wasting all the store of his pent-up energy in empty cerebration, in the hubbub of meetings with friends, and in defending and refuting more or less apt theses at soirées and dinner parties. But, in the first place, that could not last long and, in the second, it soon turned out that it was impossible to move ahead even by that path. The centers of the former associations had collapsed and friendly, intimate get-togethers were doomed to fail. The latter were particularly affected by the change in Herzen's material life and the comparatively rich furnishings of his house, which the new owners had come by, of course, without their deliberate intention. There was none of the enthusiasm that had once comprised the bouquet of such get-togethers when they would come about with everyone contributing his share, when they caused extra domestic fuss and bother. Herzen recounted how the appearance of a silver serving tray or a candelabra in his new household would seem to strike his friends dumb: cordiality and gaiety vanished the instant people encountered ready-made comfort. Herzen attributed this to that drop of democratic envy which lived in even the best of people; but such an explanation always seemed to me unfair: what was at stake was regret for the lost conditions of their modest way of life. When it now proved practically impossible to gather close friends under the same roof without seeing signs of a change in relations with them, and when it soon proved (as we shall discuss in a moment) that they were already drifting apart in their conceptions of things, as well—what was there left to do? The intellectual interests of the Moscow milieu and the Russian milieu in general had been investigated down to the last shred and the issues which had seemed important had been turned every which way. No serious work of the kind into which one could retreat and shut oneself up from the world was to be found at all, and, therefore, all that was left, of course, was to extinguish the consuming flame of activity with whatever came to hand. Meanwhile, practically next door, there existed a spacious arena, in the form of the Western world, for the unrestricted satisfaction of all intellectual needs, but access to it was shut off because of Herzen's particular situation within his homeland. He exerted a great many efforts to break the chain that held his movements in check and would not likely have succeeded if V. A. Zhukovsky had not taken an interest in his fate and not helped him attain his goal.[114]

No less noteworthy is the spiritual experience undergone at this same time by Herzen's wife. Just as her husband, she, too, chafed terribly at the discipline which the idealism then shared by the friends had introduced and undeviatingly supported. Control of oneself, relinquishment of certain impulses of heart and nature as of some pernicious element, constant practice of the same ritual of duty, responsibilities, and lofty ideas—all this resembled a kind of strict monastic initiation. As all initiations, it had the power to charm and fascinate at first, but became intolerable when continued further. It is curious that the first person to raise the banner of revolt against the creed of moral restraint and of inhibiting the freedom to give in to one's personal physical and mental impulses was Ogarev. It was he who inculcated in both his friends, Herzen and his wife (especially the latter), the viewpoint that every man had a right to do with himself as he chose, without adhering to any code of established rules, which were equally conventional and restrictive both in official morality and in the private variety that circles of friends sometimes adduce for their own usage. There is no doubt that Ogarev's viewpoint had an aristocratic underlay, giving educated people with independent means the possibility of easily and consciously ignoring the moral strictures preached by people unacquainted from birth with the charms and pleasures of complete material independence. At the basis of this viewpoint also lay respect for a person's physiological needs, to which the least recognition of all was accorded by democratic minds seeking to establish general rules and precepts even for man's organic and psychological features. Ogarev's viewpoint suited Herzen's taste when he found himself off the beaten path of his Moscow life with his friends, and that circumstance, together with the fact of his enduring tender feeling for the companion of his childhood, explains the high opinion of Ogarev that Herzen more than once expressed, calling him the freest man and cleverest head in Russia. It is a certain fact that Ogarev's influence had innumerable consequences for Herzen himself and also for his wife.

All the business of shifting from one point of view on things to another, which had begun with Ogarev's appearance in Moscow in 1846, went considerably slower in Herzen's case than in his wife's. Herzen did not readily discard his original philosophical endowment.

Despite his renunciation of the statutes of the idealistic order to which he belonged, despite his attempts, so to speak, to *secularize* his life, Herzen, for a long time afterward, retained the stamp, the manners, and the generic distinctions of his former calling. The character of an austere teacher and a moralizer remained with him even after he had stepped down, so to speak, from his chair and settled in the market place, sharing its agitations, disgruntlement and complaints. He never did disavow certain basic principles of the philosophical-moralistic doctrine he had once professed. In later time, precisely on the ground of that original sin, he even seemed to many minds and characters, who had come on the scene after him and who knew no restrictions, a half-hearted liberal and an indecisive man. On the surface, no change in the manner of his employing his life and his youth had occurred since the time he had set foot on European soil. Even before that, under no constraints from rules or principles, he had readily given himself over to the attraction of a passing fancy, to any aroused feeling or first impression, but at that time he still preserved intact the consciousness of his remaining the same person imbued with the grace of a higher understanding of life, such as his environment had fostered, of his not having lost the ability to judge his own passions correctly, and of not having sold his soul and the many years of his scientific training in order to keep hold of them. He now made just as free a disposition of his life in Paris, but with the intrusion into it of political and social passions, no reassuring fiction for his conscience any longer existed: all those things had their own regulations, which no one had verified and which were very demanding and, at times, even offensive to the ear and feelings unused to them; moreover, they still claimed to be dogmas without acceptance of which there was no access to them. The reserve of his old and never fully expended moral beliefs constituted a useless appendage on Herzen's part to those regulations; that reserve of moral beliefs had lost its value as a *regulator* of thought and existed without purpose, obstructive to his achievement of absolute faith in the moral side of things and not powerful enough to abolish them completely in the depths of his conscience as specious and unaffirmed products of a certain severe social ailment. The situation was capable of turning tragic and subsequently did just that.

On the contrary, the disintegration of old theories and conceptions was quite fully and decisively reflected in the soul of Herzen's poor, impressionable wife with her refined nature and character, and utterly made her over. In her case, the reaction against the conditions of Moscow life had begun from the instant she felt an irresistible disdain for the *bourgeois* virtues that comprised the bases for the whole way of life surrounding her, but she also added a note of passion to her criticism. She not only lost interest in but also became suspicious of the exploits of hearth and home, the domestic heroism always so content and proud of itself, and the eternal glorification of the sacrifices, labors, and voluntary deprivations which were constantly borne before her eyes to the altars of various more or less honorable Molochs who went, in her opinion, under the name of ideas. With the arousal of a craving for a wider existence, she came to despise the endless, steady march in one direction, following the sun—and explained the formation of this intolerable ceremony, resembling in her eyes the revival meetings of the Old Believers, partly by the fact that it was needed by the priests of the circle for covering up their weak, apathetic, and limited natures, and partly by the fact that it provided their generally impoverished instincts and impulses the consolation of proud self-gratification. Herzen himself had never taken so radical an attitude toward his old circle of friends, never expressed such cruelty and injustice in the verdicts he pronounced over it, and never reacted against it with such hatred, but always, despite everything, even in his quarrels with his old circle, valued the not inconsiderable efforts of its members to endure the tribulations of life of the time in as manly, sensible, and independent a way as possible. But all this had vanished from his wife's sight and had been supplanted by a sort of naive, unspiteful defamation of her former friends that took effect whenever she had occasion to remember them. Herzen's wife charged her old acquaintances also with the responsibility for the protracted boredom of her former life, whereas the real reason for that boredom was, as soon became clear, her belated, dreamy, and fruitless romanticism. Despite her constant reading of serious foreign authors, despite the philosophical talk that went on constantly around her and, of course, showed no mercy to any illusions or specious solutions of problems— her soul possessed its own secrets, kept to itself clandestine aims and fostered, in the very hubbub of skeptical effusions, furtive romantic strivings and yearnings. But wherever she turned her eyes—nothing resembling a tolerable romanticism was anywhere in evidence around her. She enjoyed the good fortune of husband, family, and friends— and suffered from the absence of the poetry to accompany all these blessings to the degree she would have liked. She would have preferred poetic afflictions, profound misfortunes in the midst of sympathetic and astonished strangers, and moments of bliss—to that unperturbed well-being she enjoyed. The goal of her life became, therefore, to find romanticism in the form in which it existed in her imagination: it was that she pursued with the passion and perseverance of the seeker after fabulous treasure troves, hoping at some future time to hit upon it and to taste the ambrosia of exalted emotions which few mortals had tried and which romanticism provides its faithful servants—to experience the bliss of the celestial sensations it purveyed. Toward the end of her life she thought she held the cup with that fabulous drink in her hands, but no sooner had she touched her lips to it than a most intense disgust and searing remorse for everything that had been done to gain possession of that precious receptacle seized her whole being and led her to an early grave.

I do not intend to rehearse here the sad details of this passion of the mind rather than of the heart, as it developed in actuality, which that nevertheless extraordinary woman possessed, but certain features of the story are important for defining the relations between the heterogeneous emigrations.

The fact of the matter is that this poetic dreamer did come to know a life in the romantic mode, which she discovered in Paris through the offices of the extremely sophisticated, polished but, also, cold and egotistically carnal personality that was the above-mentioned Herwegh's. This person was, moreover, a dual German celebrity—he was famous for his lyric songs sounding the call to arms for the masses and for the radical nature of his views on government, in general, and the Prussian Government, in particular. Under a soft and ingratiating exterior protected by a very versatile and perspicacious mind, which was forever, so to speak, on guard, and supported by an astonishing ability to perceive the slightest spiritual nuances of human behavior and to cater to them—this marvelous personality concealed within itself caches of egoism, Epicurean appetites, and needs to pamper and satisfy its passions at whatever cost and without concern for the fate of the victims that would fall under the knife of its wanton egoism. All the resources of his education and sophistication, which were, in fact, somewhat out of the ordinary even within the circle of Europe's leading people, and also the resources of his high-strung temperament, which often boiled over in inspired lyrical flashes and outbursts—all these resources, I repeat, were tried out by the extraordinary personality here described in the interest of his seducing the recently arrived dreamer and gaining a victory for himself over all the requirements of her much-demanding imagination. The long sought-after romanticism now appeared before Herzen's wife in a magnificent and dazzling form. Her Lohengrin from the realm of myths on high was face to face with her, and only by approaching closer to him did she suddenly see the terrible image hidden behind the angelic mask he had adopted—and in horror, with a last, supernatural effort of her will, tortured and mortified, she tore herself from his arms. Possibly, the seducer had in fact felt a certain sort of love and devotion for his fated victim, as does happen in the case of some persecutors; but when the victim escaped from him, love and devotion vanished without a trace, and their place was taken by rage over the failure and a craving for revenge for wounded vanity and for the offense dealt his pride and self-esteem. He undertook to throw mud in public at the woman and at her family whose well-being he destroyed, using means, in doing so, which made even his friends indignant. . . .

That was how romanticism came to an end for the poor woman who had succumbed to it and had paid for it with her life, and that was the outcome of the collision of a naive nature with a man belonging to a type of men one encounters in the West—armed head to toe both for valorous and for every other kind of feat.

What was saddest and most instructive of all in this story was the fact that Herzen had himself introduced the man of that ilk into his house and had himself installed him there. Later, Herzen spoke of his behavior toward that person as being rather that of *familiarity* than of friendship. Perhaps that is so in terms of psychological veracity, but we all saw his incessant efforts to ingratiate himself on our émigré, to exhibit himself before him in all the brilliant aspects of his mind, to curry his favor. That was the way, incidentally, Herzen behaved initially with other émigrés and celebrities of the radical world—people considerably less sophisticated than the person we have been talking about. To them, too, he had opened the treasures of his mind and heart, had squandered before them the pearls of his wit and erudition without inquiring whether they were even able to understand what was being shown them so extravagantly.

But what in the world, people will ask, had happened to Herzen's faculty for subtle analysis of character about which I spoke earlier, and his satirical and polemical *flair* that had pulsated so strongly in Moscow and had helped create such unerring, often merciless and shattering portraits of people he knew? Where had the acknowledged master of astoundingly accurate caricatures and searing epigrams that read for all the world like biographical dossiers—where had he disappeared to? These powers of his had not disappeared, as it proved later on; Herzen had not lost a single one of his old powers, but, in the pursuit of a new, spiritual homeland, he had been keeping them artificially in check, had been attempting to jam them down and hide them away in the recesses of his soul so as to acquire an artificial blindness which had now become a necessity if he was going to justify himself. He took measures against his own perspicacity and his penchant for humorous exposés; it was only on that condition that the whole world surrounding him could be retained in his mind as a real, not an illusory, existence; but that world had no wish to apprise itself of Herzen's efforts to understand it from its best side and demanded that he share with it its prejudices, its preconceived ideas, and its rough-hewn solutions and projects. Herzen bent even in that direction, and only when his cup overflowed, when reality became unbearable and shamelessly stark in its insubstantiality, did his former qualities of mind return to him—the whole force of the profound psychologist and thinker; and he set before the tribunal of Russians of the future, in the form of his well-known "Memoirs," [115] both his own person and the types of men of action who headed the political phalanxes of the time. And much else besides returned to him. . . .

On Herzen's departure for abroad from Moscow, all his friends had gathered around him for the last time and accompanied him as far as the first station on the Petersburg Road. Herzen traveled to Petersburg by stage coach—there was as yet no railroad. The farewell banquet held at the station ended, despite its noisy beginning, in a somber mood on the part of his friends—many of whom cried. What possible reason might there have been to cry on the occasion of the departure for a more or less lengthy stay abroad of a young family full of strength and hope? But with it went a man who, despite all misunderstandings, still comprised such an essential part of the lives of his friends that his loss, even for a brief period, dismayed them when the moment of parting came. What would they have said, if they had been able to guess that it was to be a permanent loss for them all? Seen off with fervent good wishes, almost passionate expressions of love and friendship, Herzen commenced his long journey under the moving impression of that scene of parting. He bore that impression with him all the way to Paris, and in the later development of his life, it more than once arose in his memory, although it could no longer reconcile him with the world he had abandoned and left far behind. Only in moments of utter moral loneliness, which he experienced especially prior to establishing his journal,[116] and also in moments of bitter reflection over his work, which, no matter what sacrifices he made for its sake, had still not entitled him to full naturalization within the band of European public figures, only then did recollections about Moscow flow in a warm, full stream to his heart and draw from him a wail of his suffering soul that even reached his friends in Moscow. He entrusted to them his children, entrusted to them the defense of his own name, and appealed for their sympathy, encouragement, and moral support. Life without his old ties with Russia, as it proved, had become an unbearable orphanhood. The crowds of people who flocked to him because of the journalistic venture he had launched for the sake of honest and of self-interested criticism, for the sake of needs of social importance and of needs of personal vengeance and injured pride—those people could not replace them.

Thus, the raging, foaming wave of European life carried that precious nugget thrown into it from some remote, unknown planet—carried it to one side and to another, pounding it to pieces, and, of course, unconcerned about where it could be placed, where made to fit.

The effect of that very same European milieu was expressed differently on another extraordinary Russian, Vasily Petrovich Botkin. Herzen had not arrived in Paris in time to see him, but I had had the chance, before his return to Russia, to spend a whole year with him and to take a trip with him, back in the summer of 1846, to the Tyrol and to Lombardy, this trip of ours having been carried out in a rather original way. Avoiding public conveyances as far as possible and also excessively hospitable inns with room and board, we traveled in carts and calashes hired from local transport suppliers, and lived for three months among peasants, boatmen, and workers in the common people's hostels, in the market places and dark alleys of cities and towns. I regret that I did not keep a diary of that trip, as it might have been of interest now after all the upheavals that have completely changed Austria and Italy. . . .

It is common knowledge that V. P. Botkin married a French woman who had come to Russia *seeking her fortune* and who never even thought about a formal marriage, as she herself made known. When Botkin's friends remarked to him that the project of marrying a girl who wished for nothing more than to live for a more or less lengthy period of time a gay life with a paramour was something somewhat queer, Botkin would become extremely indignant. "So that's where your humanitarianism and your quest for ideals end!" he said. "Exploit a woman, enjoy her, and then cast her off as soon as she bores you—fine principles!" The marriage was performed in a full church ceremony at the Kazan Cathedral, but a month later Botkin realized his mistake and immediately abandoned the unhappy woman to the whim of fate, having no wish even to hear any more about her. As always happens, he despised in her his own blunder and punished her for the sin he had himself committed. At the same time, all the garb of the extreme idealist, which he invariably had worn despite the new fashions, suddenly fell away from him as in the theatrical instant transformation of the sage Faust into a wild youth. Botkin gave himself over utterly to the sensual life and sank into the very slough of Parisian love affairs and every other sort of adventure, supplementing them with piquant impressions derived from art, in which he dug painstakingly to find the most subtle features of works, which activity was a variant of that same cult of sensualism to which he had devoted himself. He would break away from it from time to time in order to clear his head of the fumes of its heady pleasures and would return to them with even greater energy. The fruit of these *hygienic* intermissions was his trip to Spain and his superb book, *Letters from Spain,* which followed it. From the same source ensued his occupation with social and political issues in which with astounding insight he discerned, and then persecuted, the slightest features of undercover idealism or of disguised sentimentality or castle-building, which had now become for him objects of ruthless odium. It was in such a frame of mind that the change of affairs begun everywhere in Europe in 1848 reached him, by then already back in Moscow. No one was more alarmed than he over this change, and the change, what is more, further strengthened the frame of mind that had come about in him, since it could serve him in a way as a shield and a defense against suspicions of moral inclination toward Utopias. In the decline of his years, with a weakening of his energies, and at the time when he himself had become an important capitalist, V. P. Botkin assumed an honorable and distinguished place in the ranks of our ultraconservative party. But he had turned into an ultraconservative in his own fashion, which set him incomparably higher than the majority of his colleagues in convictions. At the basis of his final outlook on things he placed, aside from a sense of preservation for his social position, which was always a very lively sense in him, also the doctrines of two great contemporary thinkers—Carlyle and Schopenhauer. From the first, he drew his disdain for all the daily chatter of journalism and literary reporters and, at the same time, his doctrine on the salutary effect of subordinating oneself to the great authorities, the enlighteners of nations, and the moving forces of history, wherever they might be met. From the second, he adopted his towering contempt for the crowd and the masses of the people and his energetic damnations of the vacuous philosophizing of wits who do nothing but endlessly and aimlessly lay out the same, one idea of theirs. Thus, this extraordinary man had passed through many stages of development, and only death prevented him from seeing what form our Russian conservatism was to take and how it would end.

CHAPTER

[XXXIV]

AMONG THE DISTINGUISHING FEATURES of the Paris of those days belonged its additional important quality of providing people in search
of solitude for whatever reason the quietest spot in all of continental
Europe. One could conceal oneself in it, keep hidden and out of sight
of people, without ceasing to live the general life of a big, cosmopolitan city.

In Paris one did not need to employ special efforts to find a neutralized corner, so to speak, from which one could easily and freely
observe just the day by day creative activity of the city and of the
French national spirit in general, an occupation, moreover, of a kind
sufficient to fill whole days and months. Such corners were possible to
come by in all parts of the city—and, what is more, at comparatively
moderate expense.[117] From just one such corner I was suddenly
wrenched away by some very sad news from Russia. V. P. Botkin
wrote me that Belinsky was in a bad way and had been commanded
by his doctors to take a trip abroad, namely, to the waters at Salzbrunn
in Silesia, which were beginning to achieve a reputation for their
healing powers in cases of lung disease. His friends had taken up a
subscription for the purpose of sending the invalid there; Botkin had
written to invite my participation in that subscription. I wrote back
that I myself was going to Salzbrunn and hoped to be of greater benefit to Belinsky that way than any other. I. S. Turgenev, then in Berlin, had made the same decision. He set out at once to meet the inex-
perienced traveler, whose German was very poor and who had never
once left his own country, at Stettin where he did in fact meet him
and take him in charge. They both arrived in Ober-Salzbrunn, via
Berlin, and took up residence in a neat, wooden cottage with a cozy
little yard on the main, though far from resplendent, street of that still
poor little town.

And so, tearing myself away from all my Paris connections and putting off plans for various trips until some future time, I went off to Salzbrunn in June 1847. After having spent the night in Breslau, I found myself early the next day in a little place I had never been before and, on taking my first steps down some long street, I met Turgenev and Belinsky returning home from the waters. . . .

I hardly recognized Belinsky. Wearing a long surtout, a cap with a straight visor and carrying a stout walkingstick in his hand—there stood before me an old man who, every now and then, as if suddenly taken aback on becoming aware of himself, would quickly straighten up and pull himself together, endeavoring to impart to his appearance the look he thought it should have. The efforts did not last long and could not deceive anyone: his was an organism already half destroyed. His face had become smooth and white, like porcelain, and there was not a single healthy wrinkle on it to testify to the stubborn battle a man puts up with the years engulfing him. His terrible thinness and hollow voice completed the impression, the effect of which I tried to hide as best I could, making the effort to give our meeting a casual and unemotional air. Belinsky appeared to have noticed the pretense. "Have they brought your things to our house?" he mumbled hurriedly and as if in embarrassment, continuing on home.

My things were brought—I settled in on the tiny second story of the premises, and a long, anxious month began of hopeless treatment about which the old, broad-faced, and thick-set Salzbrunn doctor had already, it appears, formed a conception from the very first day. In answer to all my inquiries about the patient's condition and about hopes for the improvement of his health, he invariably replied with the phrase: "Yes, your friend is very sick." I failed to get any other or more enlightening idea from him.

Each morning Belinsky would leave early for the waters and, on returning home, would climb up to the second story and wake me always with the same words—"Wake up, you sybarite!" He had his favorite words and expressions to which he would become accustomed and not change for a long time until new ones were found and likewise obliged to serve for a lengthy period. So, for instance, he would usually begin his rather frequent arguments with Turgenev with the words: "Be careful, boy—I'll stand you in the corner!" There was something good-natured about these little sayings with their resemblance to a child's show of affection. The "boy" Turgenev would, however, sometimes utter some very hard truths, especially with regard to Belinsky's inability to deal with life and with regard to his failure to understand the simplest real bases of life. Belinsky would turn serious then and begin to analyze the psychological and practical conditions which sometimes prevented people from achieving full development, even though they had all the necessary qualities for development. However, many of Turgenev's words, as I came to see later, stuck in his mind and he ruminated over them to himself for some time.

No matter how lively our discussions were now and then, especially when figures and personalities left behind on the other side of the German border were the subjects, still they were not able to fill the whole monotonous summer day, and in a town totally lacking in intellectual interest, to boot. To no avail we friends rehearsed our remembrances over morning coffee, which we tried in every way to prolong, sitting under the eave of a shed which played the role in the yard of our cottage of a peculiar sort of summerhouse with no garden and no greenery. To no avail did we afterward spend the long "table d'hôte" at some restaurant telling anecdotes and relating the news from journals and remarking on books and articles we had read— there were unbearable amounts of time left over. Moreover, it soon proved necessary to tone down all these conversations. It would happen that the laughter caused Belinsky by some amusing anecdote would change into a fit of coughing which shook his chest and stomach terribly and for a long time; on the other hand, some remark taken to heart would instantly bring the color to his face and cause a lively rejoinder after which, however, physical prostration almost immediately followed. A purely vegetative, animal existence interlaced with reading and the exchange of a few ideas became a necessity; but Turgenev could not support that routine. At first, he found a way out of it by undertaking a continuation of *Notes of a Hunter,* the beginning of which had appeared some months before and had acquainted him for the first time with the taste of complete popular and literary success. In Salzbrunn he wrote his remarkable "Village Bailiff," which Belinsky liked, having listened to the whole story read and having only commented about Penochkin: "What a swine—with refined tastes!" But afterward, Turgenev could no longer coerce his restless nature and once, after receiving some letters, announced to us that he was leaving for a while to go to Berlin and say goodbye to some friends who were going to England, but that, after seeing them off, he would return to Salzbrunn. He even left part of his things behind. He did not return to Salzbrunn. We took his things with us to Paris, and he himself almost went off to London in the meantime.

Turgenev's young years were filled with examples of just such turnings aside from ventures started, which always had the effect of surprising and infuriating his friends, but it should be said that these deviations of his consistently emanated from the same source. Turgenev could not persist then for long in any one decision or set of feelings—out of fear of getting waylaid and missing out on life, which speeds past and waits for no one. He was beset with a kind of nervous anxiety whenever he found himself obliged to listen to the sounds of life from afar. He constantly rushed off to the various centers where life was most intense and burned with the desire to come in contact with as large a number as possible of the characters and types engendered by life, of whatever sort they might be. He offered many a sacrifice to this impulse in his nature, sometimes associating with people of rather paltry ambitions and continuing to share the same road with them for lengthy periods of time, just as if it were his own road and one particularly to his liking. He never shared the distaste of the majority of the people in his circle that prevented them from approaching characters and personalities belonging to a certain sphere of ideas and tenor of life—and, thereby, deprived them of a considerable share of instructive observations and conclusions. Moreover, an awareness of the variety of means to achieve success given him by his education and nature still tended to overshadow aims in life for Turgenev. During these years of young manhood and·its enthusiasms, it seemed to him that he could try all possible kinds of existence and combine in himself solid qualities as writer and artist with qualities necessary for acquiring the reputation of victor at all the marketplaces, tournaments, and arenas of the world such as any, even slightly developed, society makes available for its idle energies and its vanity. All these ambitions soon abated as much under the influence of the passage of years as of his effort at self-mastery, especially under the influence of his finally recognizing his literary calling; but his former colleagues still remember them and certain of these people remember them even with the aim of making of these long extinguished ambitions the basic features of his biography. That is why I decided to devote space here to my remembrances about the real heart of this matter—in the hope that they, these remembrances, will perhaps help in making judgments about him with a moderation and circumspection not always maintained by the contemporaries of our poet-novelist.

Even then it was already apparent, if one paid any attention, that Turgenev's true sympathies were completely clear and defined, despite his uniformly appreciative attitude toward the most qualitatively disparate elements of society, and that his true allegiances and preferences not only had reasoned bases but were also capable of being sustained at length. Afterward, all this was clearly evinced, but our circles, having become accustomed, as a general rule, to hold themselves strictly within their own limits, to regard with alarm and suspicion anything lying beyond them and adjacent to them, could not reconcile themselves with Turgenev's prodigality with regard to connections and acquaintances. The independence of all Turgenev's moves, his crossing over at will from one camp to another opposed to it, from one sphere of ideas to another inimical to it and, also, his radical revisions of his way of life, of his choice of the occupations and interest that alternated in riveting his attention—all this was a puzzle for his inflexible friends and made him subject, in their midst, to an undeserved reputation for frivolousness and lack of moral fiber. But there has been no one among us who had more often deceived the prophecies and definitions of his critics, no one who had so successfully reversed the verdicts of the public in his own favor, as had Turgenev. While the literary world was seething with eccentric anecdotes about him supposedly testifying to his propensity to rely, for the sake of securing himself an honorable place in society, more on the effect of words and actions than on their content and merit, Turgenev had nothing else in mind than to analyze the phenomena he came in possession of via experience and observation and to convert them into his mental capital—and in this work of analysis he brought to light qualities as thinker, poet, and psychologist that stunned his premature biographers. Thus, among other things, from close and friendly contact with a variety of social strata, not excluding those listed on the "index" of our circle as being strata of outcasts unworthy of attention, a certain, I dare so express myself, *need for fair play* arose in Turgenev with regard to people and with it, as its essential coloring, an attitude of goodwill toward them which forged for him another, and this time, truer reputation—the reputation of a man of extreme sympathy, benevolence, and *wide understanding* in our Russian world.

Very soon Turgenev became the favorite, for a whole literary period, of that very complex Russian world which recognized in him its agent and entrusted him with the task of representing it in all its affairs. And all those affairs were affairs of a nonmaterial character, consisting primarily in bringing to light the rights to sympathy to which the Russian world's moral and intellectual conceptions were entitled. Turgenev proved not inadequate to this task. Almost from the very beginning of his literary career he succeeded in discovering in the simple people a whole series of remarkable conceptions and a special moral code of their own, all of which was particularly valuable inasmuch as the matter concerned a timid and unassuming class of society without any skill in or the slightest fondness for talking about itself and for itself. Turning this same searching analysis on other classes of society, Turgenev became the chronicler and historian in Russia of the intellectual and spiritual torments of his entire age in the matter of its solving the urgent problems presented by an aroused consciousness of ideas and an awakened mind and heart which did not as yet know how to find an outlet for themselves and what to do with themselves.

In fact, all Turgenev's literary activity can be defined as a long, detailed, and poetically annotated catalog of ideas that circulated in the Russian land among the diverse strata of its educated and semi-educated population over the course of thirty years amid the usual setting of life and the harsh conditions of existence in which it revolved. Turgenev discovered a special kind of creativity in Russia, a creativity in the realm of ideals, and no matter how chimerical, immature, and sad these ideals might have appeared to be, and despite the character of a private, homemade affair, of uncoordinated, separate, and distinct strivings of mind and feeling that they might have borne —their instructive side consisted in their disparity with what Russian life had then been particularly proud of and what it had usually produced. But the inner meaning of ideals, even the most modest ones, exerts so strong an attraction and possesses such a power to arouse attention and sympathy that sometimes even minds well on their way up the ladder of scientific and civic development stop and dwell on it. Ideals in general are the family property of all educated mankind, and, this being so, it often happens that some insignificant thing becomes precious by virtue of the recollections and thoughts associated with it. That is why the unanimous, almost enraptured approval with which Turgenev's stories were received in the West is to be explained—aside from the narrative mastery peculiar to Turgenev, which amazed the sophisticated artistic taste of Europe, and aside from the curiosity aroused by pictures of an unknown and idiosyncratic culture—also by the fact that these stories lifted the edge of a curtain behind which one could glimpse the mystery of spiritual and universal-human productivity among a new, alien people and the work of their consciousness and of their tormented thought. We recently heard that old Guizot, after having read Turgenev's "Hamlet of the Shchigrov District," saw in this story so profound a psychological analysis of a universally human phenomenon that he desired to meet and personally speak with its author on the topic. The opinions of the philosopher and critic Taine and, also, of G. Sand on the story "Living Relics" are well known (the latter wrote the author: *"Nous tous, nous devons aller à l'école chez vous"*), not to speak of the reviewer and historian of belles lettres in Germany, Julian Schmidt, who proclaimed Turgenev—king of the contemporary short story. It would be difficult to count up all the sympathetic responses to the work of our novelist on the part of foreigners.

Turgenev did got go against the qualities of his artistry even when, later on, he brought before the public types and images of a daring, negativistic character: these cold-blooded personages, too, still showed glowing traces of the passage over them, in time past, of the same agitations, catastrophes and failures that had been caused by the idealistic strivings of the people of the preceding epoch in general. There is every justification for calling Turgenev a searcher of spiritual *treasures* hidden in the recesses of the Russian world, and a searcher in possession of unerring tokens whereby they might be procured: he dug around in a great many different kinds of existence with the aim of obtaining the concrete evidence of the idea, the *idée fixe,* that fostered them and served as their lodestar in life, and he never went away from his work empty-handed, carrying out with him, if not whole, precious psychological revelations, at least the rudiments and assays of idealistic conceptions. It was all this that made him the interpreter of his age and, at the same time, a first-class writer in his homeland and abroad.

However, the full development of all Turgenev's creative procedures, procedures which did not disdain corrosive colors, harsh words, venomous hints for the portrayal of the crudity and banality of ordinary Russian reality and which, at the same time, discovered warm and healing springs permeating that very same reality—all this creativity, I repeat, was then still ahead. Turgenev was still only collecting the materials for it.

I. S. Turgenev continued his stay abroad after Belinsky had left to return home. He lived a fairly long time, for some reason, in the provinces (in Brie and practically in the manor at Nohant, G. Sand's estate), and when he made his visit to Paris, he listened rather abstractedly to the talk of his compatriots, interested not so much in the subject matter that occupied them as in the manifestation of their characters, the psychological bases of their opinions, the reasons determining their making this or that choice of doctrines and outlooks. Study of person always stood in the forefront for him; convictions were valued not so much for their content as for the light they shed on the inner life of a man. This was a feature he shared in common with the majority of artists and, in general, with those who were psychologists by nature. He was artist and psychologist also with respect to his own person. The twofold analysis—aesthetic and moral—to which he early began to subject himself, ended by completely revising his entire moral makeup, extinguishing the vanity of trivial quests and the pursuit of affected feelings and perturbations essential for ephemeral triumphs. Europe helped him a great deal in his work on himself. Generally speaking, Europe for him was the land of renewal: the roots of all his ambitions, the bases for his cultivation of will and character and, also, for the development of his thought itself were grounded in its soil—and there they spread their roots deep down and sent up shoots. It becomes understandable why, from his early days, he preferred to remain on that soil until he had completely proved himself on it. In his lifetime, he suffered no small number of reproaches from his compatriots for this preference of his which they thought offensive; some of them even saw in it a lack of national beliefs, the cosmopolitanism of a man of means willing to exchange his civic obligations for the comfort and entertainments of foreign life, and so one and so forth. Of not a single one of the crimes brought up against him was Turgenev guilty, of course, and, indeed, no man could have been guilty of them whose literary activity—that is, in other words, the task of whose life—never gave utterance to anything other than constant, ardent meditation over his homeland and who lived on daily thoughts of it wherever he might have been, a fact which his old and his new acquaintances knew very well. It was not the lack of national sympathies in his soul and not haughty disdain for the tenor of Russian life that made Europe a necessity for his existence, but the fact that intellectual life flowed more generously there, engulfing shallow ambitions, and that in Europe he felt himself simpler, more effective, truer to himself and freer from paltry temptations than when he stood face to face with Russian reality.

It is especially important to note that, both at the time and later on, no break between Turgenev and his homeland could have existed —if for no other reason than that he always left behind there a part of his existence no matter where he went away to; this was the object of his passion, so to speak—what I mean is—Russian literature, understanding by the term artistic, critical, and publicistic activities. The other kind—scholarly literature—lived then in exclusive circles and maintained no relations with society. It was the first kind, popular literature, that was the focus of all Turgenev's thoughts. We know that at that time Russian literature was considered a stepping stone to the study of the laws and conditions of art. The people of the epoch saw in concern with art the only remaining access for them to some form of social endeavor: art virtually comprised people's salvation inasmuch as it enabled them to consider themselves free-thinking people. Never again after that was the *idea* of art understood in Russia so broadly and in so universal, political-social a meaning as during just that period of lull. Art was prized: it was the only value in circulation and at people's disposal. Each theory of art appropriating and procuring new domains for it, each extension of its jurisdiction was accepted with great thanksgiving. The more comprehensive art became in its holdings, the further back its boundaries were moved—the more emphatically was the number of subjects open to public discussion increased.

All the work of social thought was relegated to that one single agent of it, and such an understanding of art lived practically in all minds, although, to be sure, more powerfully manifested among its sworn practitioners. So it was in the case of Turgenev—his devotion to Russian literature and art comprised an organic sense which no outside temptations or attractions had it in their power to overcome. Belinsky highly valued that quality in his friend. For Turgenev and many of his contemporaries nothing, next to the Russian people, more important or more worthy of attention and study than Russian literature existed in any shape or form in Russia: it alone was what they saw there, and on it they placed all their hopes. Other voices borne along side by side with literature and, at times, insistently demanding attention and respect passed by without arousing any response in their thoughts. For Turgenev—as also, I repeat, for many others besides him—to follow Russian literature meant to follow the leading, if not exclusive, educative and civilizing element in Russia.

This conviction was also connected with the conception of the serious man of letters as inevitably a man of high moral standing: the occupation of literature, everyone believed, required, above all, clean hands and lofty character. Many examples could be cited where this opinion was voiced in the public's name. Gogol, who could not be accused of complicity with men of letters, recounted an incident in his *Correspondence* where a certain writer who was guilty of some misconduct in the provinces was sternly rebuked by an anonymous member of society, who ended his rebuke with the remark: "And a literary man, to boot!" Turgenev affirmed his passionate feeling for literature and his concern for it—in deeds. Many of his associates who witnessed the emergence of the *Contemporary* of 1847 must still remember the trouble to which Turgenev went for the sake of the journal's establishment and how much energy and aid in the form of advice and deeds he expended to disseminate and bolster it. The first issues of the *Contemporary* contained, in addition to the beginning of *Notes of a Hunter*, also several short historical and critical articles by Turgenev which have not found their way into the complete collection of his *Works*. Let me note in this connection that Turgenev's aesthetic and polemical articles always had a sort of *interlude* character about them: they displayed a distinguished mind but never possessed that fullness of content that is essential if what is said is to remain in people's memory. The same judgment can be applied to his latter-day exchanges with his critics and detractors, to his declarations of his credo (his *profession de foi*), to the amendments and supplements of his viewpoints, and the like. They did not satisfy either the people for whom they were meant or the public which was interested in following his opinions. Turgenev was in complete possession of his material and became convincing only when he explained things and himself in the arena of artistic creativity. Russian literature, which was then attached exclusively to that arena and to its various major and minor departments, became so important a phenomenon in life that in Turgenev's eyes everything else that was happening in his country was bound to, and did, fall out of sight behind it. The real matter was in its hands alone—and it was not only he who thought that way about Russian journalism, publicistics, and artistry in general, as we have already said.

That is why, among other things, Turgenev bypassed with indifference all the ideas and doctrines of the Paris Russian colony of the time: those ideas and doctrines issued from sources other than the ones in which he assumed lay real, curative powers. He still for the while envisioned the Russian "man of politics" as a first-class Russian writer who created a public around him and made it listen to him perforce.

Very characteristic for that far-off time was the fact that Turgenev's exclusive love for literature could also seem suspicious and cause him difficulties. After his return to Russia in 1851, Turgenev was stunned by the news of Gogol's death (in 1852) and sent a few fervid lines of sympathy for the expired writer to a certain Moscow newspaper, doing so after a ruling had been made in Petersburg to ban obituary panegyrics to the author of *Dead Souls*. No one has ascertained whether or not Turgenev knew about this ruling having been made and whether, supposing it was known to him, it would even be possible to consider his desire to have his brief article published a culpable act, since, in realizing this desire, he did not violate any bona fide laws and did submit his article to the usual censorship procedure, but only at a distance of some hundreds of miles from Petersburg—in Moscow. However, the chairman of the Censorship Committee of the time in Petersburg (Musin-Pushkin) descried in the article's circumvention of his jurisdiction and its appearance in Moscow a case of *disobedience of authority*, and the consequence was Turgenev's arrest and month's confinement at a certain police station and, following that, banishment to his country estate. Owing to this measure, the police station where he was kept (near the Bolshoi Theater between Ekaterinsky Canal and Ofitserskaya Street) accidentally entered into Russian literature and became an *historical* police station. There, amid the various domestic tribunals of the police (then still in full bloom) but in the quarters of the Chief inspector himself, to which he was moved on orders from the heir to the throne (now the reigning monarch), Turgenev wrote a little chef d'oeuvre of his which even to this day has not lost its ability to arouse the reader's appreciation—I mean, the story "Mumu." The day following his release and before his departure for exile, he read it to us. The story he brought out from that police station created a truly moving impression by virtue both of its content and of its calm, though melancholy, narrative tone. That is how Turgenev responded to the punishment meted out to him—he continued without letup the work he had begun of *artistic* propaganda on one of the most important political issues of the day.

Now that this digression, which seemed to me absolutely essential in view of the contradictory reports about an extraordinary man engendered by that same epoch of the 1840's, is over, I turn back once again. And so, after Turgenev's departure, Belinsky and I were left face to face, alone in each other's company in Salzbrunn.

CHAPTER

[XXXV]

DURING THOSE DAYS of long conversations and hourly exchanges of ideas, I saw Belinsky in an entirely different light. His passionate nature, no matter how undermined by his racking ailment, was far from resembling an extinct volcano. Under the crust of his outward calm, the fire still glowed in Belinsky and sometimes suffused his whole organism. True, Belinsky was now beginning to be afraid of himself, to be afraid of those still unquelled powers which were alive in him and could, bursting forth by chance, destroy· in one blow all the gains of diligent treatment. He took measures against his own impressionableness. I had many, many occasions to see Belinsky, in silence and with a pained expression on his face, slump back on his couch or in his armchair when he received an impression that cut straight to his heart and found it necessary to break away or free himself from it. Those moments were something like a special sort of mental agony added to the physical agony, and they did not pass quickly: an anguished expression remained for quite a long time afterward on his face. It was to be expected that, despite all his precautions, the instant would come when he would not be able to control himself—and indeed, such an instant did come for him at the end of our stay in Salzbrunn.

One must know what Belinsky was during the half-year before his death in order to understand the full brunt of that instant which had very important consequences and from whose further and final results only death liberated him. I have in mind here Belinsky's famous letter to Gogol which has now lost much of its original color but which, in its own time, rang out through intellectual Russia like a trumpet blast. Who would believe that, when Belinsky wrote it, he was no longer the champion in search of battles that he once had been, but, on the contrary, a man half subdued who had lost his faith in the value of literary feuds, journalistic polemics, treatises on the trends of Russian thought, and reviews aimed at destroying more or less rickety literary reputations?

His thinking had already turned to a sphere of ideas of another order and was concerned with the new, emerging definitions of the rights and obligations of man, with the new *truth* proclaimed by economic doctrines which was liquidating all notions of the old, displaced truth about the moral, the good, and the noble on earth, and was putting in their place formulas and theses of a purely rational character.

Belinsky had long since become interested, as we saw earlier, in these manifestations of the spirit of inquiry of modern times, but he never gave a thought to any application of them to the Russian world, where not so much as the alphabet for deciphering and understanding their language as yet existed. He had only come to the conclusion that the activity of developing the individual person in search of latitude and freedom for his thought must be accompanied by participation, to the furthest possible degree, in the study of the properties and elements of that stream of political and social ideas into which the civilization and culture of Europe had now been cast. It was for the sake of facilitating this work, indispensable for any, however slightly, thinking and *conscientious* person, that Belinsky had begun considering the idea that Russian literature should be the place to establish the fundamental points of view on European affairs from which the independent work of criticism and free investigation of all their content could begin in Russia.

There was only one thing that Belinsky could not abide: his composure and coolheaded deliberation abandoned him the instant he encountered a judgment which, on the pretext of the indefiniteness or questionableness of European theories, disclosed a covert intention to disparage the efforts and initiatives of the epoch, to ignore the integrity of its strivings, and to cover all its work with ridicule on the basis of precisely those obsolete traditions responsible for bringing everybody to the present state of affairs. On coming across rhetoricians or defamers of such a sort, Belinsky would lose his temper, and Gogol's book, *Correspondence with Friends,* was, as everyone knows, thoroughly permeated with a spirit of distrust and an outrageous contempt for the contemporary intellectual movement, which, moreover, he poorly understood. In addition, it served potentially as a brake on plans for peasant reforms then emerging in Russia, about which I shall speak below. The indignation it aroused in Belinsky had existed in hidden form in his heart for a long time, since he could not vent it fully in a printed assessment of the book in view of the conditions of censorship of the time, and, therefore, as soon as the chance to have a free say presented itself, his indignation flowed out in a fiery avalanche of anger, rebukes, and denunciations.

It is understandable, however, that, with his new attitude of mind, the perturbations and squabbles of the Russian literary circles, in which Belinsky had quite recently taken so lively a part, retreated to the background. He was even beginning to look at all his own activity in the past, at the struggle with literary opponents that he himself had lived through, where so much energy and health was expended in acquiring seeming victories and very real sufferings—to look at all this as an episode not worth remembering. That was what one was given to understand, at any rate, from his severe and unfair evaluation of himself, which I was not the only one to hear from him during the last months of his life. Belinsky became a solitary figure within his own party, despite the journal founded on his behalf, and the first symptom of his departure from its ranks was his losing all his *old antipathies,* antipathies to which his followers still firmly adhered as a way of imparting the appearance of staunchness and energy to their convictions. He had so far departed from the frame of mind of the circle that he found it possible to be fair, and he finally rid himself of all his deep-rooted, virtually obligatory aversions which formerly were accounted literary and political duties. Few of his associates understood the reasons urging him to have done with his past without leaving a single object of detestation behind—and the reason was clear enough. Goals and plans for literature were hatching in his mind which were supposed to change its direction, wrench it away from the soil in which it had become rooted and challenge enemies of a different color and, of course, of a different and more decisive and dangerous character than all former enemies, enemies who, although still ardent, were already half broken-down and harmless. . . .

I have already mentioned the strange impression produced on his closest associates on the journal by his declaration of sympathy for that part of the Slavophiles' conceptions of the people which could be accepted by any thinking person no matter to what party he belonged. It was even worse when Belinsky was moved to praise, making all necessary qualifications, Bulgarin's *Memoirs,* which had appeared then, and to observe that the memoirs were interesting for their characterization of Russian mores at the beginning of the century, of the system of public education of the time, and, in general, of the established practices of life of which the author was himself a witness and a victim. Praise of Bulgarin from Belinsky's lips, however modest that praise was in itself, seemed, nevertheless, so monstrous a thing to the journal's editors that they printed the short article only after having reworked and reworded it beyond recognition. Thereby they provoked a reproving observation on the part of the next publisher of Belinsky's works to the effect that "This article, as printed from the manuscript in the *Contemporary,* is some sort of strange re-vision." The editors had a certain moral right to desire that sort of re-vision. In the first place, no one was ready for such a violation of all the traditions of liberal journalism which associated certain names in literature with a number of issues that could only be raised *polemi-cally* in the press and that gave these names a symbolic meaning un-derstandable to everyone and requiring no further elaboration; and in the second place, it was conceivable that Belinsky would not stop at the first step in abolishing the liberal traditions of his party, a possibil-ity which threatened to leave the party itself without a cause in the future, leave it a complete orphan puzzled as to what to do. Many of his friends attributed the turnabout they observed in Belinsky to a breakdown of his mental powers and expressed the apprehension that he would undertake to destroy, piece by piece, the principles which had for so long and so vividly colored his own activity. And with it all, of course, the journal was losing one of the major emblems on its banner.

These apprehensions were unrealized but they were not alto-gether farfetched. Belinsky at times did display a grim outlook on his past literary life. I remember how once, after a particularly agonizing day of coughing and as he was preparing to go to bed, he suddenly began talking in a quiet, semimelancholic, but firm tone: "It is not a good thing to be sick, even worse to be dying, but to be sick and dy-ing with the thought that nothing will remain after you in the world —that's worst of all. What have I accomplished? There's the history of Russian poetry and literature I wanted to finish, but there's no sense thinking about that now. Perhaps someone might have remembered me in that case—but now what? I know what you want to say," he added, noticing that I made a motion to speak, "but, after all, two or three articles, half the space of which is taken up with contemporary trivialities already now of no use to anyone, do not comprise a leg-acy. And all the rest will perhaps come in handy for some historian of our epoch. . . ." And so on. . . .

I left him with a heavy feeling at heart. This doubt as to the value of his whole life's work had a tragic meaning for me. And it was impossible to write Belinsky's words off to the effect of his illness: he had obviously thought earlier about what he had uttered now— behind his words one had a sense of long preliminary deliberation. It became a matter of a man who enjoyed wide, popular renown, bur-dened, so to speak, with the sympathies of a whole generation whose mentor he had been—a matter of such a man's considering himself an apparition in the history of Russian culture and being unconvinced of the worth of the coin with which his influence and fame had been purchased. There was a great deal of unfairness toward himself in this evaluation, but involved as well were many newly arisen demands on a man of letters and, also, much grief—and not only of a personal kind.

But the interests of thought and development to which Belinsky constantly turned his attention always brought him out of his subjective mood, no matter how deep and sincere it might have been— brought him out into the world, to people and their affairs. That is just what happened now.

The now already completely forgotten book by Max Stirner, *Der Einzige und sein Eigentum* (*The Individual and His Property*), was then creating a sensation. The subject of the book, to give just the gist of it, consisted in the exaltation and glorification of egoism as the exclusive weapon whereby a private individual, beset on all sides with governmental rules and regulations, could and should defend himself against material and moral exploitation which legal statutes, society, and the state in general focussed on him. The book was one of a great number of attempts at the time to supplant existing bases of political life with others of a better make, and it achieved ends, as often happens with these attempts, exactly opposite the ones it had in mind. In advancing egoism to the level of a political prowess, Stirner's book was, as a matter of fact, working out a plutocracy (incidentally, the slight pun present in this word in Russian was more than once made use of by Belinsky in conversation).[118] After becoming acquainted with Stirner's book, Belinsky took closely to heart the problem it raised and tried to find its solution. It turned out that there was a very important moral question in it for him.

"It would be juvenile," he said, "to be frightened of the word 'egoism' itself. It has been proved that a man feels and thinks and acts invariably according to the law of egotistical urges, and indeed, he cannot have any others. The unfortunate thing is that mystical doctrines have brought the term into disgrace, giving it the meaning of the caterer to all the base passions and instincts in man, and we have already become accustomed to understand it in that sense. The word was dishonored for no good reason, since it denotes a completely natural, essential, and, therefore, legitimate phenomenon, and, moreover, includes, as does all that is essential and natural, the possibility of a moral inference. But what I see in this case is an author who retains the word's pejorative connotation, the connotation given it by mystics, and merely converts it into a beacon to illuminate mankind's way by claiming to have discovered in all the pejorative ideas attributed to the word new and different qualities of it and new rights of it to universal respect. He is simply doing the same thing with the word that the mystics had done, but only from the other end. That's where an unimaginable confusion originates: I suspect, for example, that the book will find enthusiastic appreciators in people of whose approval the author had no desire and stern critics in the people for whom the book was written. One cannot talk about egoism seriously without having set a *moral* principle at its basis in advance and without having made the attempt, thereupon, to expound it theoretically as a *moral* principle, which sooner or later it will surely become. . . ."

I have rendered the sense of what Belinsky said in the manner in which it impressed itself on my memory, using different words, of course, and not the ones he actually used. Repeatedly, on different occasions and at different times, he again returned to the problem that obviously held his attention. There could be no doubt that the problem was connected with the final alteration in the long profession of a moral credo that Belinsky carried on throughout his life, the gradual development of which we have already presented. The final statement of this credo is so noteworthy that it can justify the attempt to put his remarks together, with the help of the fragments that have remained intact in my memory, into one whole, with the necessary qualification, already made so often, that the exposition does not convey any idea at all of the ardor and the tone the author imparted to what he said or any idea of the form which his speech actually took.

"Crude, animal egoism," Belinsky deliberated, "cannot be advanced not only to an ideal, as the German author would have liked, but even to a simple rule of communal life. It is a dissociative, not an associative, principle in its elementary form and gains the quality of a vital and beneficial force only after careful elaboration. Who will not agree that the feeling of egoism, which governs the whole living world on earth, is exactly equally the source of all the horrors that occur on earth and the source of all the good it has seen! Therefore, if it is impossible to rid oneself of that feeling, if it is essential to come to grips with it at all points in the universe, in the political, civic, and private life of man, then it stands to reason that there is an obligation to make sense of it and to give it moral content. Exactly that was done for other, no less universal motivations—love, for example, sexual desire, ambition—and there is no reason to think that egoism is less capable of being transformed into a moral principle than the other, equally powerful natural urges which have already been so treated. But egoism will become a moral principle only when each individual person is able to join to his own private interests and needs also the interests of persons outside himself, of his country and of civilization as a whole, and to regard them as one and the same matter, and to devote to them the very concerns aroused in him by the necessity of self-preservation, self-defense, and so on. Such a generalization of egoism is in fact its transformation into a moral principle. We now already have examples in certain states of leading people who take as a personal insult any offense done to a man at the other end of the world and display a determination in prosecuting the unknown criminal, just as if it were a matter of rehabilitating their own honor. And it should be noted that, in this instance, love, sympathy, respect, and, in general, emotional attitudes play no role—protection is extended equally to people often held in utter contempt by their defenders—to people of the sort the latter would never allow in their company and, as sometimes happens, the value of whose very existence in the world they do not recognize. What is this, if not egoism which has been superlatively cultivated and has attained the sense of a strict moral principle? But such leading people are still quite rare—and they remain exceptions for the time being. The French use the term 'solidarity' to denote that ability to maintain oneself in others, and have even been trying to make a scientific term of it, introducing the concept it expresses into political economy as its indispensable branch. And what is solidarity, if not that same egoism thoroughly polished and freed of all the particles of raw material that went into its makeup! It is said that all ancient and modern philosophers and preachers of ideas have also taught from time immemorial that one should think more of one's fellow man than of oneself. That is true, but they did not so much teach as *command* one to believe their words, demanding sacrifices and promising no rewards for obedience other than the praises of conscience—and the success of these commandments was such that, as is well known, egoism exists to the present day everywhere in the rawest and most undeveloped form. What have we to say for ourselves? Despite age-old orders to be responsive to the sufferings of our fellow man, could we find more than a handful of persons among us who would take umbrage at blows that fell on any other than their own skins? The only firm and reliable bridle upon egoism is the one a man forges for himself as soon as he reaches a higher understanding of his own interests. The German author laments for no good reason the sacrifices which are now required from each individual person by the state and society, and endeavors for no good reason to defend that person by preaching a totally negativistic egoism: genuine egoism will always voluntarily bring enormous sacrifices to those forces that help ennoble its nature; and that is exactly what the task of every civilization is. State and society have in fact no other aim than the aim of furthering the conversion of a person's *animal* egoism into a sensitive, re-

sponsive spiritual instrument that vibrates and begins functioning at
the least suggestion of violence and foulness from wherever they might
come. . . ."

This hasty, superficial sketch of Belinsky's deliberations over Stirner's book shows that his final moral credo was now founded on the
effect of two inborn psychological forces in man which were later investigated in detail and given the appellation of *altruistic* forces. Belinsky anticipated by several years the psychologists' analysis, but
could not furnish it with all due purity and definiteness, which was
what likely prevented the exposition of his views in the press, where
not a trace of them is to be found. He was now apprehensive of direct, unmediated philosophizing and did not want to return to it after
his old experiences in that field.[119]

In close connection with Belinsky's attitude of mind was the appeal he directed to Russian artistic literature and belles lettres—to
undertake, as the final goal of their labors, service to social interests,
intercession on behalf of the lowest, deprived classes of society. The
appeal is found in Belinsky's last article before his death, written on
his return from abroad and published in the *Contemporary* of 1848,
"A View of Russian Literature in 1847." This survey constitutes something of a bridge thrown by the author from his generation to the
next—the new generation whose approach Belinsky already sensed in
terms of the problems emerging in people's minds. More than once,
even at an earlier time, Belinsky had given voice to those same ideas
—thoughts about the necessity of introducing motifs of a social character and importance into literature as a means of imparting to it
the proper degree of effectiveness and seriousness with the help of
which it could further extend the role of the paramount agent of culture belonging to it. Now the critic was inclined to require of literature exclusive concern with subjects of social importance and content
and to regard them as its sole aim. The difference in posing the problem was of no small importance and is to be explained, aside from
anything else, by the condition of minds, by the new wave of a spirit
of reform which society evinced.

It was at precisely that time that the peasant question tried for
the first time to come into the open, out from the unspoken wishes
and secret, closeted discussions: semiofficial committees formed, consisting of well-intentioned persons who were accounted partisans of
emancipation; projects to find the best solution of the problem were
undertaken and encouraged; economic studies bringing to light the
inviability of forced labor were sanctioned under the aegis of the Ministry of Public Properties, and so forth. All this activity, as is known,
lasted but a short time, weakened, firstly, by the secret counteractions

of disturbed interests hiding behind the banner of conservatism, and later coming to a complete halt under the effect of the violent storm of 1848 that crashed down on it from the banks of the Seine, devastating in Russia the rudiments of wholesome projects, predominantly. But before this unforeseen catastrophe, the favorable moment had come, it seemed, to show that all the truly great literatures of the ancient and modern worlds had no other aims than those society set itself in its striving toward a better intellectual and material structure. That is just what Belinsky did in his "View of Russian Literature in 1847," and, if we eliminate from the discourse that he engaged in then evaluation of the works of the epoch—the evaluation not being directly related to the issue—that discourse can be called the precursor and prototype of all subsequent discourses in the same spirit and direction delivered ten years later, with the exception of one feature in the earlier work which set Belinsky and his epoch sharply off from the time that came after them. This feature took shape out of a special conception of the very conditions of art, even though with à political tinge.

It can be positively asserted that when Belinsky was writing his article, considerations partly of a practical character flashed before his eyes. Imaginative literature could render assistance during, so to speak, the lying-in of the long-awaited peasant reform. No matter how persistent the rumors about the necessity of the reform having been acknowledged in official circles, no one spoke about it outrightly in the press. A number of considerations kept the reform from descending to the public square and taking the only road that would have led to its realization—the road of nationwide talk. Among these interfering considerations the weightiest was the following: not even the most modest and circumspect statement, not even the most unbiased and dispassionate investigation that might want to speak of the reasons for changing serfdom—that fundamental basis of Russian life—could get around characterizing the unwholesome aspects which it had engendered and which justified the attempts being made against its existence and against the practices it had instituted. How to avoid the bitter necessity of passing judgment on past times and, simultaneously, preserving intact the idea of reform which negated them was what constituted the crucial dilemma for the resolution of which all the energy of the innovators was wasted and which kept them constantly on the ground of cautious insinuations and hints with no compulsion to make an immediate decision. The literature of novels and stories, so-called imaginative literature, could render important service in the situation generally. It was not obliged to know about the existence of difficulties and of apprehensions in the matter of reform propaganda

and might forthrightly and boldly begin it in its own name. Camou-
flaging itself with its assumed indifference toward political problems,
concerned, to all appearances, with the most neutral of tasks in seeking out materials and dramatic plots for the public's entertainment,
this literature could enter by a secret door into the very midst of problems outside its own province, which it had already done more than
once before. *Notes of a Hunter, Notes of Doctor Krupov,* Dostoevski's *Poor Folk,* and, finally, the melodramatic *Anton Goremyka* and
The Village had already shown how works of pure imagination could
become treatises in psychology, ethnography, and legislation. Belinsky
believed that the time had come for literature to take upon itself all
the work that other agents had postponed under the pretext precisely
of inopportuneness and to prosecute in their stead the investigation of
the old conditions of Russian life that had to precede the final abolition and condemnation of them. Belinsky, at the same time, also became the supporter of the government, as can be seen in numerous
printed statements of his in 1847. The need for that kind of cooperation from literature soon passed, however, and, on the contrary, all the
work it had prepared for that purpose was even acknowledged as
dangerous. For all that, it remains certain that, if the movement had
continued, literature would have taken upon itself all the hatred of
riled interests and egotistical passions, would have given itself over to
malediction and vilification and would have at least freed others'
hands for the wholesome, beneficent, and the noble task of restoring
laws and justice to the country.

It is clear that both Belinsky's declaration of his credo and all his
intentions in this instance can be called *conservative,* in the broad
sense of the word, rather than revolutionary, as they were later reputed to be by the combined forces of the enemies of the press and of
reforms in the structure of Russian life. It would be appropriate to say
a few words here in general about the titles of "revolutionary and agitator" that Belinsky received from his enemies, both those contemporary with him and those who came after, all of them alike finding it
useful to disseminate that reputation. Not one of his obsessions, not
one of his judgments, either in print or in conversation, entitled anyone to see in him, as his detesters were so very desirous of doing, an
admirer of terrible social upheavals, a wild dreamer nurtured on
hopes for the downfall of the society in which he lived. Those outbursts of Belinsky's to which his defamers pointed in the interest of
confirming their words always were the products of a mind and heart
offended in their moral being, in their *idealistic* nature. Only in that
way could he alleviate his torments of mind and, at times, take vengeance for a rude affront to some humane feeling of his; but only mis-

apprehension or malicious mistrust could have supposed that behind all that lay a craving for immediate reprisals, sudden convulsions, and liberty for personal vengeance. Never, even in his thoughts, did he accept the defense of those destructive phenomena which sometimes pass through history and take effect in it with the blindness of natural forces, often without any moral foundation under them and comprising a sort of terrible and, at the same time, senseless improvisation of life exacerbated to the utmost degree by misfortunes and sufferings. Belinsky himself on numerous occasions, when talk turned to epochs of that sort, which the history of Western European nations called to mind, acknowledged that he would have been at such times a completely ineffectual and confused person, good only for increasing the number of the victims those times usually left in their wake. Everything lacking the imprint of an idea, lacking intellectual character and expression, instilled fear in him. Belinsky easily and rapidly understood daring ideas and daring decisions that stood in some, even remote, affinity with principles—and was nonplussed when faced with the *contingencies* of fate that so often set life on a course athwart man's expectations. He never put any store by them and never included them in the sphere of his conceptions. Remaining the same idealist in his comprehension of the conditions of historical progress as he was in his own life, he was distinguished by an inability to acknowledge the necessity for telling lies even when doing so would have had a soothing effect on agitated minds; he felt an irrepressible aversion for catering to shallow people and trivial matters, even if they were active within the ranks of his own party. Belinsky did not have the least, the rudimentary qualities of the revolutionary and agitator that some people wanted to repute him to be, and still do repute him even now, people in dread of his honorable candor and the inner truth of all his convictions. Instead, he had all the features of a true man and representative of the 1840's—and among these features, one very prominent feature to which I now pass on.

This feature consisted, as has already been remarked on, in the special conception of art as a vital element for forging the psychological aspect of human life and, through life, for developing in people an ability to perceive and create ideal notions. It was with this feature that Belinsky drew a sharp demarcating line between his epoch and the one following it, with which, otherwise, it had many points of contact. By dissolving and obliterating the old aesthetic aphorism of art for art's sake, by transferring all of literature's task to the grounds of service to society, by placing art and the imagination in the vanguard, so to speak, of the valiant army of volunteers fighting for high-minded ideas, which meant—in terms of the critic's thinking—to fight for the properly understood interests of each individual in the state, Belinsky wanted this force to be equipped with a dependable weapon, and that kind of weapon for him was always poetry and creativity. He admitted the role of simple exposés of evil, of simple, stark negations, but he regarded them as something like hand-to-hand combat, which might be indispensable in certain instances but which never by itself decides the matter and never by itself overthrows enemies. Only creative talent overthrows enemies or, at least, inflicts fatal wounds on them, since it alone could gather the millions of atrocious contingencies running through life into an integrated, powerfully impressive picture, and it alone was able to extract from the thousands of persons arousing our indignation to one or another degree the full-bodied type in which they were all reflected. There is no need to repeat here what he said on this matter, but it is essential to note and bear in mind the basic principle of his literary-political theory. That principle was the fundamental conviction that the creation of artistic types indicates through both its positive and negative aspects the road which the development of society has taken and the road it should take in the future. Clear signs of this conviction were left in the critic's article "A View of Russian Literature in 1847," where anybody can find it.[120]

I have already said that the article was the last link in the development of a period in our literature to which were joined and by which were fastened the first links of the new trend following it. There was no discontinuity in this case, as, it seems, there is none in any of the epochs of our Russian history, but the character of things was marked, in the beginning, by significant omissions and dissimilarities. Ten years after Belinsky's death, the doctrine on the social aims of art was accepted from among his theories of beauty and all the additional postulates of his system were put aside.

The new generation, which had managed to survive the ominous interval of time from 1848 to 1856, undertook an investigation of the forms of Russian life, its inadequacies and its antiquated practices, as soon as the possibility was presented of speaking to people about themselves.[121] A period of exposés ensued. It is understandable that the generation undertook this task using the means of production it had already available to it and had no reason to expect the arrival of elegant and refined armament (les armes de luxe) of art for the initiation of their work. With the passage of time, hands became so accustomed to the simple tools of belletristic manufacture that many people, even gifted connoisseurs in the matter, began even to doubt the value of installing more advanced tools of production which had the disadvantage besides that not everyone knew how to use them and how to earn his bread with them. One had to get used to living without creativity, inventiveness, poetry—and this was done during the existence and full-blown activity of such artists as Ostrovski, Goncharov, Dostoevski, Pisemsky, Turgenev, Leo Tolstoy, and Nekrasov, who continued to remind the public about them with every one of their works!

Criticism came to the aid of the perplexed public. It is common knowledge that, following the first glimmers of our revived literary activity, we witnessed the onset of a period of *regularization* of the convictions, opinions, and trends which had become confused during the long period of stagnation. The Russian literary world still remembers with what energy, with what talent and grasp of its objectives the work of bringing ideas and concepts to order was carried out. The historical and political sciences, philosophical and ethical theories were summoned to its aid. All the old banners and mottoes, under which people had been accustomed to gather, were opposed with different and new ones; but through it all, art consistently proved to be the one thing least amenable to regularization, always being by its very nature the least obedient pupil of theory. Only stringent religious systems had succeeded in subordinating art and making it the obedient servant of one dominant trend, but even in that case not fully, inasmuch as it was impossible fully to quell art's tendencies to change paths, to distract attention by its capricious ways, to make light of the school and to devise its own solutions of problems. Art was what comprised the element of disharmony during the period following Belinsky. To allow it the privilege of leading a life apart and completely on its own at a time when collective and obligatory labor in a common spirit and for a common cause was being proposed for everyone, meant to risk finding art blocking the way and in opposition to oneself. Strict discipline in criticism for the analysis and concomitant evaluation of the artists who had accepted its program and who had subordinated themselves to it became a necessity. However strict the discipline introduced by criticism might have been, it could not prevent society from being captivated by uncertified examples of creative art. It was then the decision was made to move art altogether to the background, to explain the genesis of its laws and its beloved procedures by the helplessness of a mentality which had not grown strong enough to be able to understand and expound the phenomena of life directly and simply. The scope of occupations condescendingly reserved for pure art was defined with extraordinary frugality. What was reserved for it was the communication of fleeting impulses of the heart, caprices of the imagination, states of sensibility, the shades and colors of physical nature—everything that lay outside science and exact investigation. All art's other claims to an active role in the development of society were eliminated, serious themes were taken out of its province and distributed among sections of philosophy, scientific criticism, and the specialized studies appropriate to them. Thinking society was painstakingly protecting itself against the influence of the very agent that most successfully prepares the soul of man for the reception of seeds for civic as well as other kinds of ideals. From time to time, of course, protests against this injustice arose, and voices rang out, calling attention to the importance of artistic works of literature in the matter of forming characters, of turning minds in the direction of moral goals, and of raising the level of ideas, but they passed without making a mark. And just what they deserved! All those attempts to call to mind the effect of the ideal and the beautiful on people's hearts, on their mentality, on all their acts large and small, could not have had any success, if for no other reason, even discounting the greater or lesser degree of their dialectical feebleness, than that the new generation had first of all to bring its cause to its end, to express all its own essential meaning, and then, and only then, could it look back and fill itself in with all that was lacking.

It would seem that different conceptions of the problems with regard to art ought not to have drawn an especially sharp dividing line between two time periods of national development, especially when they had so many points of contact in everything else. And nevertheless, these problems were sufficient to weaken significantly the bonds connecting them, to give each of them a particular expression of its own and to separate them one from the other at a considerable distance. This happened not because there proved to be variance in the matter of defining the beautiful theoretically, but because there proved to be a difference in *world outlook*. Arguments about art, as about all truly great problems of science and civilization generally, are especially instructive for the fact that, whatever their relative importance might be, underneath them, flowing like an invisible stream, is always one or another world outlook. It should be mentioned in this connection that the history of the genesis of various outlooks, which in their time answered the needs of deeply felt strivings of whole generations among us, has rights to our fullest respect, whatever our personal standpoint regarding its content might be.

Now that thirty years have passed since Belinsky's death, clear judgment can be made about his world outlook without discomposure over the influx of occasional attitudes that sometimes colored him in their particular, but short-lived, tints. Belinsky's whole outlook consisted in the conception of life and civilization as forces ordained to furnish man with the *fullness of spiritual and material existence.* He judged the relative merit and importance of epochs, of people and their works, according to the quantity of ideas and notions able to promote the realization of that fullness of rational existence which hovered before his eyes in the form of an ideal. Any reservation, omission, or concealment of any one of the elements essential for the attainment of that fullness, whether a premeditated act or the consequence of oversight, equally aroused his critical alertness. He himself constantly and conscientiously undertook the analysis and definition of genuine and spurious psychological and social agents claiming to satisfy all the needs of the mind and of development. In his evaluation of the one and the other kind, he was liable to be excessively excitable at times and to classify their colors, under the influence of enthusiasm or indignation, with a certain lack of proportion, but the documents on which his judgment was based were always authentic ones, fortified with the evidence of history and by rigorous investigations of the science concerned with the ideal and real needs of human nature. The satisfaction of these needs, without intentional exclusions prompted by the calculations and requirements of various theoretical constructs, was what he considered the task of civilization and its mission. Turning from general expression to the particular applications of this same outlook, it should be said that Belinsky demanded of each idea, image, doctrine, and literary work in general that came to his attention a fullness of content eliminating the very possiblity of questions and supplements. But such totally integrated manifestations of art and thought were rare occurrences, and for the most, one had to make do with works which were far more notable for their number of omissions rather than of discoveries in the area of themes they had selected. Strictly speaking, all his literary criticism—no matter how hard it tried to hide behind diplomatic qualifications and evasions, to which Belinsky, as the times required, had recourse no less than anybody else—was, in fact, nothing but a series of reinstatements, restorations, and justifications for various forgotten or artificially debased features of civilization, psychological and cultural necessities of individual and communal existence. This work became part of Belinsky's habitual thought and—what is particularly important—was often directed by him onto his own person, which fact readily explains his frequent changes of points of view on things that so astonished and perturbed his enemies.

It is common knowledge that masterful works of both artistic and scientific literature possess the quality of providing precious little profit for scavengers of the author's distractions and oversights, the quality of exhausting their subject and presenting such a stronghold of inferences and conclusions that its destruction, or the destruction of even its smallest part, would require almost the same power and ability as was in the possession of its creator himself. It was over works of that type, both of the ancient and modern world, in translation and in the original, that Belinsky spent his days and nights: for him they never grew old; no matter how often he reread them, they could never say their final word to him. As in the case of an ascetic of a different order of ideas, he felt the necessity of approaching the altar of great works every day and of immersing himself in the mysteries brought to pass on it. Constant contact with the great specimens of scientific and imaginative literature exalted his spirit to such a degree that people felt themselves better and freer of trivial concerns in his presence and came away from him with purified feelings and kindly remembrances, whatever may have been the nature of their conversation with him. Figuratively speaking, people always presented themselves before him as if for a *ceremonious occasion*, in their best attire, and there was no appearing in his presence as a moral sloven without incurring his indignation and his bitter and burning remonstrances. Such was the man who first pointed out to Russian literature the way to realism, even, I believe, before Europe gave it thought, and who now was summoning that same literature to the political arena, to concerns with problems of a civic, social character. What was it that motivated this aesthetician par excellence? Of course, primarily his noble heart in search of means to render assistance to the primary, urgent needs of progress, a progress that had still not even begun for the mass of his fellow countrymen, and, after that, the whole selfsame search for the fullness of an ideal and real model for life and thought. Behind this supposed literary activity, there opened for him the whole vast field of European civilization with its elaborations and accretions gained over the course of so many centuries. He never took his eyes from it. Not a single one of the experiments—old or new—that had been applied there, not a single positive result already given by those experiments would this passionate soul have been willing to do without. The final goal of all his requirements and guidance consisted in forging Russian life into a full-fledged worker for enlightenment, in endowing it with all the powers and educative principles which formed Europe's best and surest workers. It would hardly seem necessary to add that all those far-ranging plans proved in reality to be a daydream; but no one will be in a position to judge Belinsky's age aright unless he understands and acknowledges that all daydreams and fantasies of that type were at the time positive and very serious matters.

I return to my story.

The time was approaching for the course of treatment to end and for us to leave Salzbrunn. Belinsky was feeling much better, his coughing decreased, his nights became more restful—he was already making remarks about the boredom of life in a backwater. Almost on the eve of our departure from Salzbrunn for Paris, I received a totally unexpected letter from N. V. Gogol, who made it known that the publication of *Correspondence with Friends* had brought a pack of troubles down on him, and that, though not expecting I would respond favorably to the book, he would like, nevertheless, to know my real opinion of it, as the opinion of a man who seemed not to suffer from conceit and self-worship. This was the first letter I had received from him after that superciliously didactic letter of his I have already spoken about and the first after our brief meeting in Paris and Bamberg. It quite clearly evinced on Gogol's part a desire for, if not commiseration and support, at least a quiet talk. At the end of the letter Gogol suddenly made mention of Belinsky and added that he was sending him friendly regards together with a letter addressed directly to him in which he reproached him for his angry review of *Correspondence* in the second issue of the *Contemporary*. That was what provoked that famous letter of Belinsky's concerning Gogol's last stage, a letter of a sort to which Gogol had not yet been exposed, despite the host of pens engaged in educing the faults of *Correspondence* and in rebuking and reviling its author. When I began reading Gogol's letter out loud, Belinsky listened in a completely disinterested and abstracted way—but after scanning Gogol's lines addressed to him, Belinsky flared up and said: "So he doesn't understand why people are so angry with him—someone must spell it out to him—I shall answer him."

He understood Gogol's challenge.

That very day, the small room adjoining Belinsky's bedroom, furnished with a small couch and a circular table in front of it—the table on which we engaged in our rather dreary after-dinner exercises in piquet—was converted into a study. An inkwell and paper made their appearance on the circular table, and Belinsky settled down to write his letter to Gogol, as if it were a piece of work to be done, and went about it with the same ardor with which he used to produce his urgent journal articles in Petersburg. It was indeed an article, but one written under a different sky. . . .

For three days in a row Belinsky omitted climbing upstairs to my attic room on returning home from the waters and passed directly into his improvised study. He was reticent and preoccupied during all that time. Each morning, after the obligatory cup of coffee awaiting him in his study, he donned his summer surtout, sat down on the couch, and bent over the table. He continued working until our one o'clock dinner, after which he did no work. It will not seem surprising that he took three mornings to compose his letter to Gogol, if I add that he often broke away from his work when intensely agitated by it and rested from it, slumped back on his couch. Moreover, the very process of writing the letter was rather complicated. Belinsky started by writing a draft of the letter in pencil on various scraps of paper, then wrote it out legibly and neatly on clean paper and, after that, made a copy of the finished text for himself. It was clear that he attached great importance to the matter he was engaged in and seemed to understand that he was composing a document over and above private, intimate correspondence. When the work was finished, he sat me down at his circular table and read me his composition.

I was alarmed both at the tone and the content of this reply, and, of course, not on Belinsky's account, because it was then still impossible to foresee any special consequences from correspondence between acquaintances abroad; I was alarmed on Gogol's account, for he was the one supposed to receive the reply, and I could vividly imagine his condition the moment he would begin to read that terrible tongue-lashing. The letter contained not only a denunciation of his opinions and views—it attempted to bring to light the vanity and repulsiveness of all Gogol's ideals, all his concepts of good and honor, all the moral bases of his existence, as well as of the brutish character of the milieu which he had come forward to defend. I wanted to explain to Belinsky the full implications of his impassioned discourse, but he knew them better than I did, as it turned out. "What is one to do?" he said. "One must use every means to save people from a man gone mad, even if the madman be Homer himself. As for offending Gogol, I never can offend him as much as he offended me in my soul and in my faith in him."

The letter was sent and, after that, there was nothing more to do in Salzbrunn. We left for Dresden en route to Paris.

Anticipating myself for a moment, I shall say here that on arrival in Paris, Herzen, who had already been expecting us, came to the Hotel Michot at which we stopped, and Belinsky immediately told him about the challenge he had received from Gogol and about the reply he had sent him. Then he read him the copy of his letter. During the entire reading of the letter, already well known to me, I was in the next room where, seizing an opportune moment, Herzen dashed in to whisper in my ear: "That is a thing of genius—indeed, that, I believe, is his testament."

CHAPTER

[XXXVI]

BELINSKY'S UNSOCIABLENESS seemed to grow greater abroad, as time
went on, instead of decreasing. He lost all desire to make contact with
people, even contact of the momentary sort with strangers; on the
contrary, the further time advanced, the more engrossed he became
in thoughts of his family, which definitely overshadowed for him the
whole foreign scene. Exception was made in the case of two- or three-
year-old German tots—he gazed at them eagerly, and many a time he
would point out to me some particularly outstanding specimen, adding in a low voice: "I had one of just that kind at home." In short, his
family became for him a cozy corner in which he mentally shut himself up the instant the possibility for doing so was presented. What is
most curious is that he wanted to leave the world and the people
around him ignorant of that refuge of his, and when talk turned to it,
he would respond in an indifferent way, only making no effort to conceal what it was impossible to conceal—his adoration of his children.

This biographical detail is, I believe, worthwhile stopping to consider. Belinsky married in 1843, at a time when the romantic period of
his life had already passed and when he had become entrenched in
the idea that he had nothing further to expect from fate and chance,
that he was doomed not to know the sympathy of a woman's heart
both on account of his supposedly unattractive exterior and of qualities of his temperament which were supposedly not at all ingratiating
to the feminine nature. It is a remarkable fact, however, that, from as
far back as 1838, he did not cease inveighing and lashing out against
the solitude to which he appeared to have so decisively assented. In
his eyes and in his diagnosis, a strict solitude, if true to itself, was an
unnatural, artificial, and, therefore, also an immoral phenomenon no
matter what the attitude of mind from which it originated. Exceptions
to the rule, such as the artist Ivanov and people like him, he, too,

acknowledged, but he thought that even in their case one had to judge only according to the importance of the idea for the sake of which they had made the sacrifice. He abandoned his own system of solitude the instant a pretext for doing so presented itself—and abandoned it with an incredible haste that astonished his friends. People at the time explained this fact by his having encountered a devotion which had dealt a blow to his skeptical conception of himself, withstanding the test of a considerable period of time. The unexpectedness of such a discovery was so strong that it led him to the idea of restructuring his whole way of life. Be that as it may, he put his decision into action under the puzzled gaze of friends who foresaw in this step new difficulties in life for him. Once married, Belinsky did not, however, relinquish his views on *affinity of souls and aspirations* as the sole element making the state of matrimony legitimate, and confessed that his own marriage lacked ideal motivation and was devoid of poetry. He expressed this opinion without embarrassment in front of everybody, out loud, and often, and here the dignity of the reply he received to his outbursts must be acknowledged. The wisely contrived or temperamentally ingrained dispassion of the most interested party concerned allowed these protestations and critical observations on the accomplished fact to flow freely; they did not interfere in the slightest with the other party's carrying on the business of a family in an even spirit, steadily, calmly, and correctly. Toward the end, with the onset of debilitation of his physical energies, Belinsky was exposed to that invincible, enormous, leveling mightiness of *monogamous* cohabitation which quells all a man's transports, dreams, and fantasies. In his domestic hearth Belinsky now saw, as it were, the healing power for his sick heart, and in the hand that calmly served him—as it were, the hand that held him in the world.

What now became for him life's primary blessing was that busy tranquility, that vigilant quietness of domestic life which enabled him to think his own fervent thoughts to himself, to be sick at heart without interference. The sharing of bitter thoughts and feeling oftentimes becomes an incitement to them, and Belinsky no longer had need of that. He had need of something different, namely, of unobtrusive but sympathetic watchfulness over his expiring life. Belinsky's family knew how to arrange watchfulness of the kind that did not make itself felt and never questioned him about the course of his illness, did not solicit his acknowledgments or expression of faith, and did not force him to recount his sufferings. It had accustomed him to an existence reduced to the greatest possible simplicity and adapted as much to the condition of his mind as to his physical condition. It is understandable that after that the usual features associated with a journey—namely, crowds of people, the diversity of life, the unremitting impingement of external phenomena on one's attention—now seemed to him intolerable by the fact of their constituting a new and superfluous addition to his own personal world, an addition he did not at all desire. That is why he wrote long letters from abroad, often furtively, not to his friends in Petersburg, but to his wife, to the woman who, in his opinion, was at a total loss when it came to a sphere of ideas the least bit different from ideas to which she was used; and that is also why this poet at heart, reared on the reading and study of masters, but already a tired man, saw neither the monuments of culture nor the handiwork of nature's creativity on his travels, and often stood before them mute, abstracted, obviously engrossed completely in other thoughts having nothing to do with them.

Belinsky felt a particular aversion to casual conversations which so often are struck up with strangers during travel. This aversion of his sometimes came out with rather comic effects. At one of the stations en route to Dresden, a very animated and, to all appearances, good-natured Pole jumped into our carriage. Upon hearing Russian spoken, he turned to his neighbor, who, unfortunately, happened to be Belinsky, and began the following brief conversation with him which I transcribe word for word:

"You are Russian?"

"Yes."

"Direct from Russia?"

"Absolutely direct."

"And, of course, you speak French well?"

"Not at all."

"Only German, then?"

"I don't know any German, either."

"You mean," persisted the loquacious Pole, now with a saddened look, "you speak only Russian?"

"A little, and even that unwillingly," replied Belinsky, turning away and leaning back in the corner of the carriage. The look of astonishment on the questioner's face had to be seen: I could not help laughing and deflected the conversation to myself, starting over from the beginning. . . .

We stopped in Dresden for a week. Belinsky ordered some linen made for himself and, for the most part, lay on the couch in his room with a book in hand. He took desultory strolls along the bank of the Elbe, looked at the city disinterestedly, stopped in at the Grüne-Gewölbe, where the luxuries and expensive children's toys aroused his attention with the effect almost of making him indignant, and, finally, visited the Picture Gallery once or twice. There, following the established custom of tourists, he, too, sat in front of the "Sistine Madonna," but he came away with an impression entirely contrary to the one people usually experienced in this situation and later described. He was the first, apparently, not to go into ecstasies over her celestial tranquility and equanimity, but, on the contrary, to be horrified by them, which was also an indirect acknowledgment of the master who had created the type. In the same Dresden Gallery, he experienced a second aesthetic hardship: he came across that little chef d'oeuvre by Rubens, "The Judgment of Paris," in which Venus and her two unclad rivals were represented by three Flemish beauties painted from life with astounding faithfulness and realism. Belinsky, accustomed to conceive Venuses and Greek women as the realization of ideal beauty on earth, found himself standing before three naked matrons, bursting with health, well-nourished, and bounteous, like the orchards and gardens of their homeland—the mothers of robust burgomasters and manufacturers. This realism in painting aroused revulsion in the ardent admirer of realism in literature. He could not bring himself to appreciate the picture despite his having had pointed out to him the stunningness of its colors, the animation of those bodies which seemed still to give off a warmth, as did also the velvet brocaded garments of Utrecht make that they had just discarded, the harmony, the relief of the picture's parts—Belinsky stood perplexed and continued to call Rubens a butchers' poet. Only a little later, when he was shown, in a large engraving, another picture by the same master, "The Triumph of Bacchus"—that feast in which all the figures, from the inebriated tiger to the last of the bacchantes, are seized equally by the intoxication of the grape vine and the boundless joy of young life discovering the possibility of delight on earth—only then was Belinsky struck with amazement at the power of composition, of boldness of motifs, of the idea brought to the utmost degree of its élan and expression. When he was informed that the picture belonged to the same hand as had produced "The Judgment of Paris," Belinsky good-naturedly observed: "Well, I guess I pulled a boner. But, then, you can't expect much from me—after all, I'm an oaf when it comes to such things."

I had occasion more than once to encounter misconceptions of that type later on, as well, and to hear—from Herzen, for example—witty sallies against the manner of Catholic painters in placing saints on clouds in a *sitting position,* in bringing angels down to earth and obliging them to play harps, lutes, and violins, and so on and so forth. All this seemed extremely unnatural and monstrous to the very people who were not the least disturbed when, in literary works, they encountered descriptions of dreams, of the secret interviews of lovers, of momentary inner sensations, all of which should have remained, in point of fact, a secret also from the authors who themselves could not have seen or heard anything of the sort.

The fact seems to be beyond doubt that for an understanding of creations both of literary and plastic art, it is essential to habituate oneself to their customary devices, to reconcile oneself to the illogicalness of some of them and to acknowledge in them authoritative power for their own idea. But acquiescence of that sort is especially disagreeable when it appears not in the form of a habit acquired long ago but is required from a man above all as a principle of wisdom without which there is no access to making judgments about works of art. Perhaps that fact is what prompted Belinsky's curious decision, when, having reached Cologne, he had no desire to see the famous apse of its cathedral, the cathedral itself being still under construction then. He looked at it in passing, from the outside, when we were already on our way to the railroad station, and only said: "A huge place, no question about it, for the Catholic idea that is supposed to be dwelling in it."

Paris proved to be more than Belinsky could tolerate. From his very first days there, the feverish movement of the crowd, the noisy cafés and stores, brilliantly illuminated both by day and by night, the commotion and the din which arose early in the morning, the cross fire of talk ringing out from all sides—all this weakened him sooner than I had expected. After having driven through the streets and squares of Paris, having attended a few times (briefly) its operas and theaters, he felt almost instantly a need to hide away somewhere from that unabating fête. He found two refuges: at the desk in his room where he spent much time writing a great deal to his wife, first, and at the Herzens', where M. F. Korsh and his hostess surrounded him with their solicitudes and succeeded in smoothing away the wrinkles caused by fatigue at the spectacle of madly rushing people whose aims and intentions it was impossible to guess.

The impression produced on him by Paris was, in general, one, so to speak, of sad surprise. "Everything in it," Belinsky maintained, "has to assume huge dimensions: greed, vice and silliness every bit as much as the cultivation of ideas and knowledge, noble impulses and aspirations. But getting to the bottom of this quagmire and finding out what more it has in it—that is no easy matter." He repeatedly questioned his friends: Does civilization really need such vast and stupefying centers of population as Paris, London, and others?

Of course, Belinsky's acquaintances hastened to reveal to him the sources from which the activity of Paris, which so struck him, drew sustenance: I mean—its museums, lectures, meetings, and so forth. Belinsky obediently followed his guides but obviously regarded doing so as something of the fulfillment of a duty, like the formal *calls* one pays one's superiors on holidays. It was easy to detect his look of gratitude each time he was liberated from this special kind of hasty, on-the-spot instruction and was treated instead to a summary account of one or another point of interest in literature, science, or life. He was interested most of all in the question as to what result was to be expected in the future from all these beginnings and to what positive conclusions one might come regarding the further development of civilization at that very moment on the basis of existing data—in short, how great was the sum of universal human hopes borne inside all this visible culture? A great many answers were received, answers, for the most part, of the most favorable kind for future generations, with the exception only of Herzen's opinion on the subject, which did not reveal any particular faith in the power of contemporary people and of their capacity for progress. Belinsky was thus left between two opposite judgments about the subject that interested him. Not considering himself adequately qualified to decide the question by his own thought, he left Paris with no clear notion as to what it was the city was up to. And indeed, who then could have seen clearly what was being hatched in it or have foretold what the immediate, oncoming day of history would bring it?

In general, the more tolerant Belinsky became toward the Russian world, the more severe and demanding was his attitude toward the foreign one. He had an experience that was later repeated numerous times with many of our most zealous Westerners when they became tourists; they regarded Europe reproachfully, as if it had not kept the promises it had showered on them in secret. This not unusual state of affairs is easily explained. A dry, businesslike, often limited and ignorant, and always small-minded, rascally crowd of new people was the first to meet the travelers abroad, and held them, as tended to happen, for rather long periods of time in its milieu before the travelers moved on to phenomena and practices of a higher tenor of life. But by then they were already disposed to demand that the latter account for all the banality they had already seen and to place upon it the responsibility for all the repulsiveness and paltriness which had not been obliterated by its influence. Belinsky was not exempt from the common fate of travelers. Under the effect of the tedious process of his treatment and, especially, under the effect of the spectacle of the enormous human mass without the least suspicion of the ideas and principles proclaimed to the world in its name, Belinsky gave a grim account of his life and experiences abroad to his friends in Moscow—and gave them a scare. They believed that he might return home a skeptic with respect to European culture in general and that, in his continued work, he might, in such a frame of mind, even if unwillingly and despite himself, promote the spread of the disdainful opinion of Western civilization already existing in Russian society. These apprehensions were communicated even to Belinsky himself. One of those concerned—V. P. Botkin—wrote:

Moscow. July 19, 1847

Today I received your letter from Dresden, my dear Vissarion. . . . I understand the disgust you feel for Germany, Belinsky—I understand it very well, even though I do not share it. I cannot live in Germany because the character of German social life does not suit either my convictions or my sympathies, because its ways are gross, because it has so little proper sense of the real and the actual, and so forth, but I do not pronounce the sort of verdict on it that you do—and with regard to the good and bad aspects of nations I hold a somewhat eclectic point of view. I understand your boredom; I, even healthy, would have become ill from boredom, after having spent a month and a half in Germany, and you, what is more, spent time in Silesia, in Salzbrunn! Paris will, I hope, uphold its own. But why should you see there only constitutional scoundrels? There is much there that is far more vital and far more interesting. Political eyeglasses do not always show things the way they really are, especially if the eyeglasses are made out of doctrines accepted sight unseen. Often these homegrown doctrines are what make people recite a lot of nonsense (which Louis Blanc's book demonstrates; I am in complete agreement with your wise opinion about him), and watch out for trouble if one of our sort comes to a country with a doctrine memorized in advance. . . . After receiving your letter, I ran out at once to share it with Korsh and I am sending it to Granovsky today. . . . Did you receive a letter from Gogol? Talk has it that the letter shows that Gogol has finally lost his grasp on the simplest things and matters. . . . I have just received your letter to me back from Granovsky; he is unhappy about it and is afraid that you might start writing about Germany and France from your present point of view of them once you get back to Russia. Indeed—that would be a great triumph for our ignoramuses and vipers. I expect that Nekrasov has already informed you about censorship conditions and that you, of course, know already that G. Sand now will not be read in Russian. . . ."

It was not difficult for Belinsky's companions, to whom his Moscow friends also turned with inquiries as to his state of mind and feelings, to explain that at the basis of all his censure of foreign life lay not at all a feeling hostile to Europe, but, rather, a tender feeling toward it, but only put out of countenance by the fact that it had to hold back, to keep itself in check, to restrain its outpourings.

This attitude, however, did not pass from Belinsky without leaving a trace.

So far as concerns the cerebral stimulation of the Russian liberal colony with its interest about arranging the best possible intellectual comfort for itself, in which connection, of course, the handy paraphernalia of modern discoveries could not have been overlooked— there is nothing really to say. Belinsky paid no attention to that colony as being something already well known to him by experience—at home.[122]

We heard that later, when already back in Petersburg, Belinsky received the news about the 1848 Revolution in Paris almost with horror. It struck him as something totally unexpected, something deleterious for the reputation of those intellects who had been concerned with the study of the social situation in France and had failed to see the revolution approaching. He bitterly upbraided his Parisian friends who had not so much as hinted in his presence about the possibility of an imminent political upheaval, which, as it turned out, was in fact the real business of the epoch. This lack of foresight, in Belinsky's opinion, turned people either into slaves or into defenseless victims of external chance alone. His reproaches were just, but one must add that the final form of the upheaval was something totally unexpected even for those who had organized it.

Incidentally, Herzen's wife, by instinct of her woman's heart, understood Belinsky, on his arriving in Paris, better and sooner than anybody else. She gathered together a small and well-selected collection of "educational" toys, which even then were available in Paris, though without any systematization of them, and gave it to Belinsky as a present for his daughter. Among the presents were zoological picture books with magnificent drawings of the animals of all the zones of the earth, a book which Belinsky could not stop admiring. He dreamed about educating his daughter in the natural and exact sciences. Incidentally, he found at that time a toy for himself, as well. Strolling through the streets one day, he had come upon, in a store selling ready-made clothing, a strikingly decorative dressing gown with enormous red patterns on a base of white foulard—and he fell in love with it. The dressing gown was one of those *display* articles that stores order expressly for the purpose of flabbergasting a passerby and causing him to stop in front of its shiny windows. Belinsky felt a kind of attraction to this item, hesitated a long time, and finally bought it, attempting in all seriousness to convince us that it was something he absolutely needed for his morning labors in Petersburg. This detail deserves mention because that ill-fated dressing gown caused both him and myself much trouble afterward.

As the time approached for Belinsky's departure for Russia, about which he had already begun dreaming practically from the first day of his appearance in Paris, the question arose as to the means by which it would be most convenient to send him back home, since it was impossible to leave it up to Belinsky himself on account of his lack of experience and his inability to speak foreign languages. The decision had already been made when the possibility presented itself of supplying Belinsky a trustworthy companion and, at the same time, to render a service to an honorable old man who carried out the important function in Paris of *portier*—the doorkeeper in our building. The old man, very severe to *simple* residents who returned home late at night and devoted with a sort of unqualified warmth to his Russian boarders, was called Frederick. He was a Saxonian German by birth, had taken part in the 1812 Russian campaign with Napoleon's army and had become one of the orderlies to the military governor of Moscow, Marshal Davout, which is what enabled him to return safe and sound to Paris, where he settled. He willingly, especially when tipsy, told stories about the horrors he had seen enroute to and from Russia and in Moscow. In addition, he burned with desire to visit the place of his birth (somewhere near Leipzig) where he had not been for over thirty-five years; and when I offered him, on condition that he first take my friend as far as Berlin, the chance, at our expense, to visit his fatherland and then to return back to his position, which, in the meanwhile, his wife (a large and majestic woman) would keep for him, the old man just sort of squatted, placed his hands between his knees, and, jumping up and down slightly, could only mumble several times over: *"Oui, Monsieur! Ah, Monsieur! . . ."* A reliable travel companion for Belinsky had been found who spoke both German and French and who was ready to guard his person and, especially, his purse like the honor of the flag or a password received from his commander.

Gogol's reply to Belinsky's letter from Salzbrunn also arrived in Paris. Gogol sadly commented that once again the old Russian story had been repeated whereby one groundless conviction or blind obsession unfailingly produced another from the opposite side that was even riskier and more exaggerated; he sent his critic wishes for peace of mind and restoration of his energies and interlarded all of this with thoughts about the gravity of the century concerned with the idea of a more expansive edifice of life than there had ever been before. What he meant by the edifice the letter did not say, and it was generally not notable for clarity of exposition. Belinsky harbored no malice or hatred for the author of *Correspondence* personally, read his letter with feeling and only remarked: "What muddled language; I imagine he must be very unhappy at this moment."

The day of Belinsky's departure from Paris, after preliminary consultation with his friends, was finally set. The evening prior to it, he sat again for awhile in his favorite spot, on the marble steps of the terrace encircling Place de la Concorde, and pensively gazed at the Luxor Obelisk in the middle of the plaza, at Tuilleries, the facade and dome of which loomed up from its grove of chestnut trees, at the bridge over the Seine, at the palace of the Bourbons behind it, which had been turned into the Chamber of Deputies, calling to mind the terrible scenes and dramas that had once been played out in these places. Late at night, after saying farewell to Herzen, we returned home. Everything there had been packed and made ready with the help of Frederick, and at five o'clock in the morning the following day we were already on our feet and, at five-thirty, in the coach that was to deliver us to the terminal of the Far Northern Railroad. When we were already approaching the terminal and some quarter of an hour before the train was due to leave, it occurred to me to ask Belinsky: "Did you take your dressing gown?" The poor traveler shuddered and responded in a hollow voice: "I forgot it—it was in your room on the couch." "Well," I replied, "there's nothing much to worry about, I'll send it on to you in Berlin." But to Belinsky it was an unbearable hardship to let the dressing gown get out of his hands. One had to see the sad expression he made and hear the imploring tone of voice with which he said: "Isn't there a chance now?" There was no refusing him without destroying in his mind all the pleasant impressions of the journey. I summoned up Russian dumb luck to our aid, stopped the coach and sent Frederick off to dash full speed back home on the first available hackney, to pick up the dressing gown and meet us at the station. It would have been simpler to postpone the trip until the next day, but I, too, was seized with a kind of excitement and a desire to surmount the difficulty at whatever cost. Russian dumb luck, however, played us false this time. I had hardly managed to get Belinsky a ticket and to make his baggage arrangements when the third bell rang—and no Frederick. It is a well-known fact that French railroad stations are, or were, ruled with military discipline, so that, exposed to the shouts and commands of the conductors, it always seemed to me that I was rather on the bastion of some fortress than the peaceful terminal of a railroad. On this occasion the bastion commanders were even severer than usual. When the third bell had rung, they drove a crowd of passengers through the wide open gate to the train platform with such fury that one might well have wondered whether the enemy artillery and the Cossacks weren't close behind us: *Allez, passez, dépêchez vous!* I whispered in Belinsky's ear that he should leave his address in Brussels at the station and wait for Frederick there; then he was caught up in the crowd from which he flew out onto the platform. Since I did not have a ticket, I was not allowed to go there myself: the citizens of Paris did not then, and, apparently, do not now, have the privilege of seeing their friends and relatives off. Later, from Brussels, Belinsky described to me what happened to him on the platform after that. Feeling harassed and driven to distraction by the noise, commotion, and shoving, he stopped and stood still on the platform with his ticket in his hand, breathing heavily and not knowing where to go. Then one of the raging conductors who were racing up and down the platform caught sight of him, noticed his ticket, and, with a shout *"Mais que faites vous là, sacrebleu?"* dragged him by the arm and hurled him into the first available car of the train which had already started moving. And so he made his way to Brussels, but on the way he met with a new adventure. The Belgian customs, after opening his valise, noticed the set of toys, which was subject to duty, and demanded of him a statement as to the value of the goods. Instead of an answer, Belinsky started to explain, as best he could, that he did not know the value of the item since it was a present from a certain excellent lady in Paris, etc., and finally fell completely silent. One must give the customs official credit: having taken a look at the mute and embarrassed person who stood before him, he divined that this was no smuggler he was dealing with and, banging the valise shut, took no duty from him. Belinsky explained the official's magnanimity in a different and rather comical vein: "Surmising that I was a blessed idiot," he wrote, "he took pity on me and left me in peace." The next day, Frederick, all but in tears because of the mishap, set off to deliver the famous dressing gown to Belinsky in Brussels, easily found the long-suffering traveler there and saw him safely all the way to Berlin where he handed him over to D. M. Shchepkin, the extraordinary young scholar of archaeology and mythology who died prematurely. Belinsky appeared in Petersburg, to the surprise and joy of his friends, much fresher and in better spirits than when he had left, but their joy was not to last long.

*Two Winters in the Provinces
and the Country*[123]

1849. After coming from Paris, in October 1848, the situation in Petersburg seems extraordinary: the government's fear of revolution, the terror within brought on by the fear itself, persecution of the press, the buildup of the police, the suspiciousness, the repressive measures without need and without limit, the setting aside of the peasant question only just then due for consideration, the struggle between obscurantism and enlightenment, and the expectation of war.[124] Saltykov [125] is already in custody at the Peter-Paul Fortress because of his story, his review of journalism and writers. Buturlin [126] comes on the scene with his hatred for expression, thought, and freedom, preaching limitless obedience, silence, discipline. Extraordinary theories of education are laying the first stones for a grievous corruption of minds, characters, and natures.

I and my brother Fedor hurry out to the country, summoned there by a fearfully disordered state of affairs and the proposed division of the estate with my brother Alexander, whose gambling is chiefly responsible for the situation. Katerina Ivanovna, who raised the issue, is herself supposed to come to Chirkovo. I am glad to escape from Petersburg.

The new year 1849 in the country with Katerina Ivanovna, Strekalov, my brothers. The apportionment. Terribly heavy frosts. The harvesting has just been completed. My brother Fedor is to leave afterward. Ivan soon after him with Katerina Ivanovna from Chirkovo. Katerina Ivanovna has the management of the estate turned over to her and has already conceived a hatred for our efficient Adam. Alexander is to remain at Chirkovo until moving to Skryabino where he is to build a house. I am leaving for Simbirsk until spring. Adele B., Lidiya K., Tatarinov.[127] The reign of terror has reached even the provinces. The towns and villages themselves put the finger on who is to be seized from among the so-called liberals; denunciations proliferate to the point of insanity; all are suspicious of each and each of all. The anecdote about Mikhail Longinov, who had come to buy wheat for the Department of War, was taken for a gendarme, and, by making inquiries about me, gave rise to the suspicion that I was numbered among the intended victims. Meanwhile, among the usurers, horse thieves, and the coarsest landowners, patriotism grows apace—hatred for the French and for Europe: "We'll knock their blocks off!"—and a rodomantade thinly disguising their joy that all those irritating questions about serfdom and the like are now dead and buried. Here, too, originates that feeling of enthusiasm regarding the government. A reign of thievery and complicity is emerging on an unprecedented scale. I receive an express message from Moscow. A. A. Tuchkov [128] invites me to come to Moscow on an extremely urgent matter. The matter is the arrangement of Ogarev's affairs which Granovsky, Ketcher, and others have undertaken. The matter includes giving one of Tuchkov's daughters away in matrimony. The choice devolved on me. I refused. Satin turned up: they married her to him. All this came about with Granovsky feeling extremely indignant over it. In the summer I pay visits to the Trans-Volga landowners Grigory Tolstoy, Ermolov, and others, and I send the first of my "Provincial Letters" to the *Contemporary* where my "Survey of Literature" had also been published in the first issue for 1849.

At the end of winter 1849, the new governor, Prince Cherkassky, comes to Simbirsk; the old governor, Buldakov, well known on account of the Poltoratsky incident, was an illustrious profligate, glutton, and cunning man who was feared particularly by the merchants: on his outings he used to take things from them and remained in debt to everybody after his death—to the butchers, shopkeepers, the doctor, the pharmacies, and so on.

Mention should be made of a two-day sailing trip, as a continuation of summer recreations, from Bogorodsk to Simbirsk in a fishing boat with a large company including Tolstoy, Ermolov, Chernyavsky, Postnikov, and others. At Ermolov's, back in the country, an anecdote indicative of the way things are: a certain Bakhmetev was reciting in all simplicity how Korsh (Evgeny) and Granovsky had been taken from Moscow and brought to the Fortress. All of that was nonsense, but the important thing is that rumors are deliberately set going as a way of bringing the government's attention to people.

In the fall I leave Petersburg via Skryabino, where my brother Alexander has moved. His touching request—not to forget. Meanwhile, we turned over all our income to Katerina Ivanovna on the agreement that she would distribute 150 rubles a month to each brother and use the rest to cover debts. The results were terrible. Instead of covering debts, the overweening woman failed to pay the interest to the Trusteeship Council for two years, created more new debts, and placed the noose irrevocably around my brothers' necks, mine, and her own besides, since, for the pleasure of being mistress of someone else's property, she mortgaged her own estate, Khunta.

On my way through Moscow, Sadovsky reads, at V. P. Botkin's, Alexander Ostrovski's first comedy, *Bankrupt*. Powerfully impressive. I arrive in Petersburg at the quarters of my brother Ivan in a new building of the Horse Guards Barracks on Moyka which were still being finished while a great many people were already living in them.

Winter of 1849–50. The fall of the year now ending was marked by the conclusion, finally, of the inquest into the Petrashevsky [129] conspiracy, which cost all of the society entirely innocent of conspiracy so many hardships and terrors. The proclamation about the conclusion of the inquest and the verdict, which affected people who, on Petrashevsky's famous Fridays, merely read their projects for the emancipation of the peasants, for the improvement of shipbuilding and observations on the real internal state of Russia, and even people who were fond of his excellent dinners on those same Fridays, as well as affecting Petrashevsky himself and the framers of a future constitution, such as Speshnev and others, were written by Sukovkin, the state secretary. It is surprising that the proclamation included the information that, supposedly, the conspirators who organized the secret society themselves called it the society of "perverse ideas"; the fact of the matter is that they called it the society of "progressive ideas," but someone had written in the margin the polemical notation "of perverse ideas" and that is the way it came out in the proclamation which I first heard news of at the apartment of a very frightened Nekrasov. . . . The verdict was carried out—with a battalion on the ready for the execution, shrouds for the condemned prisoners, a ditch behind them, and so on, at the Semenovsky Parade Grounds—with all the trappings of a political execution commuted to the well-known amnesty. F. Dostoevski got five years in the penal work brigades for distributing Belinsky's letter to Gogol written in my presence in Salzbrunn in 1847. As a moral accomplice in not having made a report to the government about it, I also could have found myself in the penal work brigades. The verdict took effect under the horror of the February Revolution, from which dates the beginning of the reign of darkness in Russia, which grew increasingly greater until 1855. Just as I, or even more luckily, Nikolay Milyutin was saved—he who was then a section head in the Economic Affairs Department: the conspirators had designated him a minister, but the testimony against him, thanks to Milyutin's connections with Perovsky and Kiselev, was suppressed or even, some said, stolen by the well-known investigator, I. Liprandi, who made up for this indulgence on other people. I saw one of his victims, Balas-Ogly, the author of an elementary Russian textbook, who went mad while imprisoned in the Fortress; he had never been very easygoing. The innocence of that evening visitor of Petrashevsky's was so obvious that Leonty Dubelt, during Balas-Ogly's confinement in the Fortress, himself went and climbed up to the attic dwelling of his wife in order to leave her a contribution of his own. The terror completely blanketed society. Rebinder, later to be governorgeneral of Kakhtin (the person who made up the tale about the imminent secession of Siberia in 1851) and after that the superintendent of the Kiev District and a senator, was pale and distraught when he talked about the inquest into the Petrashevsky affair at the home of N. Tyutchev. Later, I had the chance to read the inquest commission's report to the emperor and learned how it had discovered the conspiracy. A police spy, Antonelli, was sent to the evening gatherings at Petrashevsky's and wrote down everything that was said there and even more; in the same building, another spy had opened a tobacconist's shop and kept watch over the comings and goings of people and engaged them in conversation; a third spy, whose name I shall not mention, appeared as a new recruit and later worked in the printing works of the *Russian Herald* run by Katkov who had no inkling as to whom he was harboring, and so on.

Thus arrives the year 1850, at the beginning of which I. S. Turgenev returns from abroad. Around this time Evgeny Korsh arrives from Moscow, having been dismissed from the *Moscow News* for his liberal editorship. He now obtains a position as editor on the *Police News,* and that thanks only to Frolov, the brother-in-law of the police commissioner, Galakhov. It is at his house that I became closely acquainted with the Milyutin brothers, Nikolay and Vladimir, with Arapetov and the Petersburg party of progress.[130] A resident at Kavelin's then was Egunov, who had seemed on the point of coming up in the world with his journal article about commerce in old Russia but who was soon beaten down and covered with ridicule by refined democratic officials for his awkwardness, his crude tastes and his behavior with its pretensions to specious dandyism.

From lack of anything to do, I write my "Provincial Letters," and my story about Bubnov enjoys the approval of my friends but goes no further than their circle. The censorship is operating with a harshness that is almost savage. The censor Krylov, for instance, uses all his intellect to devitalize a writer's expression and to render works insipid, calling this "blood-letting for a case of stroke," but the censorship was still far from having reached its limits in this matter. That year and during the years following, our press saw the establishment of censorship of various jurisdictions, aside from its own proper one —financial, ecclesiastical, communications, theaters, Imperial Court, mining, and so on; moreover and above all, there was also a "secret committee," consisting of three members, on which, in addition to Annenkov and Gamaleya, Modest Korsh also served. The committee kept track of the general trend and punished publishers and writers for articles which had been passed by all other sections of the censorship. But literature, nevertheless, did not die out, it held fast and did not perish utterly under the dreadful oppression, as any other literature might have. Its youth stood it in good stead, and that vital force, which even the government felt, exacerbated it still further.

An anecdote comes to mind. Somewhat later than this period, in 1854 I believe, in the lobby of the Mikhaylovski Theater, I met Egor Petrovich Kovalevsky, then still a colonel, who had also been held in custody . . . at a guardhouse, for some utterly innocuous remark about the severity of Asiatic governments or something of that sort in his *Guidebook by Land and Sea*. Kovalevsky [131] was strolling up and down the hall with none other than Annenkov [132]—the secret Annenkov—and stopped to say a few words to me. The secret Annenkov asked him my name, and in response to his reply that I, too, was an Annenkov, a literary man, my namesake made the following interesting comment: "Tell me—why do these people waste time on literature? After all, we've decided not to pass anything, so why should they go to the trouble?"

As was to be expected in such an atmosphere, the Ministry of Public Education was the first to be fundamentally altered. Buturlin, himself a writer, as is known, insulted by our criticism (of his *History of the Time of Troubles*), is a *man of the age*, and had he not died soon after that fateful epoch, he would have acquired a great name in history as an extinguisher and, perhaps, the influence from whose effect two generations in a row might not have recovered. That man, who recorded in excerpts and notes all the horrors of our past literature, the criticism of Belinsky and of the new *Contemporary*, and who was moved to say finally that, if the Gospel were not so widespread as it was, it would be necessary to ban it on account of the democratic spirit it disseminated—that man came to the conclusion that Uvarov's motto, the motto defining his activity as minister of education—"Orthodoxy, Autocracy and Nationality"—was an out-and-out revolutionary formula. The enlightened and sapient Sergey Stroganov, under the effect of old injuries at Uvarov's hands and the recent affair concerning the translation of Fletcher that he had passed and Uvarov condemned, joined forces with Buturlin. All Stroganov's aristocratic liber-

alism, the liberalism he had so vaunted, gave way to a thirst for revenge and turned the free magnate into a sinister purveyor of insinuations, gossip, and even slander. Thus the old historical temperament
of our aristocracy made itself immediately manifest in this situation.
There were stories at the time about a scene supposedly occurring in
the tsar's study with the tsar desiring to hear for himself the charge
and the explanations of the enemies. The scene might have been very
effective, if it is true that Stroganov accused the administration and
Uvarov of planting the seeds of democracy everywhere in their ambition to level all classes of society through education and in their prop-
agandizing immoral liberalism from the very lowest strata of society
through the secondary schools. It would have been interesting to have
had a look at Uvarov trying to prove that he had always been a zealous absolutist and had demanded a kind of learning that would eradicate all the practices then existing. Be that as it may, Uvarov vanished
and his place was occupied by the utter simpleton Shikhmatov, and a
simply unimaginable creature became the superintendent of the Saint
Petersburg School District—Musin-Pushkin. The latter could see absolutely nothing but disobedience; a poem, an article, a lecture—everything was disobedience if in the slightest degree new. The anecdotal
side of his term of office, as well as of Shikhmatov's handling of
affairs, contains a fabulously rich store of buffoonery which posterity
will hardly believe. The major manifestations of this whole administration led by the secret committee, by Buturlin and many other persons (even the ambassador Brunov, arriving in Petersburg around that
time, had a chance to express his horror over the press and Russian
social development, and spoke with the emperor about means of
stamping out as quickly as possible that pestilence which was breaking out in the state), were, aside from the censorship, the abolition of
all university privileges such as election of rectors and faculty consul-
tations, limitation of the number of students to a set figure (300 for
each university except the University of Derpt), the closure of departments of logic and philosophy and their transference to departments
of theology, persection of foreign booksellers and the virtual destruction of intellectual ties with Europe through the foreign censorship,
and, finally, the peremptory recognition of rights to education only for
the gentry and the wealthy, and to top it all off—the abolition of
classical education in the secondary schools, the introduction of the
narrowest of programs for the humanities, and the institution in them,
as well as in the military schools, of a vast system of corporal punish-
ments. Somewhat later on, I. I. Panaev visited Count Uvarov, brought
into his company by the young count, his son. Panaev recounted that
the retired minister, now a sick man, listened to his account of the

goings-on of the censorship and new administration in silence and only observed: "Our age is especially fearful for the fact that, out of fear of it, most likely, no one will keep records of it." Panaev was a great teller of tall tales but he never made anything up: he only embroidered on an already given canvas.

About that same time, A. A. Tuchkov, N. P. Ogarev, and N. M. Satin, accused of communism in monetary and matrimonial affairs and of liberalism, were brought to Petersburg, as was also. . . . Ilya Selivanov, on the strength of a denunciation from the governor of Penza, also concerning his free-thinking. Good Lord! The first three knew how to talk around their interrogators from the Third Section, but Selivanov, taking severe fright, did not even raise his eyes to look at his judges. In that condition they appeared before the chief of the Third Section, Count Orlov. This verily perspicacious gentleman, releasing them "under supervision of the police," since no offense could be found of which they were guilty, declared, turning to the first three: "You, gentlemen, can look me straight in the eye because you have made a forthright statement of your convictions, but as for you, M. Selivanov, I can't say that about you: you must have a bad conscience and you can't look straight at me." [133]

It is difficult to imagine how people lived then. People lived as if they were in hiding. The police, both the official police and a merely amateur variety, lorded it in the streets and everywhere, while appetites for embezzlement, appropriation, and making fortunes through the state and one's position developed to an incredible degree. They were even encouraged. What did not happen then under the mask of fine rules, impeccable career advancement, and dignity of high office! The three million Politkovsky stole from the pension fund, virtually under the noses of all the authorities, was a mere nothing compared to what high-ranking dignitaries were doing in general.[134] They owned gift shares in mines, insurance companies, industrial enterprises, and constituted a safeguard for them in all cases of swindling, in cases where the directors robbed shareholders, and so on. No enterprise could exist without inviting the grandees of the time to take shares in them free of charge, since any enterprise, no matter what its character, could count on success once they were with it. They took their cut of state monopolies, of inheritance litigations, and of state properties. O., for example, had himself given some 270,000 acres, 1500 rubles in quit rent, I believe, in Samara Province, and that without any reassessment in the future. Embezzlement of military funds, especially of soldiers' pay and equipment of all kinds, reached truly Roman proportions toward the end of the reign. General E. sold forty horses from the front for 4000 rubles each to his own and to other officers, replenishing them with remounts for which the Treasury allots 175 rubles.[135]

A sepulchral silence reigned over this whole world of malefactions and, needless to say, efforts were made in the higher echelons to secure this silence for all time to come. Even then it was already obvious to thinking people that the first political jolt would expose all the abomination of this dereliction veiled in false majesty, lustre, and legitimacy and would reveal all the helplessness of the young and strong, but pillaged and insensible, state; however, no one foresaw how soon that jolt would come and that the net results of the forgotten brutality and violence would be totaled up before our very eyes. We remarked about the silence. But silence was not sufficient. The police kept their eyes on all those who remained silent and did not take advantage of the troubled state of affairs, who did not intrude into anything and who looked at what was going on from the side. They were dogged every step of the way, suspected of being enemies. It was extremely difficult to live. Some people of the nervous breed, such as V. P. Botkin, who had then moved to Petersburg as the safer place to be (Moscow had been handed over to Count Zakrevsky for his unlimited exploitation, and orgies of banishments, briberies, and so on took place there)—these people all but cracked. The gentleman mentioned feared for every hour of his life. . . .

But enough about him. At that time Mme Lansky, a Pushkin by her first marriage, whose affairs my brother Ivan was managing through friendship with the family, got the idea of publishing a new edition of Pushkin's works, which had had only one edition, in 1837. She turned to me for advice and sent two trunks full of his papers to our house. At first glance at those papers I saw what treasures lay still hidden among them, but the idea of taking upon myself the labor of preparing the edition did not enter my head then. I only communicated a plan to her which seemed to me the way the edition ought to be handled.

Winter 1850–51 in the provinces. With the beginning of spring, I set out for the country and, owing to the sad state of our affairs, spent at Chirkovo and in Simbirsk not only the summer but also the fall and the whole winter of 1850–51, responding as best I could to the needs and to the claims our creditors presented us from all sides.

An upheaval had also occurred in Simbirsk, and society was up in arms. The new governor, Prince Cherkassky, had come there with ambitions to eradicate malpractices, bribery, extreme serfdom, and instantly found himself at odds with the marshal of the nobility, a venal, shallow, and vicious man behind whom stood an enormous party of brutish landowners to whom he catered: to their number were joined the old and now comfortable sinners from among the local assembly representatives and the new ones still in the process of procuring themselves honorable ease by cleverly and vigilantly robbing everyone and everything they could. A good-sized rumpus was set going, and the main instrument of the intrigue against the governor was, as might have been expected, the public prosecutor (an alumnus of the Law School), a man from the Baltic provinces who displayed all the energy proper to a German in his hatred for and persecution of a person interfering with a tranquil and successful career in dignified swindling. Unfortunately, Cherkassky was a visionary, but he left behind an endearing memory on the strength alone of his desire to cast light into that cesspool and, later, his construction of a highway down to the Volga which exists even now. As is the rule with reformers, both those who are successful and those who are not, Cherkassky brought young people to work with him—M. O. Trubnikov, N. Samarin—and associated with the party of the liberals in the city, that is, more precisely, he frequented the Alexander Tatarinov house, the Yazykov house, and so on. All the liberalism of this circle, however, consisted in its chief, Tatarinov, wearing a beard, in forcing the young people in its entourage to rack their brains over boring books such as the "Political Economy" of Smith, Say, and Bastiat, which completely addled them, in resisting the marshal's efforts to control the money and affairs of the nobility without making himself accountable for his actions, in disdaining minor officials, in despising young swains with poor educations and no interest in literature, and in feeling terribly bored, bored to the point of apathy, self-oblivion, and madness.

It was at this same time that the manifesto declaring war on the Hungarians in Austria thundered out. Perhaps never before was a declaration of war received so coldly in Russia as this one was. Even the most callous and utterly mundane attitude toward all that was happening in the world was not immune to doubts about the usefulness and gloriousness of this aid to Austria, and the common people felt nothing more than that it meant conscription into the army. Even the manifesto's exclamation, calculated to produce a special effect—"It shall not be so!"—became a popular saying with a thoroughly double meaning. Later, Shering, the doctor attached to the Guard's headquarters (a fanatic homeopath, by the way), told me that he had himself heard Grand Prince Mikhail Pavlovich, who did not approve of the war, enunciate for all to hear the prophetic words: "We've got ourselves in something that's not our affair—now we shall have to expect guests coming our way." The first movement of troops to the theater of the war could have opened eyes to the miserable condition

of our army, a condition to which it had been brought by embezzlement and administrative impotence, but no one wanted to take a look.
On its way from the western provinces, the army left behind during
its first marches whole regiments of stragglers, the weak and infirm.
The horrified emperor sent Adjutant-General N. M. Efimovich to as-
semble and regroup these soldiers and, at the same time, to find out
the reasons for such adversity. . . . Efimovich (as he himself said)
only hinted to him—since there was no necessity to spell it out in detail—that at the camps among the ruined landowners and impoverished peasants of Lithuania and Belorussia the soldiers had had
nothing to eat but plain cabbage soup and not always even that.
When they had had to resume their march with packs and rifles on
their shoulders, half of them had fallen down like children.

I returned to Simbirsk. Here, in the cathedral, after the Bishop's
celebration of the liturgy, when the manifesto was read by the arch-
deacon in his deep bass voice, right at its high point, at that famous
and above-mentioned "It shall not be so!", a terrific yawn was heard
in my vicinity, let out by some tall and grey-haired muzhik. As if from
nowhere, the chief of police came flying up to him, and between them
ensued the following half-whispered, ethnographic conversation:

"What's the matter with you—gone crazy, have you?"
"What's up?"
"Don't you hear? They're reading the tsar's decree—and you
with your big yap wide open!"
"You don't say! And here I was thinking that the service
was still going on!"

After having spent the winter, almost without going outdoors, at
the home of the intelligent Mme K. and [ ] [136] the cross fire of in-
trigues and slanders of the town parties, I visited Tatarinov's country
estate in the spring, drove over to Aksakov's and, on returning to my
estate, received the visit of Mme Pfeller with her daughter and companion. It had been decided among us at that time to resettle a part
of the Chirkovo peasants in Vasilevskoe. We could not get our affairs
straightened out. Although income from the estate did come directly
into our hands, it was needed for things that had been neglected earlier
and almost nothing of it was left. It was a difficult time. News came
from my brother in Petersburg that the Horse Guards had embarked
for the Hungarian campaign and that my brother Ivan had been
made the commander of the regrouped squadrons of the Guard Cui-
rassier Brigade that had been left behind in the city; second, that he
intended to acquire from Lansky the rights to publish an edition of

Pushkin (news that staggered me by the immensity of the task of carrying out the plan in a worthy manner); and third, that my brother Fedor, who had been appointed to serve as second commandant in Moscow back in 1850, had arranged quarters for himself in the Kremlin. In the fall I set out via Skryabino to go and see him in Moscow, where my brother Alexander also soon arrived from where he had been. This was in August 1851.

Fall 1851 in Moscow. Moscow was in a commotion. Emperor Nicholas was coming, first, to celebrate the twenty-fifth anniversary of his reign (from August 1826) and, second, to open the new railroad on that occasion. As heralds of his appearance and symbols of the future importance of the railroad, he had sent on ahead of him the Guards Infantry battalions and the combined squadrons of the Horse Guards and Mounted Guards that had been left behind from the Petersburg troops sent to the Hungarian campaign. My brother Ivan, then a colonel, commanded the latter contingents. Both they and the other contingents were met by the governor himself, Zakrevsky, at the terminal. The city's merchants had contributed various refreshments for them, the nobility did not lag behind either, and a certain glass-factory owner (I have forgotten his name) offered to supply a cavalry brigade with a hundred or so drinking glasses. Zakrevsky, who directed all these contributions and who encouraged them, made an interesting note on the slip of paper announcing that particular feat of patriotism: "Why not enough for the whole brigade?" The factory owner, it is said, hastened to make up for his oversight. Following the troops came the whole Court and, as usual, the German princes, who angered even the builder of the railroad, Kleinmichel, (he said so himself) by their appetite at the stations and their refusal to see anything on the railroad except refreshment rooms and bottles of the famous Court wines. On the day of the arrival, in the evening, there was already a great crowd of people on the Kremlin Square. I saw the emperor looking grim and weary: he had considered it his duty to spend some time under each of the bridges and to inspect all the railroad's embankments and constructions. The next day the bells pealed; the Kremlin was deluged with people; a parade for the troops was in progress on the square; uniforms gleamed; shouts, music, and drums intermingled; and there began that terrible, useless commotion of all the people, people in and out of the service, of actors and spectators, in which the deceased emperor loved to live and which seemed to him an important matter and part and parcel of the majesty and superiority of Russia over all the European world.

Needless to say, I found myself mainly in the circle of Granovsky,

Frolov, Ketcher, Kudryavtsev, of the literary men and scholars who
lived in the shadow and under the influence of Moscow University. At
that time they still did not fully understand how the pamphlet written
by Herzen and published in 1850, called *Du Développement des
idées révolutionaires en Russie,* could have managed to pass by without carrying away someone among them or all of them together.
The fact of the matter is that the government was moderate in that
instance; the immediate fear of disorders had passed and no one had
any desire to renew the incidents of condemnations en masse, particularly Count Orlov—one must give him due credit. Nikolay Milyutin
recounted that, in a conversation with his uncle, Kiselev, Orlov had
mentioned Herzen's book and had added: "It's better than any spy in
giving people away." "But whom could it possibly give away?" objected Kiselev. "It is only about people already dead, after all." "Eh!"
the chief of gendarmes replied. "If we had wanted to, it's just through
the dead that we could have worked our way to the living."

But as actually concerns Herzen's pamphlet, with the exception of
witty and, as usual, extremely lively characterizations of historical
epochs and personages, it presents nothing more on its main theme
than arrant verbiage. It was with this pamphlet that Herzen, already
an émigré, began to put on airs before Europe, before its clubs and
liberals, using a land unknown to them, his role in it, his friends, the
secret elements seething in it, a small specimen of which was "yours
truly." Subsequently, that tendency developed to the point of a falsehood and speciousness beyond comprehension, and later, when life itself exposed the vacuity of his hypothesis and the best minds were unwilling to support it with their practical activity, he experienced a
moment of blind rage against everything, everybody, and, finally,
even against the country's national feeling—down to and including its
instincts of self-preservation. The common people remained: it was to
that factor that the publicist shifted imaginary elements of revolu-
tionism, socialism, and communism. It was easier than before: one
could make oneself the representative of the great ideas of universal
renovation existing in Russia without any apprehension or reservation;
after all, the people do not make replies: the people remain silent and
never enter into disputation with their commentators. Indeed, who
but Herzen, that brilliant and, at the same time, specious intellect,
could have taken the party of Belinsky, Granovsky, and others for a
party of revolutionaries in the European sense, and taken all their
demands and notions about easing the lot of the suffering classes,
about reducing arbitrariness, about instituting the primary principles
of civic life, about spreading enlightenment, refining mores, eradi-
cating superstitions and hypocrisy, encouraging respect for ideas and

contact with Europe and its science—for Montagnarism, Babeufism, for affiliation with the discoverers of new political horizons? By thus inflating the modest Russian noble-minded and profoundly endearing circles, Herzen naturally inflated himself but did harm to those whom he praised. He was the source responsible for people, not only in official spheres but within the public itself, beginning to think that all those stuttering efforts, so to speak, to spell out the rudiments of public life, all those efforts aimed at overcoming the murkiness, rampages, vices, and plunderings of the established administration meant revolution, cataclysm, and anarchy. It would have been all right had Herzen limited himself to the Decembrists—they could be inflated in all directions because they themselves did not know where they were going, where they came from, and what they wanted, and nobody knows even now. They wanted a change—and that was all there was to it. Think what you will about it, give it a lot of thought or a little thought: it will be a matter of your own temperament, and the Decembrists themselves will have nothing to do with it.

The one who was most alarmed over Herzen's pamphlet was, once again, V. Botkin. "Just see," he said to me in 1850, hissing out the words, "what a nice little report on his friends Alexander Ivanovich has written!" He calmed down, however, when he saw no persecutions, and the circle for a short while, until its imminent disintegration, continued to exist, only remaining under police surveillance; Granovsky, in particular, as was later ascertained from acknowledgments on the part of employees in the governor's service, was the focus of intense spy activity. They were waiting for his first thoughtless step, and they were left waiting: everything about him was serious, sedate, and correct, no matter what; there was the possibility, no doubt, of taking him in on account of his principles, but they had a bad conscience in the face of history, which, incidentally, they would have loved to dupe, all of them without exception—those gentlemen who were making history in our land.

The situation with the Slavophiles was no better. Herzen had also included them among the cohorts of the Russian revolutionaries, which was. what must partly have justified, in its own eyes, the Third Section's absurd arrest of Chizhov [137] and Ivan Aksakov in 1847. Absurdity, in general, has an amazing quality: it can associate together, like brothers, people completely opposite in character, views, and convictions—Herzen with the ingenious detective I. Liprandi, for instance. During the period of intensive persecution of the Raskolniki (1850–55), Liprandi, who was in charge of the campaign, submitted a memorandum in which, to the list of antigovernment sects existing in Russia, he also added the Slavophile sect, with Khomyakov,

Kireevsky, Aksakov, and others among its members, and outrightly termed it, moreover, the natural progeny of the schism. I myself read that memorandum, and also a memorandum by I. S. Aksakov which he composed on the *gracious invitation* of Dubelt in the chambers of the Third Section (on Fontanka), where he was being held under arrest. Aksakov's memorandum is distinguished . . . even by a fervor in defense of the principle of authority accountable to no one but God and his own conscience; it explains the Slavophiles' sympathy for Slavic peoples in general by the fact of their being under the yoke of German governments where they could not develop as freely as under the aegis of the historical and sage Russian autocracy; and, finally, it musters its biggest charges against the exercise of special privileges by the upper classes to oppress the lower orders, which constituted even an insult to the supreme authority, inasmuch as its privilege, possessed by right of law, ought to exclude all others. Emperor Nicholas must have read the memorandum very carefully, for he made notations on it in his own hand to the effect that serfdom came about through the *unpardonable stupidity* of earlier governments and the like. What likely was behind the arrest of Chizhov and Aksakov, in general, was the government's desire to find out the real theories and views of the parties which it could not otherwise keep firm hold on. It was an invitation to make candid confession and profession of belief, a sort of *invitation à la valse*. Yet, despite the ingenious tone of Aksakov's memorandum, the emperor detected all the same a streak of protest invisibly permeating it, since on the report submitted by Count Orlov, who attested the satisfaction of the document, he wrote: *"C'est le ton qui fait la musique."* Nevertheless, he decided to call off these absurd arrests, the outward pretext for which had been supplied by Chizhov's trip through the Slavic territories and Austria's complaints about him and people like him stirring up its subjects. The emperor expressed his decision in writing, addressing himself to Orlov: "Call them in, read them a lecture, give them your blessings, and let them go."

However that may have been, it is certain that the administration was in fact somewhat afraid of the Slavophiles, supposing that they had some moral link with the deepest, most hidden aspirations of the Russian national spirit. That is why it considered it highly valuable that the party make public declaration of its enthusiastic devotion to the administration on important occasions. In the present instance, it required Pogodin to eulogize the celebration of the tsar's jubilee. A draft version of just such a hymn written by Pogodin evidently kept the Third Section busy whole nights on end. It kept seeming insufficient, ambiguous, reticent; it was corrected all over, scribbled all over, returned to the author, and corrected again. I saw the manuscript which bears witness to the toilsome, tormented process and ordeal of this document which did finally appear on the pages of the *Muscovite*, where archaeologists can find and study it. At the same time, thanks to the party's outspoken enmity for European movements and its outspoken reverence for the modesty and sanctity of the Russian mode of life, it enjoyed during that period a relatively greater freedom of opinion than all the other parties, and could at times speak on subjects about which people around them were even forbidden to think. This did not, however, keep them from being placed under strong police surveillance, inasmuch as it would have been as difficult for any thinking person to escape that surveillance as for an infant to escape baptism of its own volition. The hand of the administration came down on the Slavophile party without the least inhibition whenever there was cause. Confirmation of this is provided by the arrest of Bodyansky [138] (whom and what did they not arrest!) over Fletcher's "A Description of Russia," which he had had printed in the *Papers of the Society for the Study of History and Antiquities* with the permission of the provost, and by the internment of Yury Samarin in the Peter-Paul Fortress for an article in manuscript about dealings between the Baltic Germans and the Russians, Latvians, and, in general, the populations of all other nationalities in the country. Very likely they will leave memoirs for posterity about those adventures of theirs, adventures so common in those times. I heard later from Skripitsyn, the famous director of the Department of Foreign Religions, that when Yury Samarin, on the complaint of Prince Suvorov (the governor of Riga at the time), was taken into custody for divulging official secrets (in manuscript!), he was kept waiting for trial, but suddenly, some two weeks later, an order came for him to appear at the palace before the emperor. Samarin wanted to shave and make himself presentable, but the Fortress commandant, General Nabokov, a very honorable man (according to the reports of all the numerous residents at the Fortress), prevented him from doing so, desirous that he should appear before the emperor in the deplorable shape he was in when the order reached him. . . . The emperor received him, standing, in his study, and asked him in an ominous voice whether he repented of his act, and having received an affirmative reply, embraced him, kissed him, sat him down facing him next to his desk, and exhorted him in moving terms to use his distinguished talents for honorable service to his country and to be a consolation to his renowned family. "I myself am a father," he said, "and I know how fathers can suffer for their children."

That's the way we lived in that day and age.

Meanwhile, my brother Ivan brought with him to Moscow the

news that he had concluded the deal with Lansky about the Pushkin edition and had signed a formal contract with her on it. But the edition, of course, devolved upon me. Fear and doubt as to the success of so vast an enterprise, for which were required substantial outlays of money, as well as of powers of mind and spirit, never left me even when, due to the news of the edition being spread, I became acquainted through Gogol with Pogodin, and through Pogodin with Bartenev (P. I.), Noshchokin, and other persons in possession of biographical information about the poet. Simultaneously, I began thorough research of the journals of the years 1817–25.

Gogol was living at the time at Tolstoy's house, on Nikitsky Boulevard, if I am not mistaken, and was then still constantly at work on the second volume of *Dead Souls*. At any rate, in response to my remark about the impatience of the whole reading public to see the great feat of his life and literary career finally fully completed, he said in a confident and meaningful way: "Yes . . . we'll give it a try!" I found him considerably more cautious in his opinions after the terrible storm caused by his *Correspondence* but still an optimist in the highest degree and virtually incomprehensible for me. He knew almost nothing or did not want to know anything about what was going on around him, about such things, for example, as Liprandi's recent suggestion that he be sent to inspect all the private libraries in the whole of Russia, a suggestion the government itself rejected with horror and indignation; and his reaction to exiles and other measures indicated that he regarded them as things so mildly carried out as to be even courtesies and kindnesses with respect to many of those on whom sentence had been passed. He also continued to suppose that, through lack of fortitude in the Russian character, persecutions of the press and of life could not last long, and he advised literary men and diligent people of all sorts to utilize the time for the unobtrusive preparation of serious works for a time when conditions would be relaxed. It was this same idea that he had expressed in my presence in 1849 at an evening gathering at the home of Alexander Komarov. A rather naive scene occurred there. Nekrasov, who was also present, observed: "Fine and good, Nikolay Vasilevich, but in the meantime one has to eat." Gogol was taken aback, riveted his eyes upon him, and slowly uttered: "Yes, that is a difficult matter." Instead of a sense of actuality, something he had lost abroad and in the last stage of his development, he retained, as before, an artistic sensibility in the very utmost degree. He made me promise to keep the groves and woods on my country estate intact, and one evening he suggested we take a walk around town and spent the whole time of it describing Damascus, the marvelous mountains surrounding it, the Bedouins in their Biblical dress who showed up at its walls (for purposes of brigandage), and so forth; but in answer to my question as to what kind of life people led there, he said almost with annoyance: "What life are you talking about? It's not life that one thinks about there!" That was my very last conversation with that marvelous personality who, together with Belinsky, Herzen, Granovsky, and others, adorned the years of my young manhood. When we were about to reach the Tolstoy house on the way back and were saying good-bye, he made a touching request of me to keep a good opinion of him and to militate for that opinion among the people in the party "to which you belong." After that I never saw him again, not counting a chance meeting with him in the Kremlin that did occur afterward. At four o'clock in the afternoon I was driving with my brother, the commandant, to go and have dinner somewhere, when suddenly I met Gogol obviously on his way to the cathedrals for the evening service, the bells for which were being rung. As if desiring to ward off any suspicion as to where he intended to go, he quickly stepped up to our calash and, with a sly Ukrainian's resourcefulness, said: "Here I was on my way to see you, but obviously I've come at the wrong time. Farewell!" The poor sufferer!

All my work on Pushkin and all my acquaintanceships came to a halt on account of a serious and dangerous illness—enteritis and dysentery. I contracted the disease at Arkhangelskoe where Granovsky had rented a summer cottage and where we had gotten together and had arranged a banquet, embellished, as was customary, with fireworks which Pikulin had carted along with him (he still to this day carts fireworks to parties despite his paralytic and semidemented condition). After a long and, needless to say, not exactly modest repast, I lay down under a tree and awoke only when Pikulin [139] just barely missed setting off a firecracker under my very nose. The consequence was an illness of four weeks. Among the picnic guests were Panaev and Vladimir Milyutin, both of whom had already come to despise the second-rate prophets of Moscow, as they called Granovsky's entourage—N. Shchepkin, Frolov—who were also living there at the cottage. Panaev played a role that was not altogether decent when the owner of Arkhangelskoe, Prince Yusupov, appeared there. Out of subservience before the beau monde, from which he could not refrain throughout his whole life despite his writing lampoons on his idols afterward, he began to play up to Yusupov and to try to steer Granovsky over to him. Granovsky simply did not budge, but Frolov went so far as to respond with contempt for the trade of gratuitous go-between which the editor of the Contemporary had taken upon himself. Panaev's hatred was, of course, not abolished or assuaged by this circumstance; it expressed itself very forcefully in Panaev's memoirs, written eight years after Frolov's death, where the poor journalist, ruined by Nekrasov and utterly befuddled by Dobrolyubov's and Chernyshevsky's radicalism, himself relates with remarkable lack of any sense of reserve how he peeked through the keyhole and listened at the door of Frolov's study out of curiosity to know what he was doing there, shut up in the room away from everybody for the entire time until dinner. Patrician behavior that, of course, remained unknown to the journalist's patrons!

Even lying sick in the commandant's quarters in the Kremlin, I heard all the tumult and din of the celebration which centered in that area. In the daytime, carriages and calashes with gentlemen in feathers and gold and ladies decked out in all their finery passed before me, clattering down the street; uniforms, ribbons, braid glittered in an indescribable mêlée that produced on my afflicted organism a kind of oppressive nightmare effect. The apartment was almost always empty, my brothers being constantly on duty. The glorious autumn weather outside had a painful effect on my inflamed eyes. At night, unable to sleep, I would hear the long-drawn-out calls of the sentries stationed on all the corners. There was a lavishness with guardhouses and sentries in those days. With the first light of day, all who served in offices and in the royal retinue rose up again, the earth rumbled, people dashed to and fro, doing something or other that my weary brain found hard to understand. I have distinct memory of only two scenes. The emperor was riding past my windows with one of the governor-generals, accompanied by the tumultuous shouts of the crowd. At the foot of his calash stood a shabby old muzhik and, despite the emperor's commanding gestures, evidently did not want to leave his place, holding on to the folded top of the calash with one hand and incessantly crossing himself with the other, looking goggle-eyed and with mouth agape. Another time, in the early morning, some six or seven troikas drove up at a gallop and came to a stop at the entrance to the commandant's office. In each vehicle sat one gendarme and one Pole. I remember one young man with long hair who gazed around him with an expression of intense curiosity while his gendarme ran on the double to the office, presumably to sign in. The vehicles remained at the entrance about ten minutes and then drove on further.

Recovering my health in October, I went with my brother Fedor, who had received leave, to Petersburg by mail coach. Moscow was already deserted and had quieted down once again.

Winter 1851–52 in Petersburg. I have been writing my reminiscences from memory without consulting books and documents. A great deal of time has already passed and certain secondary details possibly do figure in my account somewhat earlier or later than they actually happened, but the main details and the general character of those years are preserved accurately in my memoirs.

Turgenev, who came here from the country to spend the fall, was staying on Malaya Morskaya Street in the apartment of Mme Dumet, from which place he was taken and brought to the police station. He was a man who had worked out his moral character with extreme difficulty. He had come from Paris such an amalgam of the most endearing qualities of mind and soul and of juvenile vices—pretense, affectation, and falsification at every opportunity—that he made it impossible for one to fix on him any specific feeling or specific judgment. We were far from being friends then; at one time he even positively despised me, owing to my unconcealed suspiciousness of his every word and action, and especially of those to which he wanted to impart an air of sincerity and impassioned interest. I was rude and in the wrong in his regard; he paid me back with ridicule and epigrams, a fact which was disagreeable only on account of the joy it gave our common enemies. Only after many years of alternating affability and coolness did we come to understand that there was some invisible bond that kept us from parting company with equanimity and going each our own way. Somehow or other we kept coming back together again with evident joy, only once again to begin the old story of bitter attestation of each other's truths until the passage of years and success in the world and in literature made him a good deal more phlegmatic with respect to self-exhibition, and until the passage of those same years and weariness of life drew from me my audaciousness and totally unjustified desire to mock people. However, neither did he fully free himself from a clandestine indifferentism that permitted him to engage in innocent betrayals of friends on occasion and in complicity with the foulness of acquaintances who were, for some reason, interesting for or needed by him, nor did I free myself definitely from an inclination to consider another human being something of no account and to act toward that being with high-handed bravado. Such is our confession: reformation in both cases is proceeding slowly and is likely never to reach completion.

Notes

1. Vissarion Grigorevich Belinsky (1811–48) occupies the center of the stage through much of Annenkov's *Memoirs* as he enjoyed the center of attention among the intelligentsia during the extraordinary decade. In his classic account of Russian thought and literature, D. S. Mirsky expressed the judgment of both Belinsky's contemporaries and of later-day scholars when he described him as "the true father of the intelligentsia, the embodiment of what remained of its spirit for more than two generations—of social idealism, of the passion for improving the world, of the disrespect for all tradition, and of highly strung, disinterested enthusiasm." His entire life was one of struggle. He fought to make a place for himself, an impoverished son of a poor army doctor, among the aristocrats who largely comprised the literary and intellectual circles of the time. He drove himself by frenzied and omnivorous study to make up for an inadequate education, plunging along the way into a succession of radically opposed philosophies in a vain search for solutions to the many "accursed questions" that plagued the age. There was hardly a moment when he was not immersed in bitter controversy or straining to meet deadlines of demanding editors who became rich on his fame but provided him only a pittance. After leaving Moscow University, from which he was expelled, he began his career as a journalist and literary critic and almost at once turned these professions into effective vehicles for militant social and political criticism. His diffuse, iconoclastic, and explosive style, which earned him the nickname "furious" Vissarion, became the fashion for the Russian intelligentsia from that time on. Although this journalistic career began in Moscow, with his work for Telescope (*Teleskop*) and, in 1838, for the *Moscow Observer* (*Moskovsky nablyudatel*), his fame really dates from his articles in the St. Petersburg *Notes of the Fatherland* (*Otechestvennye zapiski*) founded by A. A. Kraevsky in 1839. He remained associated with *Notes of the Fatherland* until 1846, when he became the principal critic for *Contemporary* (*Sovremennik*). The following year he went abroad, where he wrote—under conditions so graphically described by Annenkov—his famous letter to Gogol, attacking him for having, in Belinsky's eyes, betrayed the cause of progress, reason, and freedom.

2. I. I. Panaev (1812–62), a writer and a principal collaborator on *Notes of the Fatherland*. One of Belinsky's closest friends and supporters.

3. *Report (Molva)*. A supplement to *Telescope* (See note 24). D. S. Mirsky called Belinsky's 1834 "Literary Reveries" "the beginning of Russian intelligentsia journalism."

4. Mikhail Trofimovich Kachenovsky (1775–1842). A journalist and professor of history at Moscow University. His irreverent rejection of eminent scholars, such as the historian Karamzin, corresponded to Belinsky's own audacious treatment of authorities.

5. Recounted by V. G. Belinsky. (Note by Annenkov. Hereafter such notes will be identified by the author's name in parenthesis at the end of the note.)

6. *Library for Reading (Biblioteka dlya chteniya)*. A monthly journal established in St. Petersburg in 1834 and concerned with a wide range of topics, including art, science, literature, industry, and fashions. Its editor was O. I. Senkowski (1800–1858), a professor of Far Eastern languages at St. Petersburg University. The liberal and radical intelligentsia attacked it for its criticism and reviews, designed, in Belinsky's words, to "misguide the younger generation."

7. Nikolay Ivanovich Grech (1787–1867). Author, editor of the conservative journal *Son of the Fatherland (Syn otechestva)*, and coeditor with F. V. Bulgarin of the archconservative newspaper *Northern Bee (Severnaya pchela)*. Although he had held liberal views before the Decembrist rising of 1825, he later turned to extreme conservatism and became, together with F. V. Bulgarin, a leading defender of autocracy, orthodoxy, and nationalism, the pillars of reaction during the reign of Nicholas I.

8. Faddey V. Bulgarin (1789–1859). (See preceding note.)

9. These complaints of Bulgarin's did not remain without consequence for literature. When an edition of Pushkin was being brought out in 1834, censorship difficulties arose in connection with reporting our poet's views on Derzhavin, since, previously, a ruling of the censorship board had been made to shield the names of Derzhavin, Lomonosov, and Karamzin, and the person of Bulgarin himself, as well, from unwelcome criticism. No one at the time was sensible of the offense done the first three great names of our fatherland by being thus put on a level with the person of the editor of the *Northern Bee* (Annenkov).

10. Annenkov refers here to the "Stankevich circle," one of the earliest and most significant of a long series of intellectual discussion circles around which successive phases of Russian intellectual history formed. The circle was established in the 1830's around Nikolay Vladimirovich Stankevich (1813–40) and included, in the main, students at Moscow University interested in philosophy, art, and literature. It contrasted sharply with the circle

formed around Alexander Herzen, which concentrated on social, economic, and political issues.

11. Konstantin S. Aksakov (1817–60). Critic, poet, dramatist, historian, and prominent Slavophile.

12. Petr V. Kireevsky (1808–56). A Slavophile principally interested in collecting Russian folklore and songs. Brother of I. V. Kireevsky, a more prominent Slavophile theorist. (See note 67.)

13. Timofey N. Granovsky (1813–55). Professor of history, Moscow University from 1839. A moderate Westerner who opposed what he considered Herzen's extremism.

14. Sergey Nikolaevich Glinka (1775–1847). Publisher and editor of the extreme nationalistic journal *Russian Herald* (*Russky vestnik*).

15. Koltsov had by that time been brought into the circle of Moscow friends by Stankevich. In all likelihood, it was he who was indirectly responsible for the expectations Belinsky expressed for people of the middle status (Annenkov).

16. Annenkov is referring here to the combined attack on liberal views by the so-called literary triumvirate, formed by Bulgarin's *Northern Bee,* Grech's *Son of the Fatherland,* and Senkowski's *Library for Reading.*

17. *Contemporary* (*Sovremennik*). A literary journal, founded by Pushkin and published in St. Petersburg from 1836 to 1866. Its contributors included the most prominent authors of the period.

18. According to the same source of information, Pushkin also added in secret the observation that Belinsky had lessons even his revilers could afford to learn (Annenkov).

19. *Northern Bee* (*Severnaya pchela*). The extreme conservative newspaper edited by F. V. Bulgarin (See note 7).

20. A. A. Komarov's circle was made up of art and literature enthusiasts that gathered around A. A. Kraevsky and his liberal publications. Belinsky was introduced to these Saturday gatherings by Panaev, and it was at one such meeting that Annenkov first met Belinsky.

21. Alexander F. Smirdin (1795–1857). St. Petersburg publisher and book-dealer.

22. K. P. Masalsky (1802–61), A. P. Stepanov (1781–1837), and N. V. Kukolnik (1809–68) were mediocre writers for the conservative journals edited by Grech, Bulgarin, and Senkowski.

23. "Baron Brambeus" was a literary psuedonym for Senkowski.

24. *Telescope* (*Teleskop*). Published in Moscow in the years 1831–36 under the editorship of Professor N. I. Nadezhdin. It was in *Report* (*Molva*), a weekly supplement to *Telescope* that Belinsky published his "Literary Reveries of 1834," mentioned in note 3. The journal was closed in 1836 in

reprisal for its publishing a still more famous article, "Philosophical Letters" by P. I. Chaadaev, the publication which, for many scholars, begins the Westerner-Slavophile debates.

25. *Moscow Observer (Moskovsky nablyudatel)*. Published from 1835 to 1837, at first with the participation of Pushkin and Gogol. As Annenkov states here, it was believed that the journal would oppose the conservative "triumvirate," Bulgarin, Grech, and Senkowski. The line of the journal soon changed, however, moving away from the liberal position toward that of the "triumvirate."

26. To support this publication, Gogol took upon himself the role of its propagandist and collected subscriptions from all his acquaintances in Petersburg—and did this, let us add, with extreme insistence and energy. Each of us was *expected* to have, and *did* have, his *Observer* (Annenkov).

27. In its first number *Contemporary* carried an attack by Gogol against Senkowski's *Library for Reading*. The influence of the *Contemporary* dropped sharply, however, after Pushkin's death, although it was later to be revived when Belinsky, together with Panaev and the writer N. A. Nekrasov, took it over in 1846.

28. Raskolniki. Religious sectarians who opposed some of the rituals and doctrines of official Russian Orthodoxy. Although schisms in Russian Orthodoxy occurred throughout Russian history, the term Raskolniki usually refers to those sects that either directly or indirectly derived from the widespread and intense opposition to changes in church practice introduced by Patriarch Nikon in the mid-seventeenth century.

29. Andrey A. Kraevsky (1810–89). Liberal publicist, editor of *Notes of the Fatherland* during the years 1839–67.

30. Pavel P. Svinin (1788–1839). Writer and, in 1818, founder of *Notes of the Fatherland*.

31. I. Panaev, "Literary Reminiscences," *Contemporary* (February, 1861) (Annenkov).

32. P. A. Pletnev (1792–1865). Poet, critic, and publisher of the *Contemporary* during the years 1838–46.

33. Stepan P. Shevyrev (1806–64). Poet, critic, literary historian, and professor of Russian literature at Moscow University.

34. Gavril R. Derzhavin (1793–1816), Vasily A. Zhukovsky (1783–1852), and Konstantin N. Batyushkov (1787–1855) were the leading Russian poets before Pushkin. Nikolay M. Karamzin (1766–1826) was the most prominent Russian historian of the time.

35. Alexander I. Herzen (1812–70). The most brilliant and illustrious of the Westerners. An illegitimate son of a wealthy landowner, Herzen received an education in science at Moscow University. For his participation

in radical circles, which he helped form, he was exiled to the provinces from 1834 to 1840. In 1841 he was banished again for a year, this time from St. Petersburg to Novgorod. He then resettled in Moscow until 1847, constantly engaged in the intense debates described by Annenkov. The fortune that he inherited after his father's death in 1846 allowed him to leave Russia, and in 1847 he left forever. His disillusionment with what he saw of the "bourgeois" West, exacerbated by his dismay over the fate of the 1848 revolutions, turned him for a time away from many of his earlier liberal, Western views, toward several of the fundamental precepts of Slavophilism. After the Crimean disaster, he again became an active liberal, urging reform and exposing injustices through journals he published abroad and smuggled into Russia in large numbers—the *Polar Star* (*Polyarnaya zvezda*, 1855–62) and the *Bell* (*Kolokol*, 1857–67). His liberalism in the 1860's turned the new generation of radicals against him, just as his earlier alleged radicalism had provoked the disapproval of the more moderate Westerners described by Annenkov.

36. Died while these notes were being compiled (Annenkov).

37. Vasily Petrovich Botkin (1811–69). Writer, participant in the Stankevich circle (See note 10.), and collaborator on *Notes of the Fatherland* and, later, on the *Contemporary*. His ideological career parallels that of Annenkov, becoming increasingly more conservative as the dominant currents in the intelligentsia became more radical. During the "extraordinary decade," he belonged to the more conservative wing of the liberal, Westerner circle that formed in Moscow around Herzen and the historian T. N. Granovsky.

38. Heinrich-Theodor Roetscher (1803–71). German, Hegelian literary critic.

39. Annenkov is discussing here one of Belinsky's most famous articles: "*Hamlet:* A Drama by Shakespeare and Molchalov in the Role of Hamlet." It was published in the March and April 1838 issues of *Moscow Observer*.

40. Nikolay A. Polevoy (1796–1846). Prominent writer of the period, journalist, and historian (See also note 43.).

41. The 1835 *Telescope* contained exemplary articles: "On the Russian Tale and the Tales of Gogol," "On Baratynsky's Short Poems," "The Short Poems of Vladimir Benediktov," and "The Short Poems of Koltsov." Nadezhdin, who had entrusted the publication of the *Telescope* to Belinsky on leaving for abroad, was struck, on his return in December 1835, by the high quality of the articles published in the journal and by the remissness of the staff in failing to publish a number of its issues. Such was Belinsky the "editor" and such he continued to be (Annenkov).

42. See my *Reminiscences and Critical Essays,* Vol. 1, the article about Gogol (Annenkov).

43. *Moscow Telegraph* (*Moskovsky telegraf*). Established in 1825 and edited by N. A. Polevoy. It was closed in April 1834 in response to a hostile review of a patriotic play.

44. Nikolay Ya. Prokopovich (1810–57). Poet, teacher of Russian literature, and close friend of Gogol.

45. Nikolay P. Ogarev (1813–77). Poet and radical publicist. Herzen's lifelong friend, he left Russia in 1856 and was coeditor of *Kolokol* (See note 35.).

46. Mikhail N. Katkov (1818–87). Although famous as a leading conservative after the 1860's and editor of the conservative *Moscow News* (*Moskovskie vedomosti*) and *Russian Herald* (*Russky vestnik*), Katkov was a liberal Westerner in the 1840's.

47. On my departure for abroad, Belinsky, relating the details of this scene, commissioned me to try and effect a reconciliation: "It would be a great misfortune," he said, "to lose a man like Katkov. Work especially on Bakunin—he is a *raisonneur* and more likely to come to terms" (Annenkov).

48. Aleksey V. Koltsov (1809–42). (See note 15.)

49. *Lighthouse* (*Mayak*). A conservative journal established in 1840. Because its policies were similar to those of the conservative Moscow journal *Muscovite* (*Moskvityanin*), Belinsky called it the St. Petersburg *Muscovite*.

50. An untranslatable pun occurs here: *dukh* ("spirit") also has the meaning *smell* (Translator's note).

51. The "Chinese word" is a play on Russian *sukin syn* = "son of a bitch" (Translator's note).

52. By a queer coincidence, at exactly the same time the renovated *Notes of the Fatherland* was heading in the direction about which we have been talking, the journal *Muscovite* appeared on the scene with the apparent purpose of serving as a counterbalance to the Petersburg publication. The *Muscovite* was founded in 1841 (Annenkov).

53. Needless to say, there were in this instance, as always, shining exceptions: such people as Humboldt, Varnhagen, Ranke, Gervinus, Gans, and others never evinced terror for French ideas, in general, or French society, in particular (Annenkov).

54. Nikolay G. Frolov (1812–55). A collaborator on the *Contemporary*.

55. Heinrich Ritter (1791–1869). German philosopher and historian of philosophy.

56. *Hallische Jahrbücher*, founded in 1838 as a radical, "left-Hegelian" journal and published by a group headed by Arnold Ruge (1802–80). To

escape oppressive Prussian censorship, in 1841 the journal moved from Halle to Leipzig, where it was published under the title *Deutsche Jahrbücher für Wissenschaft und Kunst* until it ceased publication in 1843.

57. *Das Leben Jesus*. Published in 1835 by David F. Strauss (1808–47).

58. Aleksandr A. Ivanov (1806–58). Eminent Russian painter.

59. Fedor I. Iordan (1800–1883). Engraver and professor of art.

60. Not to speak of the new religion of "humanity" which the fantastic theosophist, Pierre Leroux, expounded in his book, *De l'Humanité*. The book, on account of its verging on wearisome pietism and failing to sustain its ideas philosophically—things to which we were always very sensitive—did not have any particular success. I cite these various books from memory; it is possible that I have failed to give their full and exact titles (Annenkov).

61. The subject of Granovsky's lecture was the medieval history of France and England (Annenkov).

62. P. I. Chaadaev (see note 72).

63. Louis Veuillot (1813–1883). French conservative, writer and publicist of Catholic views. *Père Duchêne* was an extremist newspaper published during the French Revolution.

64. A characteristic anecdote comes to mind in this connection. After 1848, one of the Russian émigrés, Sazonov, hit on the idea of compiling a portrait album of the sparse Russian emigration of the time, which he was going to call *The Real Russia*. He solicited Herzen for his portrait. "I agree to give you my portrait for the collection," Herzen replied, "provided that a colleague of mine also be included in it—a serf-footman who recently ran away from his master in Paris" (Annenkov).

65. Among the poetic pages, of which many are to be found in Herzen, belongs his description of his last trip to Naples and his visit there to a Carmelite monastery. The painful, deeply melancholy and moving reflections aroused in him by the tranquil monastery reveal the state of his soul and belong among the most precious autobiographical remains, which should be valued as they deserve (Annenkov).

66. His enthusiastic articles about Granovsky in the *Moscow News*, 1844, and in the *Muscovite*, 1844, were also remarkable for the fact that in them he held out his hand to the Slavic party, proposing peace on honorable terms. Here is what he had in mind to gain from it for his side: "There is no position more *objective*, with respect to Europe's past, than the position of a Russian. Of course, in order to make use of it, it is not enough to be a Russian; it is requisite that one reach *universal human* development, requisite precisely not to be a Russian exclusively, i.e., to understand oneself as, not opposed to, but in kinship with Western Europe" (*Muscovite*, No. 7, 1844).

The Slavophile party accepted these conditions of peace in part, as we shall see, but with qualifications which greatly changed them (Annenkov).

67. Ivan V. Kireevsky (1806–56). Critic and one of the most eminent of Slavophile theorists. Brother of Peter V. Kireevsky (1808–56) (See note 12.).

68. We heard, however, that the gatherings at the Elagin house had to be suspended in the end on account of the ever increasing heatedness of the arguments between the people from both parties who met there. It is enough to cite one example. In 1845 the difference in judgments over N. M. Yazykov's pamphlet "Not Ours" and over the behavior of its author nearly caused a duel between P. V. Kireevsky and T. N. Granovsky, which their friends just barely managed to prevent (Annenkov).

69. Aleksey S. Khomyakov (1804–1860). Philosopher, poet, dramatist, linguist, historian and the most prominent and prolific Slavophile authority.

70. Reported by Belinsky (Annenkov).

71. Reported by T. N. Granovsky (Annenkov).

72. Reference here is to the first of Petr I. Chaadaev's "Philosophical Letters," published in *Telescope* in 1836. The letters deplore Russia's shortcomings, past and present, and lament the severance of Russian history from that of Western Europe. As a result of its publication, *Telescope* was forced to cease publication.

73. August Neander (1789–1850). Author of *Life of Christ* written in response to Strauss's *Life of Jesus* (see note 57). August-Freidrich Gfrörer (1813–1861). Church historian.

74. Mikhail P. Pogodin (1800–1875). Son of a serf, Pogodin became a famous publicist and historian. He was the editor of *Muscovite* (*Moskvityanin*), a conservative and nationalistic journal, and was later a leading theorist of Pan-Slavism.

75. The chapter numbers, with XXI and XXII missing, are those of the two Russian texts used in the translation, published in 1928 and 1960 (see the Introduction, p. xi).

76. Also a schoolmate of Gogol's at Nezhin, who was making great efforts to become a man of letters and, for that purpose, kept visiting the various literary circles (Annenkov).

77. Aleksandra O. Smirnova (1809–82). A friend of Pushkin and Gogol; author of a book of reminiscences of Gogol.

78. Nikolay M. Yazykov (1803–46). A leading poet of the 1820's, particularly esteemed by the Slavophiles and praised by Gogol.

79. Marquis de Custine, *La Russie en 1839*. An account of Custine's travels in Russia, highly critical of the Russian state and society. Published in 1843 in Paris, but prohibited in Russia.

80. In this passage Khomyakov cited, as examples of such wise and luminous eras, the formation of which did not involve formal knowledge, the reigns of Fedor Ivanovich, Aleksey Mikhaylovich, and Empress Elizaveta Petrovna, as has already been mentioned (Annenkov).

81. This daring contention of A. S. Khomyakov's, taken note of by everyone and not left without objection, demonstrated once again to what lengths his brilliant mind would go, with its penchant for decisive words and aphorisms, for the sake of producing a powerful effect on his listeners. Here is what he said further on in confirmation of his idea: "It (England) every-where appears a creation of conventional, lifeless formalism . . . but it does, at the same time, have traditions, poetry, sanctity of hearth and home, warmheartedness, and Dickens, Gogol's *younger brother*" (!) (*Muscovite*, No. 4, 1845, p. 29) (Annenkov).

82. Evgeny Fedorovich Korsh (1810–97). Journalist, translator, and editor of *Moscow News* (*Moskovskie vedomosti*) in the period 1843–48. A member of Herzen's Westerner circle in the 1840's, Korsh, like Annenkov and Botkin, became a more moderate liberal during the 1850's and advocated reforms instituted by the existing regime.

83. Among his many catchy sayings, I remember one addressed to a conversation partner of his who, on the grounds of Proudhon's writings, sought a means of salvation for modern societies in anarchy. "That probably is because," Evgeny Korsh said, "anarchy always elicits monarchy." On another occasion, in answer to a certain professor who had exclaimed in a provincial accent, "I, my friends, as you know, am a radical," Evgeny Korsh remarked, "I've always thought there was nothing else for you to *radiate*" (Annenkov).

84. Nikolay K. Ketcher (1806–86). A physician by profession, but prominent as a translator of Shakespeare, Shiller, and other West European authors. Edited the first collection of Belinsky's works. A close friend and supporter of Belinsky, Ketcher was identified with the more radical wing of the Westerners, although he became more conservative in the 1850's and came to support a reformed autocracy.

85. The notes and excerpts I jotted down at the time for my own record have helped a great deal in reconstructing this whole scene (Annenkov).

86. In Herzen's "Memoirs" [See note 115.] the story of his quarrel with Granovsky in 1846 is related in detail. The quarrel was over a rude word incautiously uttered by Ogarev in the presence of the mistress, later the wife, of Ketcher. Herzen then took Ogarev's part, not considering him at fault for the accidental, unprintable expression, but Ketcher, who previously had forgiven offhand remarks without trouble, became offended. Granovsky sided with Ketcher and shared his indignation (Annenkov).

87. Konstantin D. Kavelin (1818–85). Historian and jurist, Kavelin was friends with and shared the views of Herzen, Belinsky, and Granovsky

in the 1840's. As with Annenkov, Botkin, Ketcher, and Korsh, his Western-ism and liberalism became more moderate in the 1850's, and he actively and influentially participated in preparing the reforms of Alexander II.

88. I have kept a sheet of caricatures he did in pencil of Herzen, Granovsky, Korsh, Panaev, myself, and others engaged in one of those night-time discussions which often took place in the garden pavillion on the slope of the hill of Sokolovo's park. The circle gathered at Sokolovo lacked two very prominent members, V. P. Botkin and Ogarev. Both were living abroad in Paris. The former, according to the account given by Panaev, who had himself recently returned from there, was assiduously endeavoring to make himself French in language, way of life, and manners, and had already be-gun to distinguish himself by a violent hatred for his former idol—idealism. The latter philosophically squandered the remains of his once enormous for-tune and his robust health. However, Panaev's scandalous anecdotes about the two did not fully convey their moral content, seeing that the first, Bot-kin, after a trip to Spain, presented the Russian public with an extraordi-narily clever and picturesque description of the country; and the second, Ogarev, when he returned home in 1846, exerted so strong a fascination through his poetic personality that he became almost something of a *directeur de conscience* in two families, the families of Herzen and A. Tuchkov [Ogarev's father-in-law]. The ladies of both families were enrap-tured by his poetic-philosophical and socially lachrymose poem-cycle *Mono-logues,* and the male half of the two families, as became known later on, fell under the poet's influence no less than had the female. The secret of Ogarev's fascination consisted in a sort of apathetic, lethargic temperamental-ness which enabled him gradually to reach the furthest limits both in life and in thought and, though suffering, to tolerate all the most impossible situations with as much ease as if he were at home (Annenkov).

89. Ludwig A. Feuerbach (1804–72), *Das Wesen des Christentums* (1841).

90. Another fact is relevant here. One of Belinsky's friends had made a translation for him of a few chapters and of the crucial passages in Feuer-bach's book, and Belinsky was able to make, so to speak, palpable acquain-tance with the process of criticism whereby his old mystical and philosoph-ical idols were overthrown. I need hardly add that Belinsky was so stupefied by it that he remained completely mute in the face of it and lost the ability to pose questions of his own, a feature that had always distinguished him (Annenkov).

91. Petr N. Kudryavtsev (1816–58). Professor of history, University of Moscow, and close friend of Botkin and Belinsky. Under the pseudonym A. Nestroev, he published stories in the principal journals.

92. *Chto Delat?* (*What Is to Be Done?*). First published in *Notes of the Fatherland* in 1845–46.

93. "Iz sochineniya Doktora Krupova" ("From the Works of Doctor Krupov"). First published in the *Contemporary* in 1847.

94. During my second absence from Russia in 1846, Belinsky was possessed of almost the same feeling, I was informed, in connection with the manuscript of I. A. Goncharov's *A Common Story*—also an artistic novel. From the very first, he predicted great literary careers in the future for both writers, which was not difficult to do, but he also predicted that it would take both of them much time and effort to accrue creative ideas worthy of their talents (Annenkov).

95. Vasily A. Karatygin (1802–53). A tragic actor famous for his portrayal of Hamlet.

96. He had in mind primarily Schelling's new system (philosophy of revelation), and, after it, Buchez's doctrine on Catholic socialism, and others (Annenkov).

97. Dmitry Aleksandrovich Valuev (1820–45). An historian with Slavophile sympathies whom Annenkov knew well and whose posthumous papers he helped arrange.

98. I cite here an anecdote from those instances of self-condemnation and self-criticism to which he was prone but in which he was always also sincere. One of the editors of the time, having printed in his publication a translated novel for which he had paid the translator an agreed sum, considered himself in his rights to republish the translation as a separate book for his own profit. But he found himself up against a forceful man who, after fruitless protests, was prepared to make it a serious matter and perhaps go as far as to take legal steps such as were then available. The editor was forced to give in and to return the translator his property. Upon hearing this story, Belinsky began silently to search around in the corners of his room, found his cane there and, handing it over to the storyteller, said at the same time: "Teach me. Perhaps I, too, will get to know how one should protect one's own goods." But he could not learn to do that without ceasing to be Belinsky (Annenkov).

99. Valerian N. Maykov (1823–47). Literary critic and publicist, who focused on sociological themes in literature, under the influence of Comtian positivism. Vladimir A. Milyutin (1826–55), mentioned by Annenkov in the following note, was a professor of economics whose articles included studies of poverty in England.

100. In company with V. N. Maykov was another extraordinary young man, V. A. Milyutin, who also died young. They both could be considered the last scions of the extraordinary decade, comprising a transition to the literary period of 1850–60 (Annenkov).

101. Aleksandr V. Nikitenko (1805–77). Professor at St. Petersburg University, critic, literary historian, and government censor.

102. Nikolay I. Sazonov (1815–62). Participant in the Herzen circle during the early 1830's. He settled in Paris at the end of the 1830's, and at the end of the 1840's, the period described by Annenkov, he shared with

Bakunin virtual leadership of the Russian radicals in Paris. Like Bakunin, he was also in contact with revolutionaries throughout Western Europe.

103. Ivan G. Golovin (1816–90). A Russian émigré, he settled in Paris, where he published several books on economics and history.

104. The funniest thing of all was that he considered himself an important criminal offender. He feared deportation of his person by diplomatic means and rushed to have matters out with the minister Duchâtel, who, after hearing what he had to say, laughed and remarked: "What nonsense! Live in peace and do what you like, but if you absolutely must have my advice—then here it is: Don't get yourself so mixed up in Polish affairs" (Recounted by Golovin) (Annenkov).

105. *C tovo berega* (*From the Other Shore*). Written by Herzen in the years 1847–50 and published in 1850.

106. His preoccupation with the stream of life passing before his eyes was also reflected in his plans for writing. He had begun a story taken from the French Revolution of 1789 which included a Russian participating in it, and he had no misgivings about sending it to the *Contemporary*. Panaev later said to me in Petersburg: "Herzen has gone off his mind. He's sending us pictures of the French Revolution as if it were something we had taken account of and had forgotten." Needless to say, the story did not get published, but did appear abroad in a special collection (Annenkov).

107. Andrei Towianski (1799–1878). Religious philosopher who propagated theories of Poland's messianic calling. His influence was apparent in the works of the Polish poet Adam Mickiewicz (1798–1855), whose Paris lectures on Slavic literature Annenkov attended.

108. Galician movement of 1846. A Polish insurrection centered at Cracow against Austrian control. It was crushed with great bloodshed, partly with the aid of Russian troops, although a "Republic of Cracow" lasted for ten days.

109. Prince Adam J. Czartoryski (1770–1861). Polish aristocrat, educated in Edinburg. Close friend and adviser of Alexander I during the first, liberal years of his reign, and minister of foreign affairs until 1806.

110. "Die Reaction in Deutschland," *Deutsche Jahrbücher für Wissenschaft und Kunst* (October, 1842).

111. Joachim Lelewel (1786–1861). Polish history professor and participant in the Polish independence movement. After the failure of the Polish Revolution of 1830, he emigrated to Paris, where he headed the Polish National Committee. Expelled from Paris in 1833, he settled in Brussels.

112. George Herwegh (1817–75). German poet and political activist, associated with Marx, Ruge, Feuerbach, and other leaders of revolutionary movements in Europe. Also a friend of émigré Russians, such as Turgenev,

Herzen, Bakunin, and Sazonov. The "misery and suffering" to which Annenkov refers here concern a love affair between Herwegh and Herzen's wife, Natalia.

113. Sister of E. F. Korsh (see note 82).

114. The poet Vasily Andreevich Zhukovsky (1783–1852) met Herzen during the latter's exile in Vyatka in 1837. In 1846 Zhukovsky sent a favorable recommendation on Herzen to L. V. Dubelt, the head of the political police, and thereby helped Herzen gain permission to travel abroad.

115. Annenkov is referring to Herzen's autobiography, *Byloe i dumy* (*Past and Thoughts*) (London, 1861).

116. The journal referred to is *Polar Star* (*Polyarnaya zvezda*) which Herzen began publishing in 1855.

117. In such corners lived a great many German scholars who had come to Paris to finish their work. Among the Russians there at the time were N. G. Frolov, busy translating Humboldt's *Cosmos* and P. N. Kudryavtsev, who was finishing his dissertation "The Destinies of Italy" (Annenkov).

118. The play on words alluded to involves the Russian *plut*—a cheat, swindler, etc. (Translator's note).

119. Perhaps it was under the influence of the above-described thoughts that Belinsky formed his impression of the Sistine Madonna, which he later saw in Dresden, as an ultra-aristocratic type. He translated her *divine* tranquility, of which V. A. Zhukovsky has given us so poetic a rendition, into a simple characterization according to which her face expressed indifference toward the sufferings and needs of our low-lying world, or, in other words, a complete lack of altruistic feelings (Annenkov).

120. The reader himself may verify these words in the *Contemporary* of 1848 where the article appeared, or in *The Collected Works of Belinsky* xi, (1861), pp. 348–56 and 363–65 (Annenkov).

121. No matter how contemptuous a response criticism later gave all this store of minute observations, caustic remembrances, and bitter experience which had accumulated among us over the course of the many years of silence and patience and which had finally found an outlet for itself as being the only necessary and possible art, one must say, nevertheless, that that exposé literature, as the expression of offended personal or popular feeling, still has a value which not one historian of our society will pass over without attention (Annenkov).

122. Belinsky's attitude toward the Polish question was always from a *humane* point of view, as he believed that the victims of history and of their own sins could arouse deep compassion, as did, in general, all the extinct nationalities of earlier epochs. He never concerned himself with the political

aspect of the Polish question and continually bypassed it with indifference (Annenkov).

123. This section of Annenkov's memoirs represents a sketch of the first part of what Annenkov intended to be a volume covering the years 1848–58, which he called "the second extraordinary epoch" of Russian literary history. The telegraphic style of these notes, so different from Annenkov's prolix, flowery sentences, suits well for the theme: the oppressive security measures imposed by Nicholas I out of fear that the revolutionary wave covering Western Europe at the end of the 1840's would spill over into Russia.

124. The "expectations" were aroused by the tsar's intentions of using Russian troops to help suppress revolutions that swept Europe in this year. Russian troops were in fact sent into Hungary to crush the independence movement.

125. The writer Satlykov-Shchedrin was arrested in April 1848 for a story he had published the previous month in *Notes of the Fatherland*.

126. Count D. P. Buturlin (1790–1849). In reaction to the 1848 revolutions in Western Europe, Buturlin, a high government official and member of the Imperial Senate, was given extraordinary powers as head of a special committee to censor publications and to purge the educational system of teachers, students, and courses considered too liberal.

127. Ivan, Fedor, and Alexander were Annenkov's brothers. Katerina Ivanovna was a distant relative and companion of Annenkov's father in his last years. Strelkov was a relative on his mother's side. Lidiya N. Kashperova was the sister of the musician V. N. Kashperov, and Adel N. Beketova was his friend and later wife.

128. Aleksey A. Tuchkov (1799–1878). Liberal landowner, associated in his youth with the Decembrists and, later, with Herzen and Ogarev.

129. Mikhail V. Petrashevsky (1821–66). Organizer, in the mid-1840's, of an illegal circle in St. Petersburg which discussed programs for social, economic, and political reform. In April 1848, Petrashevsky, his followers, and individuals who had merely attended on occasion his weekly, Friday meetings were arrested on charges of intending to overthrow the government. That fall, after the inquiry was completed, a number of those arrested, including Dostoevski, were sentenced to be shot. At the last minute, the sentence was commuted to various periods of exile and imprisonment.

130. The "party of progress" comprised individuals who were associated with the government and urged reforms. Many of them, such as Kavelin and Korsh (see notes 82 and 87) and I. P. Arapetov, mentioned here, had been part of the radical Westerner circles of the 1830's but had, like Annenkov, grown more moderate and had come to regard reforms through the existing system as more realistic and hopeful than revolutionary

movements seeking radical changes in the system. N. A. Milyutin was a well-known economist and publicist. The "party of progress" was to play an influential part in the reforms of Alexander II.

131. E. P. Kovalevsky (1811–68). One time director of the Far Eastern Department in the Ministry of Foreign Affairs and later founder and first chairman of a literary fund organized to aid writers and scholars.

132. Nikolay N. Annenkov, a member of the secret committee established under Buturlin (see note 126) to intensify press censorship.

133. Credit must be given to Emperor Nicholas: his closest associates, taking advantage of the moment, demanded the complete closure of the universities, and he took a stand against that attempt, one might say, one against all, just as he alone did not succumb to the temptation of destroying general education, which, in accordance with a project of Mr. P. O., could easily have been supplanted by specialized education only for engineers, artillerists, jurists, teachers for the lower schools, etc. (Annenkov).

134. A. G. Politkovsky. Shortly before his death, this high ranking government official was accused of having subsidized his extravagant and licentious life by regularly embezzling large sums from a government welfare agency he administered. What particularly shocked society and infuriated Tsar Nicholas was that Politkovsky was a man of eminent social standing and a recipient of orders and honors, and that the theft was carried on, not in some remote province, but in the capital city itself.

135. But this feat and others like it were overshadowed by what was done later in the arsenals, in the Commisariat, in procurement of medical supplies, at the Headquarters, and so on (Annenkov).

136. There is apparently a piece of text missing here (Translator's note).

137. F. V. Chizhov, a Slavophile, was arrested in 1847 as a result of pressure from the Austrian government which accused him of agitating revolution among the Slavs in Dalmatia.

138. O. M. Bodyansky. At the time of his arrest, he was secretary of the Society of Russian History and Antiquities. He was arrested and exiled to Kazan in punishment for publishing Fletcher's book in the society's journal.

139. Pavel L. Pikulin. A doctor, relative of Botkin, and close friend of Granovsky.

Index